ARCHIE AND THE LISTERS

By the same author:

Original Aston Martin

Patrick Stephens Limited, an imprint of Haynes Publishing, has published authoritative, quality books for more than 25 years. During that time the company has established a reputation as one of the world's leading publishers of books on aviation, maritime, motor cycle, car, motorsport, and railway subjects. Readers or authors with suggestions for books they would like to see published are invited to write to: The Editorial Director, Patrick Stephens Limited, Sparkford, Nr. Yeovil, Somerset BA22 7JJ.

ARCHIE AND THE LISTERS

The heroic story of Archie Scott Brown
and the racing marque he made famous

ROBERT EDWARDS
Foreword by Brian Lister

Patrick Stephens Limited

First published 1995
Reprinted in October 1995

British Library cataloguing-in-publication data:
A catalogue record for this book is available
from the British Library.

ISBN: 1 85260 469 7

Library of Congress Catalog Card No. 94 73827

Publishers Note: The Scott Brown family name has appeared in both hyphenated and non-hyphenated form. The writer is using the latter as it appears correct through family useage.

Patrick Stephens Limited is an imprint of
Haynes Publishing, Sparkford, Nr Yeovil, Somerset BA22 7JJ

Designed & typeset by G&M, Raunds, Northamptonshire
Printed in Great Britain by Butler & Tanner Ltd, London and Frome

Contents

To Sarah

Foreword

TODAY, many authors who write about past heroic personalities tend to demean them. This book justifiably enhances the character of a racing motorist who, despite his awful physical handicaps, was unbelievably quick and was already held in the highest regard by his peers and fans for his skills, sportsmanship, good manners and character.

I first met Archie Scott Brown in competition at a timed sprint around an aircraft dispersal site circuit at Bottisham just outside Cambridge. He was driving a standard TD MG, a most unsuitable car for such an event. My car was a Tojeiro with an air-cooled JAP engine, and it would have been difficult to find a more suitable sports car for that meeting. Nevertheless, Archie was very close to my time, and with that performance he convinced me I was wasting my time driving competition cars. I therefore offered him my car for the rest of the season. So began a partnership which in five years became what has been referred to as a legend of motorsport.

By the way, the third member of that partnership made FTD at that meeting at Bottisham on 19 October 1952. At the time he was an underrated but gifted engine development engineer. His name was Don Moore.

During World War II, private and competition motoring had been banned. The freedom to use cars after the war was a new experience for my generation, and we had an advantage over previous generations of competitive motorists in that scores of redundant airfields were available to test and race motor vehicles.

There had been great advances in engineering techniques during the war, and these were now being incorporated in vehicle design and construction. The '50s were a very exciting decade in motor racing, new makes of car were appearing regularly in the paddocks, some now famous – Cooper, Lotus, Tojeiro, HWM and Lola. Other names, familiar then, have now faded into the mists of time, but all contributed to laying the foundation of a new industry for the UK. That foundation led to this country becoming the world centre for the design and construction of competition cars.

I am proud to have been part of that movement, inspired as I was by Archie Scott Brown, and greatly assisted by Don Moore and my own team of craftsmen at the family engineering company. Looking back it seems almost providential that Archie moved to Cambridge in 1951. Had it not been for his presence, it is doubtful I would have built cars to my own design. I realized then that here on my doorstep was a naturally gifted driver who was world class. Even so, the whole enterprise succeeded beyond my wildest dreams.

Within four years of producing my first car, the Lister-Jaguar was being described by *The Autocar*, the UK's principal motoring magazine, as 'Britain's fastest sports car'. Notwithstanding all our successes, we remained a very happy team. A major reason for this was that Archie was so undemanding, either for money or special attention of any kind. I thought this remarkable at the time, but since reading the proofs of this book I have experienced a deep feeling of humility, learning for the first time the extent of the problems he had with his legs and feet when he was young. He did not talk about his problems and effectively hid any difficulties even from close associates like me.

The team seemed to go from success to success on what appeared to be a never ending road of achievement until that fateful and tragic day at Spa in Belgium on 18 May 1958.

I can remember saying to Don Moore as we left the hospital where Archie had just died: 'Some day someone will write the story of Archie', little realizing that the individual destined to be that author was, as I spoke, a three-year old boy living in Malaya. He had just been given a model of the Vanwall racing car, which he treasured. The wait of 37 years has been worthwhile. Robert Edwards has done his research well and tells this moving story with the same resolution, pace and urge that characterised the driving of Archie Scott Brown, a Scottish gentleman and one of Britain's greatest racing drivers.

Brian Lister
Cambridge

Acknowledgements

THE list of people who have assisted in the preparation of this book is a long one. Obviously, Brian and Jose Lister's patience and enthusiasm have been priceless to me, as has their picture archive. Don and Babs Moore and Edwin 'Dick' Barton gave much of their time, and their undimmed enthusiasm for the subject was a great help. Dick also provided a portfolio of colour pictures which gives a rare documentary insight into the events described and adds great depth. Tony Murkett, despite the short notice he was given, rose to the occasion wonderfully. Brian and Don also checked the draft manuscript for technical errors, always a minefield in a work of this nature, and for that I am particularly obliged.

Roy Salvadori, Bruce Halford, Tony Brooks, Tony Crook, Mike Oliver, Stirling Moss and Jack Sears all seem to be blessed with total recall, as does Peter Riley, one of Archie's closest friends, as was the late Duncan Hamilton. Cavendish Morton, Louis Klemantaski, the late Frank Costin, Henry Taylor, Peter Nott, Archie Butterworth, John Tojeiro and Rodney Tibbs were all extremely helpful, and the total consistency of their recollections was a tremendous reassurance to me as I tackled the early stages of this project.

Many thanks are due to Merchiston Castle School for their assistance in contacting their alumni, of whom Duncan Simpson and Iain McWilliam deserve special mention. Gordon McLachlan, Alan and Gray Mickel and Marion Reynolds were of notable help in putting Archie's early life into perspective. Marion was particularly supportive and helpful.

There is one man to whom I owe a particular debt of thanks, and he is Paddy McGarvey, who was preparing a biography of Archie when he was still alive. Without Paddy's carefully taped and transcribed interviews, which he generously provided, I would not have had the benefit of knowing what Archie's parents and many of his early friends had to say about him. Again, the consistency of their input gave a satisfyingly empirical flavour to the research, and banished idle speculation. Paddy's input and enthusiasm for the project was truly invaluable.

Elsewhere, I received encouragement from every quarter. Mike Lawrence and Raymond Baxter were particularly supportive, as was Mick Walsh of *Classic and Sportscar* magazine. My thanks also go to Charlie Pierce and Jed Leicester for the chance to trawl through the archives at *Autocar* and *Autosport*. Doug Nye, a respected authority on all matters pertaining to British motor racing as well as a fan of Scott Brown and the Lister équipe, was massively helpful and encouraging, particularly in terms of archive material.

My thanks also to Robert Benjafield and Margaret Humphries (BP Archive), Mike Petty of the Cambridge Collection, Keith Challen, David Ham, Jonathan Evans of Toronto, Syd Silverman and John Harden of the Sportscar Vintage Racing Association. Harry Handley of the Sports Car Club of America, who put up with my pestering with imperturbable charm, made a great contribution, giving me insight into the Cunningham effort.

Such is my confidence in the accuracy and veracity of all contributions that I make no hesitation in claiming that any errors there may be will be mine.

The sources of picture material are many; Brian and Jose Lister, of course, Peter Riley, Roy Salvadori, Edwin Barton, the LAT archive, *Autocar*, *Motor* and *Autosport*, Doug Nye, Gordon McLachlan, Marion Reynolds and Moira Scott Brown all contributed pictures, for which I thank them very much.

Naturally, I am grateful to Patrick Stephens, Darryl Reach, Alison Roelich and Flora Myer, not only for their patience but for their unfailing support. I had eloquent testimony from other would-be biographers as to the chances of actually finding a publisher who would produce a book on this subject. I count myself lucky that none of them had contacted Patrick Stephens.

Not only has this been a fascinating piece of research for me to undertake, but I have made friends doing it.

Preface

ON 3 April 1954, just over 40 years ago, the product of an unlikely union first took to the track at Snetterton circuit in Norfolk. It was a Lister-MG sports racing car. It went well, winning by a country mile, and the name was not out of the press for the next five years. It was driven on that day by an expatriate Scottish amateur, who at the time made a living as a travelling salesman. His name was Archie Scott Brown, and he became great. He was also dreadfully handicapped. This is his story.

Robert Edwards
Ditchling, E. Sussex
1995

'WHATEVER one says about Archie, it would be most difficult to exaggerate his impact on the motor racing scene. Not only was he one of the truly greats of the sport, he was also a gentleman, and these two qualities do not always co-exist' – Roy Salvadori

Prologue – 1916 The Western Front

A MAN OF CHARACTER IN PEACE IS A MAN OF COURAGE IN WAR.
– Lord Moran

IF Second Lieutenant Bill Scott Brown was pleased to be posted to No. 11 Squadron, Royal Flying Corps, then he was probably mistaken. It certainly seemed better than wallowing in the trenches around Arras, which is what he had been doing up to Christmas 1915. His life expectancy was only marginally increased by the transfer but, at least, now he was able to see the battle from above.

His job, as observer in a Vickers FB5, had three functions – those of navigator, air gunner and photographer. His enthusiasm for the photographic element had already landed him in trouble, for taking air-to-air pictures. His pilot, Second Lieutenant Bill Phelan, from the RFC Special Reserve, was really just the driver.

Bill's route into the RFC was not a particularly unusual one. He had enlisted at the outbreak of war in August 1914 as a despatch rider, a job description easily fulfilled, as he had brought his own conveyance with him – an Indian motorcycle, hotted-up for racing. He was to remember being grateful later that he hadn't turned up on a horse. He applied for a commission at the same time, which was gazetted in December 1914, whereupon he joined the Renfrewshire Territorial Battalion of the Argyll and Sutherland Highlanders, where his brother had already been posted. As a junior lieutenant, he was given the job of Battalion Machine-gun Officer. The Argylls were part of the 51st (Highland) Division, which was training at Bedford.

Since he was a territorial, he remained behind when the Argylls went to France as part of the British Expeditionary Force; that dubious privilege having been denied to reservists at that stage of the war. He put in for a transfer to the regulars more or less as they embarked for France and was posted to the 2nd Line Battalion, accompanying them to the Western Front in the late spring of 1915, spending seven months in the trenches. As a Machine-gun Officer he had much to do and, like many, rapidly sickened of the work. He sought a transfer to the RFC, and news of his quickly granted request reached him at Christmas 1915, while he was home on leave. The speed of his acceptance should have made Bill just a little suspicious; losses were mounting at such a rate that, by the end of 1915, the life expectancy of a junior flying officer was little better than that of a subaltern in the trenches.

His first job in the RFC was teaching observers to shoot straight with an American Lewis gun, the second as observer in Phelan's plane. The FB5 was a 1913 design 'pusher' plane with the occupants sitting in a gondola sandwiched between two 36 ft. wings with a 105 hp Gnome rotary engine fixed to its rear. Outside the radius of the airscrew, a steel tube framework, substituting for a proper fuselage, ran rearwards to the tailplane. It could have been built by the Wright brothers.

Fully laden, the Gunbus weighed 2000 lb., and flat out at 5000 ft. could just scrape 70 mph. It was already an elderly design, the nemesis of which came from Dutchman Anthony Fokker (designer of a monoplane scout in 1913), whose interrupter gear enabled the pilot of a front-engined plane to fire through the area occupied by the airscrew.

Britain was a little behind in the development of this technology. The Bristol Aeroplane Company, which has a part in this story rather later on, had developed the 'Bullet' Type D before the war, which had been used as both military scout and air racer, most famously by Lord Carbury. The company had tried out various types of interrupter gear on it by 1915, but never with the sanction or approval of the aeroplane establishment, already firmly, but famously wrongly wedded to the 'pusher' layout.

On the morning of 23 April 1916 – St George's Day – Second Lieutenants Bill Scott Brown and Bill Phelan took off at 8.45 a.m. in their FB5 Gunbus (serial number 5079) to photograph German troop concentrations around Douai. They may well have been wary; the casualty rate of the Gunbus aircrews was quite high – 11 Squadron having taken its fair share. Lieutenants Kemp and Hathaway had been shot down in January, the former wounded and the latter killed, flying a similar machine. The two Bills' Gunbus, one of the last of its type, lacked the new profiled Raf-wires, which cut down wind resistance, it used a crude wheel-and-skid undercarriage and it would generally have been tired. It enjoyed the aerodynamic qualities of a picnic basket and constantly struggled to stay above stalling speed. Without it, though, this book would not have been written.

Across the lines, two men named Max were also preparing themselves that morning. They both flew Fokker EIII scouts, with twin machine-guns and 180 hp Oberursal engines, weighing less than 1000 lb. each. By common agreement, these planes, despite their obvious shortcomings compared with what was to come, were the snake's eyebrows. Half the weight and twice the power of the Gunbus.

One Max was a Prussian toff – Max Ritter, von Mulzer. The other, of lower military rank, a Saxon bourgeois, son of a minor industrialist who manufactured paper and cardboard packaging, was Max Immelmann.

Immelmann was not as famous then as he was to become. His regular commission had yet to be confirmed and he was as junior as you could be while still an officer in the Kaiser's army. Technically he was a subaltern in the Royal Saxon reserve and would not become a full lieutenant until a fortnight later. His unit was KEK II (Douai) a temporary outfit carved out of Feldfliege 62, recently despatched to the Eastern Front. In a parochial sense, he was something of a local hero, having shot down 13 aircraft, including the unfortunate Lts. Kemp and Hathaway, as well as Capt. Darley and 2nd. Lt. Slade (also flying a Gunbus) the previous October. Immelmann was already known as the 'Eagle of Lille', by the Germans at least. The form book was not in the Bills' favour should they encounter a Fokker 'Eindecker'.

Well, they did. Mulzer found them first. He made several passes at the Gunbus and succeeded in puncturing the fuel tank. The tank was pressurized, and Phelan, sitting immediately forward of it was doused in the best part of eight gallons of petrol. Wisely, he cut the engine and headed for a cloudbank. The plane was possessed of a huge square footage of wing, and the faint hope was that they would glide about, hidden from view, edging westward towards safety.

Inevitably, avoirdupois took over and they fell out of the clouds at about 3000 ft. where Immelmann found them. Mulzer courteously allowed the Eagle of Lille to deliver the coup de grâce, which he uncharacteristically failed to do. The Gunbus, now lightened somewhat because Bill Scott Brown had heaved out camera, machine-gun, ammunition, gunsight and nigh everything else that was not nailed down, jinked clumsily to avoid the rounds that Immelmann was loosing off at it. The pair had recognized the markings on Immelmann's plane and had wisely decided not to engage the enemy.

According to a letter which Immelmann wrote to his mother, he fired 120 rounds, or about one third of his ammunition, at the Gunbus. None of them hit either of the Bills, and by dint of a great deal of good fortune and not a little skill, Phelan put down in a fairly rough and ready fashion on a meadow near Monchy. The Gunbus stayed right side up (which was about all) courtesy of the skids at the front of the undercarriage, and the pair gratefully scrambled out.

Their first task was to destroy the plane. Never mind that its construction would probably have had the Fokker and Albatros engineers rolling in the aisles at the Johannistal proving ground – they had to burn it. It had come to rest nose down in a depression and Phelan manfully triggered the self-destruct device, which came apart in his hands. It was a suicidally brave thing to do, given the shower of fuel he had received, but that was his duty. Scott Brown had already thrown the Very pistol out, so it really came down to Bill's Vestas.

The fuel-drenched Phelan then wisely allowed his observer to strike the matches and throw them, flaring, at the plane. It, too, was soaked in petrol and the doped canvas caught fire relatively easily, erupting just as a troop of German Uhlans cantered up to rather irrelevantly, but with firm courtesy, demand their surrender.

Immelman joined the crowd shortly afterwards. The public relations opportunity offered by an enemy wreck on the right side of the lines was a hard one for an ace to pass up, particularly a career soldier like Max Immelmann. Photographs were taken and the serial number was clipped from the tailplane (which was, of course, isolated from the fire) to add to the KEK II collection of trophies, which was growing at an impressive rate.

But, the Eagle of Lille wanted rather more than that. Bill Scott Brown was wearing a bespoke leather flying coat, to which he had sewn a fur collar. He had bought the garment from a Canadian airman and treasured it greatly. Immelmann wanted it. Bill, using most unofficer-like language, refused. To be downed in an unarmed plane with a dead engine under withering fire was bad enough. To then have the unsporting foe try to annexe your overcoat was truly beyond enduring. Immelmann had no right to take it, of course, and the matter ended there and then. As events transpired, Bill Scott Brown was to need it.

Immelman would not have. He was killed less than two months later on 18 June 1916. The Saxon ace was credited with 17 victories in total, which cost the lives of 15 men and wounded nine others, so that Phelan and Scott Brown were, actuarially, remarkable.

The Royal Flying Corps communiqué, published with its usual and commendable speed on the evening of St George's Day, using information received courtesy of the Red Cross, put the encounter in its baldest possible terms:

23rd APRIL

2nd Lieutenant Phelan and 2nd Lieutenant Scott Brown started on photographic reconnaissance at 8.45 a.m. Their machine was brought down as a result of a fight in the air and the pilot and observer were taken prisoner.

Bill

BILL and his pilot spent the night of 23 April in the town jail at Douai. The next morning they were entrained under guard and sent, via Mainz and Essen, to a hastily-erected hamlet of wooden huts in the grounds of a winter sports hotel near Holzminden, in the Harz mountains. The idea was that they would be locked up for the duration.

Bill, however, disliked inactivity. He was an inventive man, as he had proved as a teenager when he motorized his grandfather's bath chair, rather to the old boy's concern. Straightaway he became involved in a tunnelling scheme which was almost ready by September 1916, but was betrayed at the last moment. He had to cool his heels until Christmas 1917 before he made another attempt.

Others had noted the resemblance which he bore to the second in command of the camp. Bill exploited this by dressing up in a home-made German uniform and strolling out through the front gate in the company of a Navy man, Lieutenant Wainwright. They wore dyed uniforms, spurs made from biscuit tins, cardboard medals and Army-styled cap covers over British uniform hats. The distinctive round badge of the German Army was replicated using the centre from a gramophone record, so they were clearly possessed of at least some creature comforts while in the camp.

Bill also made his partner's outfit; a British Army overcoat soaked in blue-grey paint, a tunic front, like a boiled shirt 'dickey' and a wooden sword. A huge false moustache completed the disguise.

They successfully got out of the camp, after which they removed their outer clothes, under which they were dressed as seamen on shore-leave. They buried the greatcoats and waded up a tributary of the river Weser to put off the dogs which they knew were coming. Behind them they could hear the alarms going off as the real officers had appeared, to the confusion of the sentries. They evaded capture during the night by hiding in a pigsty. The next morning, as they tried to board the 10 a.m. train headed for the Baltic coast, they were apprehended at the barrier, presumably for understandable olfactory reasons. Their greatcoats had been found by the camp dogs and the Commandant was particularly outraged by the subterfuge involving the cardboard medals. The two were confined to solitary for some weeks before Bill was consigned to another camp at Holzminden itself run, by a strange coincidence, by the brother of his erstwhile gaoler. Bill, along with others, was exchanged almost exactly two years after his encounter with Immelmann, via neutral Holland, for German officers of similar rank.

Holland, like Switzerland, was a clearing house for many Anglo-German dealings during the War. Industrial concerns from Britain, France and Germany all did business there on a large scale. By use of this, Carl Zeiss sold optical equipment to the Royal Navy, and Krupp sold patent fuses to Vickers, punctiliously invoicing them on a regular basis. It was also in Holland that the deal was done whereby British Tommies found themselves caught up in British-made barbed wire at the Somme. With such a community, the simple swap of a few prisoners was easy. Bill waited patiently in the Hague, his German counterparts in Rotterdam. Both sides were on the strictest parole, of course, the rules of war being sacrosanct.

Bill reported back for duty in Paris, where a pleasant surprise awaited him. He had accrued two years' of flying pay; which he did not find it hard to spend. The process may well have exhausted him rather more than his two years of incarceration, but he had strength enough to end up at Norwich as a gunnery instructor in the newly-formed Royal Air Force. To his disappointment, he was given his discharge a year later and he went back up to Glasgow to consider his options.

He was hardly broke – the family business was coal: mining it, storing it, distributing and selling it. It was a business which had done very well during the war. The family was one of a host of little dynasties which had been created in the Victorian age, the result of a union – merger, really – between mine-owner Scott and haulier Brown. There was no hyphen, except when it suited.

Although theirs was a heritage of coal, others in their peer group owed their wealth to engineering, ceramics, textiles and, most famously on Clydeside, shipbuilding. Newer money, already a thing to be sniffed at by the 1880s, came from stockbroking, real estate speculation, retailing and commercial banking. Few of these little tribes were truly grand in either the clan-based Scottish sense, or in the land-based English one. Glaswegian feudalism was based upon industry and commerce, not agriculture. A modest day's pay for a hellish day's work.

As we have seen, Bill's young manhood was rather mislaid during the Great War. He had been extremely well-educated at Fettes school and the Glasgow Academy and was intent upon a career in engineering, as his early experiments with the motorized bath chair suggest. To further this engineering objective Bill had worked as an apprentice at the John Brown Shipyard on the Clyde as well as holiday work with Armstrong Whitworth's in Newcastle, both of whom were customers of the family firm. A family background in coal was wonderful financially, but it was not an activity which suited Bill.

He had been born on 13 January 1894. The family home was at Giffnock in Renfrewshire which, rather like Paisley where Bill would later live, was a comfortable oasis of middle class calm on the edge of the hurly-burly of an industrial city. A long-time friend and close neighbour was Jeanette Watson, to whom Bill instinctively turned upon his reappearance in 1919. The two were comfortable in each other's company, made closer by their mourning of several mutual friends. One in particular, to whom Jeanette had been engaged, was an especial loss, as Bill had introduced them. He had died on the Somme.

Over the months Bill and Jeanette (always shortened to Jay) reached an understanding that they would eventually get married. There was no formal engagement, not uncommon then, as people struggled to become used to new friends and future partners, so great had been the slaughter. It was a state into which they drifted easily, almost imperceptibly and at no surprise to anyone.

The decision to liquidate the family firm, taken in 1919, was to prove both timely from a commercial perspective and convenient for Bill. He was now quite rich. In order to avoid death duties it was decided to pay out those with an expectation on the spot. Bill received about £60,000, a colossal fortune when a middle class occupation in the professions would possibly bring in £300 a year. It allowed Bill the luxury of broadening his experience somewhat. He opted to travel for a while, but in a working capacity. Armed with a letter of introduction and recommendation, he set sail for Toledo, Ohio, the home of the Willys Overland company, to learn more about engineering. He had quickly calculated that the apprenticeship which he had started at the Glasgow shipyard was more in the nature of cheap labour than a learning process; certainly he was to return from Toledo with a much more developed sense of engineering than he would have picked up at John Brown's.

He spent about a year in Ohio, before returning to Glasgow in 1921 to embark upon his career as a great engineer. His duties had been light, working in the area which now would be called quality control, but he learned much, particularly about automobiles, as the Americans called them. He already knew quite a lot about engines and had proved his enthusiasm for speed, so it was rather strange that he indulged his ambition first by the acquisition of a local company, A. J. Craig, which manufactured printing presses. It was not a success, as the post-war slump was already beginning to bite hard and he had clearly paid the wrong price for it. He closed it down after something of a struggle; the difficulties of filling the order books at anything like profitable margins soon becoming apparent to him. He was reluctant to lay off his men, but eventually he was forced to.

All around him Bill had observed the disaster of the post-war economy. Hordes of men, many disabled, blinded or deranged by their experiences, looked for work, any work. They busked by the battalion on street corners, they sold bootlaces, matches, anything they could. They begged if they could not work. Gardening was a favourite, construction another (not that much was being built), for many were possessed of at least one major skill – they had unrivalled experience with pick and shovel.

Bill and Jay married on 7 March 1923. Craig's was replaced by a garage business, the first of which he built in the Glasgow Road, Paisley. The newlyweds moved there also. Paisley was a town rather less depressed by the plight of the working class population than was its larger neighbour. Bill acquired agency arrangements for the sale of Lagonda, Alvis and Frazer Nash cars, and later on, Standards.

He was soon firmly set up in the motor trade. Better, the cars he sold were powerful and expensive. It gave both Bill and Jay the excuse to go racing, an activity at which Bill proved skilful. He drove a few times at Brooklands for the Alvis team, partnering Phillip Fotheringham-Parker, and Jay had several goes at the ladies' relay races which were common then. There seemed to be little thought of children, which set the fingernails drumming with impatience in Giffnock, but the two seemed to be having fun and were content. If Bill was a little slow on the uptake to claim his conjugal rights, then Jay was far too well brought-up to make an issue of it.

When it finally came in the autumn of 1926, the news that Jay was expecting a baby was greeted with predictable glee in both the Scott Brown and Watson households. To celebrate, Bill built another garage, in Bothwell Street, Glasgow. The businesses were going well, even if the roaring twenties were just a little muted north of the border. The war seemed almost forgotten, so starting a family was, in the opinion of their friends, just what they both needed. Jay's brief illness in the early winter of 1926 was of only slight and passing concern, so minor was its effect on her. She shrugged it off and pursued her social round with the same keenness as before. She had in fact suffered a bout of German measles.

Nothing much was known about rubella within the medical profession, its impact not being formally identified until 1941, with no vaccine for it until 1963. The mildness of her affliction, a light rash and a slight temperature, gave neither Jay nor her doctor any real cause for concern over and above the natural worry of the effect of any disease on a pregnant woman or her baby. Even if a more timely alarm could have been sounded, there was little that could have been done; therapeutic abortion was a thing of the future.

Chapter 2

Archie

A fortnight before Jay's term was due, Bill took a trip to the local cinema. While driving there, top down and flat-out as usual, he had been soaked to the skin by a sudden downpour and developed a bad cold. This rapidly transformed itself into raging pneumonia. He was immediately consigned to bed where he was to remain until after the arrival of his child, so was not able to be present at the birth. He was the recipient of rather more medical attention than his wife, who stayed serenely in bed while Bill literally fought for his life across the landing. It was his condition, not hers, which ensured that the house had more medical staff than family and servants in it by the time the child was due.

The baby, a boy, was born on Friday 13 May 1927. He weighed in at 8 lb. 2 oz., which was a remarkable weight considering how little there was of him. His mother did not see him for 24 hours, so quickly did the midwife whip him out of the bedroom. Jay's bout of German measles had wrought massive damage to the unborn baby inside her, the most obvious result of which was a significant underdevelopment of three of his limbs.

There was no proper right forearm, merely an elementary thumb and palm, which started below the elbow. A similar condition affected both legs, but marginally less badly. Neither leg had a shinbone; only a fibula. Both legs were radically twisted and bowed, and the club-feet were tiny, with no discernible toes. The right foot was twisted outwards about 90 degrees, and the left was almost back to front. Only the left arm was normal.

When, finally, Jay was shown the baby, her first reaction, she remembered, was one of despair. She hit the bottom, but bounced back fairly quickly once she was able to share the load with Bill – but that wasn't to be for another two weeks. She recollected finding that the hardest thing was not being able to show the baby to all her friends and family; she had to look to Bill for a strategy upon which they could both agree. The behaviour of the medical people present, she recalled, gave rise to more of a sense of shame in her than anything else.

When Bill recovered, the pair of them left Archie in capable hands and sailed off to Norway for Bill to recuperate and the pair of them to discuss what was best to be done. There was no apparent discomfort for the baby – on the contrary he was a very cheerful little fellow. They had named him William Archibald, after his father, but whereas the father was always known as Bill, the son was never to be known as anything but Archie.

The parental options were depressingly few. The consultant surgeon at the Glasgow Royal Infirmary recommended amputation and the fitting of artificial feet. But, despite the advances which had taken place as a result of the war, both parents felt it to be an unthinkable thing to do; as was the option of lifetime care in an institution, which was a quite normal route for those for whom money was little object. The alternative which eventually offered itself was to seem little better for a while. Both parents viewed the prospect of introducing pain into their son's life with something close to horror, but they had to look ahead to his future. Left as he was, he would never even have the chance of walking, let alone doing anything else.

After a search which lasted 18 months, the Scott Browns discovered Naughton Dunn. He was a specialist orthopaedic surgeon who worked from 105 Harley Street, but also at the St Gerard's Hospital in Birmingham and the Robert Jones and Agnes Hunt Hospital in Oswestry, a few miles to the West. He had qualified as a doctor in 1909 from Aberdeen University and served as a Major in the Royal Army Medical Corps during the Great War as surgeon in charge at the Birmingham Military Orthopaedic Hospital. As a result of his experiences, he had emerged as one of the foremost orthopaedic surgeons in the country. As well as holding these posts, he was consultant at the Hartshill Cripples' Hospital in Stoke-on-Trent and at the Royal Cripples' Hospital in Birmingham. Already the author of several published and authoritative texts on the subject of bone grafting and limb surgery, the first of which was published in 1918, he was an eminent, calm and sympathetic man. Fortunately for little Archie, Dunn was prepared to rise to the challenge; even better, Bill and Jay could afford him.

Jay first saw Dunn in London, where he said that he would begin in the spring of 1929. 'All young things do better in the spring' was how he put it. So, more or less on Archie's second birthday, Jay and her son arrived at St Gerard's Hospital, Coleshill for the first part of Archie's ordeal. It was all a huge risk, of course, but they felt that they had little choice but to take it. Bill and Jay both agreed that it was liable to be a make or break exercise in terms of their son's character.

First, Archie's legs had to be straightened, which involved breaking and resetting them before putting them in plaster. The underdevelopment and absence of the bones in the lower leg always suggested that

22

later growth would be a problem, but straightening them out was an obvious first step. After months in plaster casts, after which his legs were lined up as correctly as they would ever be, work could begin on his feet. They had to be virtually amputated, rotated and reattached the right way round, without damaging the nerves. The toes, the last of the problem, were present but undeveloped, X-rays had revealed. It was important for the baby's future sense of balance that as many as possible were teased out, and Dunn found three on one foot, and nearly four on the other. Most important, the big toes were made to articulate properly; vital in ensuring both locomotion and balance. The whole process was to take a total of two years and no less than 22 separate operations, with another year in plaster after that for good measure, mainly to immobilize Archie, who was showing signs of a healthily aggressive nature by the time he was four.

The gamble worked. Archie came out of the ordeal, in Bill's words, as a '… joyously cheerful and ambitious child, with an immense zest for life.' As he was in splints and plaster for most of the time, the nurses used to push him around in a small cart, which Archie quickly decided he could manage to steer himself.

Jay's determination to be at Archie's side as much as possible was reinforced by the fact that Bill was starting to behave most oddly. He was a man already prone to introspection and occasional self-pity. Unfortunately, he was also a ferocious boozer, and the two characteristics seldom mix without disastrous results. He had learned to drink in the RFC, assuming he needed teaching, and it was now to the bottle that he was starting to turn. Basically, he was lonely. His prosperity and marriage had promised great things, and the hurdle thrown up by Archie's plight was obviously a hard one to clear. A slight resentment of babies by their fathers is by no means unremarkable, given the demands which they naturally make upon their mother's time, but Jay's complete absorption in dealing with Archie did cause Bill problems.

But he had other problems. The Stock Market collapse in October 1929 was less than helpful as his investments fared no better than anyone else's; and the economic decline which it obviously heralded was to treat him badly. Worse, a condition which had first appeared when he was a prisoner of war at Holzminden started to accelerate – blindness. He had started to suffer from cataracts at quite an early age, possibly compounded by the virtually third world living conditions in the POW camp. Bill had started to take the route which many would follow in the next few years, a relentless decline into alcoholism.

Jay had always been aware of Bill's drinking. Glasgow was a hard-drinking place at every level of society and no-one, not even the most naïve and well brought-up girl, could have failed to notice the role which the consumption of alcohol played in the fabric of the place.

Alcoholism was rife after the war anyway, which was a particular irony if you had been a soldier, given where the Haig family fortune came from.

It had been said that Bill was something of a cad and that his drink problem stemmed from a sense of shame at Archie's physiology. That he was shattered by Archie's plight is not hard to believe, but that it tipped him towards the bottle is improbable. More likely, as if it matters now, is that the combination of his sense of guilt at wealth and surviving, compounded by his genuine concern at the state of so many of his fellow soldiers, as well as missing those who had died, depressed him greatly. His eye problems and Archie's condition served to push him from being merely a heavy drinker to someone who had a genuine clinical dependency.

When Jay brought their son back to Scotland permanently, she resolved to meet his problems head on. There was no question in her mind of keeping him hidden; on the contrary, the whole extended tribe of assorted cousins and friends were encouraged to spend as much time as they wished at the Scott Brown house. She clearly felt that her son had as much right to a place in society as anyone else.

The children of the extended family were, of course, curious to see their new peer. He had been more or less absent for two years, after all, and Jay allowed them to help bathe little Archie, so that they would all be familiar with his appearance. If this seems a brave way of dealing with a heartbreaking situation, then it should also be remembered that many handicapped children were locked away in institutions then, to receive special care. The fact that Jay took such a modern approach, rare even today, to introducing her son to the world goes a long way towards explaining how it was that he became so hugely self-confident. He was brought up to believe that he was merely built to a different set of plans from others. He was to learn, painfully and quite soon, that not everyone shared this view, but the experience bolstered his ego usefully at a time when he was in great physical pain, and probably quite confused. It was also basic to Jay's approach, as she had been warned by Dunn that there was no certainty that the work which he had done would last for ever, that Archie's development, indeed his whole life, should be dealt with one day at a time – a process of discovery. She instilled in Archie the idea that little would be easy and that he should expect nothing. As he started to achieve, he would get more pleasure from his successes than most people ever do. This view rather moulded Archie's character, although sharp reverses were to hurt him as much as they hurt anyone, as unavoidably he became prepared for the next high point rather than the next low one.

We should not confuse Jay's attitude with anything so crass as political correctness; if such a doctrine existed then it would be called plain common sense – addressing the problems and difficulties of the handicapped required rather more than the invention of a few slick euphemisms. War had produced legions of handicapped people and they were a part of everyday life. Children, pragmatic as they always are, grew to accept them as mere curiosities. For Jay, though, all it took was a quick glance at a limbless soldier selling bootlaces to put into brutal relief the plight of the crippled, whatever its cause.

By 1933 Archie was walking, after a fashion. His method, encumbered first by plaster casts, then callipers and surgical boots, was simplicity itself. He would trot, bottom sticking out, body leaning forward and close to toppling over, arms waving to retain balance. By the time he was eight he had mastered locomotion, but it became clear that his lower legs were not going to grow any more. Although he was to limp badly, with a rolling flat-footed sailor's gait, he managed to get about quite well, but all his life he walked as little as possible, preferring to save his energy, which was always limited, for more enjoyable activities on the sports field and, later, on the dance floor. There was no denying that Dunn's work had been groundbreaking in more ways than one. The success which he had with his little patient was to allow that patient to set standards of excellence which few able-bodied people would ever match.

Educating Archie was a formidable obstacle. The first step was to address the basics, for which a governess was required. Bill's best friend was Iain McWilliam; he had a son, also Iain, born in August 1928. It was agreed that the two should share the services of one Miss Margaret McLaren, and that Archie should go to the McWilliam house for his lessons. A good reason for doing this was that Bill was in danger of turning the Scott Brown residence into a replica of the Western Front. On one occasion, the story goes (and it may even be true), he produced a service revolver and blazed away at the 'wildlife' which he saw emerging from the wallpaper. Poor Bill, in the iron grip of delirium tremens, was fast deteriorating into a potentially huge liability. Jay was totally unequipped to deal with this. If Archie was going to survive childhood, then he had better spend as much time as possible out of the house while catching up on the years which hospital had neatly sectioned out of his life.

He was an amiable little boy, quick to make friends and skilled at keeping them. He and Iain McWilliam became almost inseparable; they were to go through primary, prep and public school together and remain close all of Archie's life.

Despite his occasional incapacity, Bill remained capable of acts of great sensitivity as far as his son was concerned. On one trip back home from a lesson with Miss McLaren, Archie had witnessed the brutal maltreatment of a pony by its owner, a coal haulier, which had distressed him greatly. Bill ventured forth to track down this dismal little equipage and, on squiffy impulse, bought the horse. It was, unsurprisingly, a bad-tempered brute, which Bill promptly christened Jimmy; his brother-in-law's name. It was not a flattering comparison. The creature was a retired pit-pony, one-eyed, undernourished and quite vicious. It was a crossbred Shetland, which, as anyone who knows will testify, is a gene pool that was missed when the nice natures were thrown in, and the pony's years of abuse had not improved it. Archie, however, loved it. It occupied a place in the Scott Brown garage, which was rather dangerous for Bill's car collection, as it was a prodigious kicker. To everyone's amazement, little Archie started to ride it. Or, rather, he started to try.

He was kicked off several times, and bitten more than once, but per-severed. None of his friends could get anywhere near it, but after some weeks Archie was allowed to stay in the saddle, and he began to use it as everyday transport, riding to the McWilliam house daily for his lessons. Jimmy was turned loose in the McWilliam's garden while Archie and Iain were introduced to the three Rs. Years later Iain remembered:

> I was warned beforehand that the child coming to lessons in our house had a hand missing and to treat him with due deference, but after a few days together, I forgot about the missing hand completely, and everything else.

Miss McLaren was fascinated by Archie:

> Archie's handicaps were terrible to see in so small and handsome a child. He had a beautiful face as an infant and enjoyed coming to classes on his pony, but it really was too slow for him. He had a craving for speed even then; he taught me a great deal in perseverance.

Miss McLaren spotted one huge problem immediately. Archie was, behaviourally, right-handed. That he had no right hand at all created probably the biggest obstacle of all. It was one which, if he was to accomplish anything, had to be addressed as an urgent priority. That she taught him to write left-handed was a signal achievement, as she had no formal training in the field of therapy. Archie's writing was always to be one of his lesser skills, uncharitably described by a later colleague whose own efforts at calligraphy are no monument to the art as 'bloody awful'; which misses the point, I think.

Miss McLaren was right, though, about Archie's craving for speed. Jimmy the pony not only got Archie around for a while, but saved his callipered legs from the dreadful punishment which he routinely dished out to them; but only for a while. Archie had also discovered cycling. A close neighbour, Mary Rose Harper, who was a little older than Archie, was in the habit of riding over to help Jay bathe him and afterwards snip out the lint pads which he needed to prevent his cal-lipers from chafing. For this noble dedication, Archie rewarded her by pinching her bike, a fairy cycle with a single brake. Of course, the brake was on the right side of the handlebar, so Archie quickly learned to push his coat sleeve over the end of the bar and pull backwards to slow down. It was a little rough on the coat sleeves, but seemed to work well. Soon afterwards Jay bought him a tricycle of his own with blocked pedals, so that Mary Rose's bike was allowed to survive. Archie happily careered around the streets with little thought for his own safety, nor indeed for anyone else's, and he taught Mary Rose how to ride hers almost as fast.

Archie pushed himself ridiculously hard, possibly in the belief that being aggressively active would change something. It did not, of course, but his unusually harsh physical regime was to build him into something of a tough. Always in a scrape, always daring others to best him, always ready with a small hard fist to punctuate any belittling remarks unwisely made by others; Archie started to grow up as a perfectly normal little boy.

When the basics had been mastered under the benign eye of Miss McLaren, the two boys were sent, in May 1935, to the local pre-prep. school, Dardenne, at Kilmacolm, about five miles away. The place was an oasis. Adam Fraser built the grounds within the environs of Birkmyre Park. It was laid out in a distinctly Alpine theme, with chalets, pavilions and cottages. It was Fraser's descendants, neighbours of the Scott Brown's, who had recommended it. The journey to school was usually undertaken by Jay, frequently assisted by Archie sitting on her lap, as Bill was often in no condition to drive – although this never stopped him trying. Archie loved the place, and after a term rather startled his mother by asking to become a weekly boarder. He was eight. He understood her reluctance, but charmed her into allowing it. He craved not only speed, but company. Iain McWilliam, preferring the comforts of home, stayed as a day boy.

This afforded Archie's parents an opportunity to seek a cure for Bill's worsening cataracts. While Archie was at school, and looked after at the weekends either by the McWilliams or Scott Brown cousins, Bill and Jay flew to Switzerland to an eye clinic. After two visits, one for each eye, the problem was fixed. His cure did not stop him drinking (this was not to happen until later), but he did make several attempts. By now he was swigging whisky straight from the bottle, which was a hard habit to break, but like many alcoholics, he did achieve long periods of relative sobriety.

At school, Archie was capitalizing on Naughton Dunn's hard work. He had already developed a prodigious sense of balance, which he used to great effect on his bicycle. He won fast and slow bicycle races for three years in a row. This latter is a little-known activity now, but really consisted of hopping aboard and going as slowly as possible. Archie could just about stand still on his bike, making tiny invisible adjustments to the handlebars in order to stay upright. He participated in every sport except rugby, for which he was simply not fast enough. He played in goal on the five-a-side soccer field, though.

At home, the transportation question was being addressed in a thoroughly grown-up manner. A pedal car was acquired for Archie which he used at weekends and during the holidays. He drove it recklessly of course. A close friend was Kate Shanks, whose family owned the now-famous bathroom fittings business. Kate used to drop in at the Scott Brown house to play with Archie, play the piano and watch him race about. Archie managed to collide with the Shanks's family Rolls as it swept through the gates of the house, which could have killed Archie, and certainly frightened its driver. The pedal car was taken away, which action the ten-year old Archie accepted philosophically.

Now that Bill had his sight back, he could drive again with some confidence, particularly after a sharpener or two. His stable of cars included a Frazer Nash BMW, a couple of Bentleys (one of 4½ litres and one of eight) and an Alvis tourer. He started to introduce Archie to driving on the roads around Paisley, which were almost entirely innocent of traffic, and to demonstrate some elementary race techniques. That it was all quite illegal worried Bill not at all. He had a purpose in mind.

He was in the middle of building a proper car for his son. It was under construction in the workshops of the Paisley garage under the supervision of the foreman, David Browning, and Bill worked on it in spare moments. He had seized upon his mother-in-law's motor mower, up for replacement, and removed its Villiers engine. The car was to have worm drive steering, made from an Armstrong Siddely car jack, and the rear axle was a miniature replica of a chain-driven Frazer Nash type. The body was simple, but professionally put together. It was no toy, this. It had solid wheels at the rear 'to absorb the torque', with wire ones on the front.

Unfortunately, Bill was still drinking hard. He was playing golf as well. The two do not mix well, and while out on the links one day he managed to break his leg. He failed to notice the fracture, anaesthetized as he was, and a blood clot formed which nearly carried him off altogether. He pulled through in the end, his constitution still massive despite the ravages of the POW camp, the pneumonia and the drink. Browning finished the car and delivered it to its pleased new owner in time for his 11th birthday. It carried a 'registration' ASB 38, which presumably dates it. Archie was able to apply all the lessons from the quite illegal sessions he had enjoyed in his father's cars, and within weeks had mastered the machine. Every weekend he practised around the gravel roads of Castlehead and Paisley, learning the niceties of the racing change and the four wheel drift. The clutch was rudimentary, so clutchless gearchanging was a useful skill, and the brakes, wooden blocks acting upon the wheels, wore out quickly. Archie never used them much anyway. His enthusiasm for cars, as opposed to 'stink bikes' never left him after that. This first car was to have a hard life. Quite soon after it was finished, Archie managed to smash into the wrought iron gates at the entrance to the drive, hard enough to bend them.

Bill and Jay continued to map out Archie's academic career. Iain McWilliam had been put down for Clifton Hall prep. school in Newbridge, Midlothian and Archie was also sent there in 1939. The pair stayed there until 1941, when they went to Merchiston Castle School, Edinburgh. It was at Merchiston that Archie came across the rough and ready curiosity which characterises schoolboys of all types. Bluntly, he was asked what kind of accident he had had, to which he replied that he had laid down under a train, and his gullible inquisitors were so awed by this that they asked no more. He became a minor celebrity instantly.

School food was predictably iffy. It is seldom a culinary tour de force, but school food under rationing can hardly be expected to improve. Archie was rather shy of having it cut up for him, as he ate only with a fork, à l'Américain, as it were, but the burgeoning strength of his left arm allowed him to slice even the toughest of iridescent liver with the edge of it. Not surprisingly, omelettes were a deal simpler, even if they were usually made from reconstituted dried egg, so it was a slightly eggbound Archie who took to the sports field. The staff, continuing Miss McLaren's noble efforts, could see that his polarity was still a problem – anyone who read one of his essays could work that one out – so they encouraged him in games to improve his dexterity. He practised, too. Determined to get it right, he frequently deserted the dormitory so that he could practise with a cricket bat out of sight of his peers, but not, of course, out of hearing. He became an adept at cricket and tennis. Fencing, which suited the aggressive side of his nature, was pleasing, although he tutted somewhat at the ritual. Golf, the sport which nearly killed his father, had to be played backhanded with right-handed clubs, which was fairly tortuous, but he became competent at it. Physically, he became absurdly strong on his left side, which went a long way towards compensating for his lack of a sound right hand even if it meant that he looked even more asymmetric than he had before. The hand/eye co-ordination which ball games gave, coupled with supernatural balance and an unerring sense of timing, allowed him to evolve into a natural sportsman. He missed his little car, though.

Back in Paisley, Jay was struggling to keep the business going. Bill had been called up to the Clyde Patrol, a marine Home Guard keeping an eye out for German mines, which was a piece of cake to him, as he knew the waters well since he owned a 12-ton ketch, the *Judith*, which he regularly sailed from Fairlie up to Colintraive, where the Scott Browns had often taken a house in the summer months. Sailing was good for him as it kept him sober. His later posting, up to Scapa Flow, was rather less of a sinecure.

The War brought compromise to the Scott Brown family, as it did to many others. Jay locked up the family home and moved in with friends, the Marshalls. The garage works were taken over by the services in 1943 as a repair facility, and it was not until Bill returned from Scapa Flow that they lived in the family house again.

At Merchiston, Archie was doing rather well. Cecil Evans, the headmaster of Merchiston, awed by his attitude to his problems and quick to spot promise, ruthlessly piled responsibility upon him, to which he responded as well as 'the Blog' hoped he would. School teams, away matches, extra lessons, school duties, as well as an appointment as a prefect – an authority which Archie carried off rather well – all combined to build Archie's sense of self-esteem, which was not exactly retarded anyway. Evans was also very concerned for him.

It was a well-intentioned manoeuvre by Archie's maternal granny which nearly unmanned him. She was concerned at the thought of the lad looking so odd, and insisted upon an artificial hand. This was, of course, what had been suggested by some at the time of his birth, but he greeted the prospect with horror. She was insistent; Jay gave in and sanctioned it. Dutifully, Archie tried out the prosthetic forearm and hand, even pretending some technical interest in the wretched thing, but Evans noticed that it 'crippled and humiliated him'. He was compelled to write to Jay, recommending that Archie be allowed to throw it away. She assented, and gleeful he was as he discarded the 'toy hand', none too carefully, and reverted to being 'normal'. It was understandable, if naïve, meddling on the part of his granny, but she was to play an important, if posthumous, role in another phase of Archie's life much later on.

Archie also discovered girls. He had built, with Evans's de facto connivance, a modest personality cult about himself. When Archie, with fellow pupil Morrison Low, discovered that the fire service had been unwise enough to leave a Royal Enfield combination stored in a shed in the school grounds for the duration, they resuscitated it, cadged some fuel, no mean feat in wartime and got it started. Evans was tolerant in the extreme when the pair were seen actually riding about on it, but put it out of bounds, nonetheless. There were *some* limits.

Archie reached them quite easily. Having discovered the local girls' school, he invited, without permission, a large contingent to the school sports day at Merchiston. Reluctant to make a formal protest to Jay, Evans chose to be diplomatic and mention to McWilliam's parents that this was possibly a bit off. Jay reacted rather badly to this indirect approach, responding that it was all open and above board, young people must mix, and so on. She was perhaps missing the point. Evans had a boys' boarding school to run, after all, and such behaviour was, if perfectly natural, perhaps the thin end of a very awkward wedge, the kind of risk that in those days would have made even the most liberal thinker wake up sweating in the small hours.

Jay, though, had all the instincts of a lioness as far as Archie was concerned. No perceived slight was too small to ignore, whatever its underlying intent. Evans had diplomatically passed a polite hint through unofficial channels; he was to wince somewhat at the response.

In truth, Evans had probably been astonished rather than anything else. The sight of Archie being such a roaring success with the ladies, many of whom preferred him to the more conventionally built Spartans of the sports field, was not something he may have been prepared for. The manner of his communicating this to Jay, as a mere hint really, suggests that he was not prepared to make a fuss about it; he and his wife thought the world of Archie.

There was another problem, though – Bill. Archie's parents were having a difficult time, and at school speech days, the sight of Jay concentrating solely upon her son, and Bill concentrating on nothing much in particular, forced Archie into an agony of divided loyalty; and it distressed him, and therefore Evans. Bluntly, Evans suggested that the best thing they could do was to separate, for Archie's sake. If this seems little short of breathtaking, then bear in mind that Evans, taking his job *in loco parentis* very seriously indeed, probably felt quite within his rights in expressing his opinion. So, apparently, did Jay. Bill was almost past caring, really.

The unhappy pair were attempting, constantly, to reconcile their differences, right up to the steps of the court, but to no avail. The grounds were adultery, accomplished, in the seamy manner of the time, with a hired female accomplice, a private detective and a hotel apparently used to the procedure. Bill and the accomplice allowed themselves to be photographed coming out of the room by the detective and that was considered to be proof positive that a decree should be granted. In Presbyterian Scotland, adultery was probably a more acceptable reason for divorce than drunkenness, and anyway, amazing to relate, drunkenness was not considered to be grounds for divorce at all. Bill never hit Jay, after all, merely allegedly discharged a pistol in her presence. He hadn't been aiming at her, so it would probably have been a nice legal point. No; adultery was all it could be, fiction though it was.

Broken home or no, Archie passed his School Certificate. He also took the Oxford and Cambridge Exams and elected to go for a place at Pembroke College. The war was nearly over now and Archie lined up, with 54 candidates for a place to read Economics. He did not get one.

The Master of Pembroke, A. C. Roberts, was impressed enough by Archie to be moved to write a letter to Jay offering to help him get a place somewhere else. St Andrews was the lucky establishment chosen, albeit at full fees and not for a year.

To fill in the time, Archie, with Cecil Evans's assistance, got a job for the academic year at Ardvreck School in Crieff, a popular prep. school which provided many Merchistonians. Theoretically, Archie was supposed to teach History and Maths to nine-year olds and, up to a point, it went well. He found the scrutiny of so many kids rather hard to bear, and dealt with it by showing off with the trusty cricket bat, hammering balls over the school buildings to the uncritical approval of all concerned, staff excepted. His time there, despite his popularity, left him with a mild dislike of staring infants. For handicapped or sick children, though, he couldn't do enough.

The period back at prep. school was a useful filler and earned him enough money to run his three-wheeler BSA, known by all as the biscuit tin. He was allowed a special petrol ration because of his disabilities – the only time he ever exploited them – so drove everywhere. He needed mobility in order to rush back to Kilmacolm where he had spotted someone who he wished to get to know rather better. She was called Marion Armour. Marion later remembered:

> He started to take me to school in the morning. His car was a three wheeler and very noisy, and I used to hear it returning for me, phut-phutting around the school, and I used to go scarlet, but continue writing. The whole class would turn round with a look. I don't know why I wasn't expelled; he was always sitting there when I got outside.

As Archie departed Ardvreck and went up to St Andrews, a little chap called James Clark entered the portals of Clifton Hall for the first time. Clark was not to go to Merchiston, but instead to Loretto School, where he too would excel at games, but little else. The two would eventually meet much later on.

Archie had, to the relief of the family, survived the ordeal of childhood very well. He had turned out to be possessed of great charm, inherited from his father, and seeming endless determination. He was perhaps prone to overreach himself occasionally, particularly when competing, but also had, as a result, a realistic attitude towards his own limitations. Above all, he was able to enjoy life more or less on his terms. The awesome gamble which Jay, Bill and Dunn had taken had paid off handsomely. It was a very well-adjusted Archie who set off to St Andrews. He was not to manage to live in Cambridge for some time yet.

Chapter 3

The outside world

IT is probably fair to say that Archie's star did not rise far in the acad-emic firmament. This is not to suggest that he was thick – far from it. He merely had little time for work. He had started off reading Economics, then Accounting, but actually read *The Autocar* more than anything else. He also had a lot to prove physically, in spite of the sav-age contempt with which he occasionally treated his problems. Of less irritation to him was the fact that left arm bowlers around the wicket are often at a premium at all levels of the sport and, although his physique precluded real all-round success, he quickly became a stal-wart of the second XI.

Archie's gene pool, inherited from both sides, contained impressive physical skills, and all he lacked was a way of expressing them. He lived in the same digs as Desmond Titterington, the son of a Belfast flax merchant, who had come from Glenalmond School in Perthshire. Happily, the two got on well, having both background and interests in common. Many of their fellow students were just back from the forces and they tended to keep to their own set. Titterington acted as a sort of unpaid mechanic to Archie, fascinated as he was by motors. Despite Titterington's ministrations, the biscuit tin expired from the cruel and unusual treatment which it received, and Archie promptly replaced it with a Morgan three-wheeler, which fared little better. The BMW 327 which he eventually acquired was his first fast car. Actually, the BMW was Bill's. He had gone off to South Africa on a cruise, the first, but unsuccessful, stage toward rehabilitation from alcohol, a step he final-ly took after a ferocious course of aversion therapy. Archie revelled in the power of the BMW, sliding it around the rough roads in the area. He lasted at St Andrews about a year, then left. Despite the fees he was paying, it was thought that places were too important to throw away on dilettantes, however deserving. He would, however, meet up with Titterington a few years later under very different but entirely agree-able circumstances.

What Archie *had* managed to do during his short spell at St Andrews was, in effect, to reinvent himself. Gone now was the boister-

33

ous, under-sized asymmetric. In his place appeared a moustachio'd cavalier, quick with a joke, very handsome, a little on the short side, right arm inevitably shoved into the pocket of a nicely-cut tweed coat. A little raffish, perhaps, even a hint of the fighter pilot about him. An Irvin flying jacket helped. The trouble was, he had no way to make a living. The family wealth was severely depleted by Bill's extravagances, medical bills, the depression and the war and he was reduced to a modest allowance. He needed a job.

At this stage, Archie was in great danger of amounting to little more than an agreeable, sporty, clubbable under-achiever. Having dropped out, or been pushed out, of University at a time when the job market was flooded with young men, many of them as handicapped as he, returning from the war, he could easily have been subsumed into the crowd and lost for ever. At this time, the family business could not support him as it had been requisitioned by the RAF for the duration of the war and, anyway, because of chronic raw material shortages there were no cars to be had for home sale – certainly not Lagondas, as they were tottering towards bankruptcy after an ill-advised court case with Rolls-Royce, and about to be taken over by Aston Martin; and certainly not BMWs either, for obvious reasons. His father Bill couldn't be bothered with it anyway. Archie's eventual route into the motor trade was to be rather more convoluted than normal.

For a few months Archie entertained semi-serious thoughts of going into the RAF. It was a fairly hopeless endeavour, despite the fact that he actually had 'flown' a plane – Bill's de Havilland, in which Archie had at least held the controls, was one of his father's many and expensive indulgences. It is not inconceivable that this attempt by Archie was the expression of a desire to prove that he could succeed in the same field as his father, but if that was his intention, he was to demonstrate it much more forcefully later on.

The RAF were polite, but firm. They were demobbing people, not taking them on, and anyway ...

Another possibility was selling, or travelling (as it was known). Glasgow was replete with industrial concerns which needed salesmen, and the Scott Brown family knew most of them. One such magnate, in the soap business, upon request offered Archie an interview. It went something like this, according to an interview which Archie gave to a magazine at the end of 1957:

Magnate: 'Now, Mr Scott Brown, just let us bring our minds to bear on the problem of selling foam. In the first place, how does it strike you as a creative career?'
Archie: 'Bloody awful, I'm afraid.'

If there is a Baderesque flavour to this, it was probably intentional on Archie's part. Archie was destined to go through the assault course of humdrum business in much the same way as the fighter pilot had had to before the war, before re-discovering his true calling.

George Dobie and Sons was a largish tobacco company, whose flagship product was the Four Square brand, and the war had not done them any harm. War is supposed to be 90 per cent boredom and ten per cent terror. During the 90 per cent, soldiers smoke. The return of so many customers postwar triggered a small expansion in the firm's operations. Archie was fully qualified for the task in one respect – he was an inveterate smoker, having taken it up at school, like so many then and now. After taking him on in 1948 as a trainee rep, against their better judgement but under pressure from Scott Brown family friends, Dobie's were eventually delighted with his ability to communicate on so many levels. The old-fashioned expression for this is the 'common touch'. Archie had it in spades. After the induction process, they despatched him to represent the firm in East Anglia, complete with a Ford Anglia car, which came in an unpleasant shade of brown.

His mother went, too. There was little for her in Paisley. By this time, Bill had simultaneously taken both the pledge and a pub, complete with its own landlady. Archie was thus delighted to go south, and set to it with a slightly wary confidence. His second residential spell south of the border was to be rather less painful than his first. He was probably unaware that East Anglia had and has a well-earned reputation for being something of a salesman's graveyard. The family influence which had got him in through the door of Dobie's was not of sufficient clout to ensure a secure living. That, he would have to make for himself.

Archie and Jay established their first base camp at Colchester in a rather shabby apartment block known as Crouch End Court, Lexden Road, which really suited neither of them particularly well. Given that Archie's patch ran from the Thames to The Wash, they realized quite soon that a move to East Anglia proper was going to be necessary. They were there long enough for Archie to take at least one significant step.

His grandmother, architect of the scheme to equip him with an artificial hand whilst at Merchiston Castle, had died. She left him a legacy of around £1000 and, like many a young man before and since, Archie's first thought was how he was going to spend it. Of course, he blew it – on a car.

The MG TD, XS 6931, which Archie bought in 1950 was, to the average undergraduate, the last word. His ownership of it guaranteed, if that was necessary, membership of the Eastern Counties Car Club. He had already put his mother's Standard 8 saloon to good use in rallies and a few driving tests. His first club circuit race was to take place at Fersfield, an airfield circuit borrowed by the ECCC before they adopted Snetterton. The ECCC was not the only motor club in East Anglia, though.

Archie had acquired the car just in time to avoid double purchase tax, courtesy of his friend McWilliam, who by happy coincidence now worked at Abingdon, where MGs were made. McWilliam recollects that there were no MGs to be had for the home market that year; all the production was designated for export. Archie's old friend, however, was able to pull some strings, and Archie was provided with either a South African or Australian specification model.

The MG dealer in Colchester was mortified. He had virtually no cars of any type for sale, except pre-war models, and could not persuade any serious buyers in through the front door of his showroom. He was so desperate to be seen to have stock, he offered to garage the car during the week, waxed and polished, to bring in the punters. It was to be hard work for him, as Archie proceeded to thrash the car unmercifully at weekends. His extra petrol allowance, and he used every precious drop, was a godsend.

There were also ways to save petrol. One commodity which was in reasonable supply was paraffin, or domestic kerosene. Another, for Archie at least, was Ronson lighter fuel. He hit on the idea of running the Anglia on paraffin – of course, it had to be started using the lighter fluid, but ran tolerably well on the witch's brew of petrol, paraffin and Ronsonol. Actually, the low octane 'pool' petrol which was available then wasn't really that much better. If Archie was concerned at breaking the law, it didn't really show, as his little economy was an open secret. The petrol which he saved, at the risk of calling the Customs and Excise down upon his head, he put in the MG's tank, to be used for racing.

The decision that Archie and Jay took to move to Cambridge was a pivotal one, and by that curious process of Brownian motion which seems to guide so many events, the pair found themselves in a rather nicer flat than they had left, at 163 Hills Road, Cambridge. At one end of the road, in Cambridge Place, was the workshop of Don Moore, which he had just set up after leaving his job as service manager at Ted Salisbury's garage after a war spent defusing bombs. A few miles away Brian and Jose Lister, married on Summer Solstice, 1951, were installed at Brook Cottage, Histon. The stage was set for the start of one of the most remarkable synergies that motorsport will ever see. The three protagonists were in place, but yet to work together.

Upon enquiry, Archie divined that the Cambridge University Auto Club met regularly at The Rose pub, in Rose Crescent, Cambridge. In fact, it did little else, having neither a home circuit nor very much petrol to use – a problem compounded by the fact that ownership of a car was against the University rules for all but the most senior undergraduates. He wandered in one evening early in 1951, leaving the rakish MG parked outside. Inside, he met Peter Riley, later to become a works Healey driver. The assembly not unnaturally took him for a demobbed pilot, an impression Archie made no initial attempt to correct. Archie's dashing moustache, the way he carried himself with the panache which was often an assumed trademark of the type, and the fact that he was very short, as pilots often are, all served to make him look the part.

After a few hours, it was suggested that a brief test be organized soon at Bottisham, another of the multitude of suddenly abandoned wartime USAAF air bases in East Anglia. However, it was not simply a matter of driving in and getting started, as in an unofficial meet. The barbed wire had to be negotiated first. There was also a small delay as the various cars were retrieved from their lock-ups, barns and side-streets to converge upon the place. Riley owned an HRG, and a contest between the MG and the 'Hurg' was anticipated as a potential tale to relate.

Riley and Archie went around the perimeter at a fair old crack. Archie was quicker, and offered Riley a ride round. It was only when a tight part of the badly-surfaced route tested Archie's skills a little further that Riley realized that he was basically one-handed.

At this stage, Riley had known Archie at least a week; they had met socially on several occasions and neither Riley nor anybody else had noticed that Archie had only one hand, so adept had he become at concealing it. All had remarked upon his shortness, also his limp, and had assumed that at least the latter was the result of a war wound. It was only when they did some elementary arithmetic that they worked out that this, given his age, was most unlikely. Archie always looked rather older than he really was, anyway, which rather perpetuated the confusion.

Archie and Riley became the closest of friends, and Peter is now the custodian of many of Archie's most personal possessions, bequeathed to him by Jay Scott Brown when she died, he being a founder member of the 163 Club, a Scott Brown appreciation society. This group was to become the pivot of Archie's social life in Cambridge.

The band took its name from the number 163 Hills Road. When expressed in Roman numerals it became CLXIII, and inevitably, Clixy. The core of the Club was a group of seven; Peter Riley, Martyn Noble, Peter Nott, Tim Woods, Mottram Rankin, Michael Hilton and Leslie Hawkes. These young men, Mr Toads all, were to follow Archie's ascendance with initial disbelief, a sense quickly supplanted by something akin to hero worship. Women, of course, were permitted in the Club, subject to Jay's approval, but were mandated to wear only black and grey. No-one can remember why this was, but there were certainly no sinister connotations. There really wasn't anything more to it than a desire by the members to live a social life not entirely driven by the University, and to share costs going to and from motor races. There was even a Club tie, in a suitable shade of racing green.

Chapter 4

Brian Lister

WHILE Bill Scott Brown was disentangling ASB 38 from the
wrought iron garden gates at Castlehead, just after delivery to its
first owner, a boy almost one year older than Archie was rather warily
beginning his secondary education at the Perse School in Cambridge;
he had already attended the Perse Preparatory School. He knew perhaps rather more than he wanted to about wrought iron gates – they
were one of the many areas of expertise of the family business which
his father ran. Not unsurprisingly, he was fascinated by motor cars, but
had long ago discarded his own pedal car – aluminium body, polished
steering wheel and all. He was experimenting with car construction of
the Meccano school, along with the inevitable and enviable Hornby
train set.

The firm of Lister, Flatters and Branch had started as general engineers in Abbey Road, Cambridge in 1890. After the Great War, which
had treated the family rather more gently than the Scott Browns, it
became George Lister & Sons, when brothers Horace and Alfred
joined. Brian had been born on 12 July 1926, the year of the General
Strike. The firm undertook most types of engineering, from architec-
tural ironwork to general machining. After restoring the massive
structures outside St John's College, Bill Scott Brown's little problem
would probably have been but an hour's work. Like many such concerns then, consistency was the key to building the business – consistency in quality, that is. Virtually any project would be addressed with
the same underlying approach, the doctrine of the 'proper job', delivered on time. It is said, but memories fade, that even the legendary
Chitty-Bang-Bang was once repaired there.

Brian would pore through the pages of *The Autocar* which his uncle
Tom Howard slipped him, and gaze longingly at his Uncle Tom
Arnold's SS1 tourer, not to mention the MG P-Types that the senior
and wealthier undergraduates at the University parked carelessly near
Midsummer Common. Some of these had become famous racers;
Whitney Straight, Prince Birabongse, Richard Seaman. Seaman, who
had died racing at Spa in Belgium before the outbreak of war, would

touch Brian's life much later in a weirdly tragic coincidence.

While he didn't find school an ordeal, Brian was not an outstanding pupil. He was something of a comedian and relished asking awkward questions, particularly of the science masters, which made him popular with his fellow students if not the school establishment.

He left the Perse, with a small sigh of relief, aged 15½ at the end of 1941, and began an apprenticeship at George Lister & Sons. He had already discovered jazz (or, more correctly, swing) as early as the age of eight, so was particularly happy when the sound was introduced to East Anglia by the hordes of American airmen who descended upon the place to man the air bases which had sprouted everywhere as launch pads for the USAAF daylight bombing raids on Germany.

The precision of drumming in a rhythm section attracted Lister for a number of reasons; setting the tempo being merely one of them. The disciplines imposed on the performer by the need to operate as conductor (driving the soloists on) as well as player, but which allowed a degree of interpretation as well, pleased him. Percussive sounds were, after all, part of his upbringing, and jazz was to become something of an obsession for him. He was lucky to have a talented tutor in George Hackford, who performed in a five-piece band at nearby Waterbeach aerodrome; Hackford was one of the best technicians in the music business, having played with both dance bands and the BBC military band. Brian practised for hours every evening and landed a job with a local dance band. By late 1943 he had helped start 'The Downbeats', which flourished, winning *Melody Maker* contests for the next few years. British audiences, though, did not necessarily appreciate 'swing' as much as American ones did, often preferring strict tempo music, but the war would change that. Brian actually won the individual drumming prize for south-east Britain at the Hammersmith Palais. Such success led him to consider seriously a career as a professional musician.

In terms of the engineering training which was given to him, it was thorough and comprehensive. Welding and machining, the core skills of the firm, were the two main areas of his curriculum, and being the boss's son made little difference to the arduousness of the work, least of all to the boss, Horace, who is remembered as a slightly Edwardian figure by those who worked for him. He set and demanded high standards of work and punctuality, and although not without humour, tended towards the Goldwynesque: 'You get the surprise of your life when you die,' was one of his best-remembered aphorisms. His own engineering training had been formidable; during the Great War he had worked at Brotherhoods of Peterborough, making torpedo components.

Horace had made few demands on Brian's efforts at school – he barely read Brian's school reports and held the view that success at school indicated little in terms of later life. He reckoned that if teachers did their jobs properly, homework should be unnecessary, and approved wholeheartedly of Brian's interest in jazz, even if it meant that it interfered with prep.

By the time Brian's apprenticeship at Listers had concluded in the year the war ended, he was as good an engineer as the firm could make him. A short period of time would reveal how good. He was now eligible for call-up, but having decided that he wanted to get into the RAF, as they had the best bands, he circumvented the process and volunteered. The possibility of spud bashing at Catterick, or something equally dismal, held little attraction.

National Service did him no harm at all. After initial training at Wilmslow, a posting to RAF St Athan followed, to be followed in turn by Colerne, Waterbeach, Beaulieu, Locking, and, as a matter of strategy, back to Waterbeach before his discharge in March 1948. He had met his future wife, an attractive redhead called Josephine Prest, always known as Jose, who he would marry three years later. Jose's family, like Bill's, had also owned collieries, but in Northumberland, not Scotland. She had moved down to Cambridge and shared Brian's interest in motorsport. Together, they were part of a group which was instrumental in forming the Cambridge '50 Car Club, another member of which was an oddly diminutive Scot.

Brian had also worked with some very fine machinery indeed, and seen closely how a proper airframe was constructed, for example. It had taught him much. He had also bought his first car. Like many young men who have followed their hearts in the matter of buying cars, it was not the cleverest purchase; an ex-police MG TA which must have done at least 500,000 miles during the war years with only the most routine servicing. It was, to say the least, ever so slightly shagged . . .

It was replaced by a Morgan 4/4, FHU 351, which he was able to enter in the sort of motoring gymkhana events which were popping up all over the place. The posting to Locking, near Bath, was particularly handy as the Bristol Light Car Club were active at organizing events. Once he was back as a Lister employee, though, he was able to improve it a little, mainly by lightening it. His father was slightly uneasy at the prospect, not unnaturally, but did not interfere. After all, most young men are interested in messing about in sports cars, and no doubt it would pass. Brian continued competing and sprinted a little with it, but it was clearly uncompetitive.

Down at Surbiton, Surrey, John Cooper had just announced the Cooper T14, available in chassis form. They sold very well, and Brian bought one. He fitted it up with the assistance of Edwin 'Dick' Barton, a Lister apprentice, and registered it JER 547. The car used an 1100 cc MG engine, which later blew up at Silverstone. The cost of a rebuild was prohibitive, so badly was it damaged, and Brian was already looking elsewhere, so he sold it to Peter Reece.

In 1951, a quiet man called John Tojeiro, just out of the Fleet Air Arm, had set up business in a leaky shed in the village of Arrington, a few minutes' outside Cambridge. He was, ambitiously, designing his own chassis. He had driven a TA type MG in club events and had more or less sorted out the mechanical side of it, but felt that the handling lacked precision. For a few of the parts which he needed for his new chassis he had become a George Lister customer. It seemed to be a reversible process, for the second Tojeiro ever made was sold to Brian Lister. It was an adaptable device, having the added advantage of being cheaper and much lighter than a Cooper T14 chassis, and Brian had the idea of adapting it to accept the JAP 1100 V-twin motorcycle engine. It would, he thought, make a fine lightweight sprint car. The JAP fitted rather well, in fact. Better still, an enthusiast called Bartlett, whose intention of fitting the JAP engine into a trials car had been written up in *The Autocar*, had produced a small run of bellhousings for the JAP engine so that a Jowett Jupiter sports car gearbox could be fitted. Had it not been for Mr Bartlett's enthusiasm, Brian Lister would probably not have bothered. Lightweight bodywork and mudguards completed the set-up. Road registered KER 694, Brian grandly named it The Asteroid. 'Haemorrhoid's more like it!' contributed some wag. It reverted to being a rather more modest Tojeiro JAP. It was hard to persuade into action, but it was fearsomely quick when on song, despite an apparently insatiable appetite for valves.

One of the first events which Brian entered was the CUAC sprint around the perimeter of the aircraft dispersal site at Bottisham aerodrome. Brian was confident, and had every reason to be. He had reckoned without one of the opposition, a fellow clubman who lapped the tiny circuit almost as quickly in his rather battered-looking MG TD. Don Moore actually won, in his very quick and very modified MG PB.

Archie had won five events with his MG since his first race at Diss, Norfolk in 1951. He was one of Don Moore's customers, and so was Brian Lister, who needed help coaxing a consistent performance from his vicious and temperamental JAP. Archie seemed fascinated by the machine. Perhaps it reminded him of ASB 38 – they had something in common, after all. It didn't take much persuading for Brian to offer him a turn at the wheel the next season. To the local participants in East Anglian motorsport, Archie's physical problems were a matter of record by 1953 and didn't merit comment. Everyone knew, or came to know, how quickly he could drive, and thought no more about it.

Archie had developed his MG, 'Emma', about as far as it could go, which had involved taking her to Cliff Davis, the moustachio'd extrovert in London's Goldhawk Road, owner/driver of a rather quicker Cooper MG than Brian Lister had owned, for an overbore to 1380 cc from 1250 cc. While Davis was attending to the bottom end, Archie took the cylinder head to Don Moore for gas-flowing.

Davis had achieved real prominence in JOY 500, a Cooper-MG which he had bought from Lionel Leonard. Leonard had had it bodied as a Ferrari barchetta lookalike in 1951, but had had problems with the Morris XPAG engine. The root of his difficulty lay in the fact that he had overdone the compression ratio, shaving too much off the cylinder head, with the predictable result that the valves fouled the pistons. Davis had rebuilt the engine and had never looked back, which, given that Leonard was something of a guru in MG circles, despite the fact that by profession he was a market gardener rather than an engineer, gave Davis the reputation of a demigod on the club circuits. The car was one of the many small legends of the post-war racing scene.

Archie, who was really no mechanic, had modified 'Emma's' bodywork, fitted alloy cycle wings and done all the 'boy racer' tuning that he could, such as removing the carpets, taping up the lamps and fitting an aero screen. Most of this work was carried out in the street in Hills Road and took an inordinate amount of time. One passer-by who seemed fascinated by the antics of this would-be Fangio was Anthony Armstrong-Jones, later Lord Snowdon, who, out of curiosity and an eye for the bizarre, took some photographs. Sadly, they are lost now, but he became an admirer of Archie's, although never a close friend. One decorative non-essential which Archie added to 'Emma' was a chrome female nude which he optimistically bolted to the transmission tunnel. It may have served to indicate to female passengers what might be in order if they played their cards right! When his mother saw it she ordered him to paint at least a pair of knickers on, which he did, reluctantly, but with loving neatness and typical enthusiasm for accuracy. He was later to acquire a different, more conventional mascot. Unfortunately for Archie, but happily for Lister, all the work on 'Emma' had, between the Goldhawk Road and Hills Road, basically used up all his money. He was near enough broke when Brian offered him the drive in the Tojeiro-JAP and was in no position to refuse if he intended to carry on racing. He had come extremely close to giving up, despite his obvious skill and potential. He had even started doing odd jobs for Don Moore around the workshop in order to make ends meet.

The most obvious paper benefit of the Tojeiro driver change, encouraged by the car's designer, was the weight saved by having Archie in the cockpit – he was only five feet tall and quite slim, whereas Brian was more heavily built as well as being taller. There was more to it than that, though. Archie's level of skill was altogether of a higher order. On 2 March 1952 Archie tried the Tojeiro JAP in anger at the Cambridge University Auto Club meeting at Bedwell Hay. The car was in the 750–1100 class; he won the 1100–1500 class. He was to repeat this trick five times in 1952. He competed in his own MG in parallel, of course, buoyed by the success he was having in the Tojeiro, and he frequently contested three or four events at the same meeting.

Such was the success of this new car and driver combination that there were accusations soon flying about that Lister had not built a car in the 'spirit of the sport'. Brian's response, as that of any successful entrant, from Ferrari to Williams, was straightforward; he shrugged and made even more entries.

The next season was little different for Archie. He started it driving a Bugatti Type 35 (readily loaned by its trusting owner as it was not quite the cherished machine then that it is now) at the CUAC sprint at Bedwell Hay, coming a depressing third. Third again at the Aston Martin Owners' Club meeting at Snetterton cheered him even less, as he was driving his beloved 'Emma', but on 25 April Lister handed the Tojeiro over for the first time that season, after the ministrations of Don Moore had smoothed it a bit over the winter, and he romped home first in both class and handicap events. He repeated this trick at the Maidstone and Mid-Kent Motor Club meeting, held oddly at Silverstone on 16 May. The next day he drove it off to Prescott and won the 1500 cc class at the Bugatti Owners' Club meeting. A weekend after that he won the 1200 cc event at the Bristol Motor Club meeting at Thruxton. In total, Archie piloted the Tojeiro to 11 outright or class victories in 1952 and 1953. The machine frequently won its next class up, and often lapped all comers, even in five lap events.

Oddly, the engine seemed to prefer competition rather than road use once Moore had tuned it. On the two occasions when it dropped valves after Don's ministrations, it was being cantered along the public roads with Archie at the wheel. The JAP engine was so unreliable, possibly overtuned, that Brian, Jose and Archie usually had to tow the Tojeiro to races using a solid tow bar at the back of Brian's side-valve Morris Minor. Near Prescott, the poor Morris gave up the unequal struggle going up a hill. Archie had to start the Tojeiro's engine and push the Minor up from behind.

Its lack of meaningful springing made it an ordeal to drive anywhere at all, but at least there was some point in competition. It was a dismal sports car. Brian disposed of it after the Thruxton meeting, via Archie's good offices, to Archie's friend Peter Hughes, the Editor of Scotland's *Top Gear* magazine. Hughes was to return the favour, if that is what it was, by investing in Archie later on. Hughes became a great friend of Brian and Jose's, too, right up to his death in a road accident on the Scottish border a few years later. It was to be the first time Brian and Jose lost a friend, and the experience shook them.

The racing successes seemed to be something of a trend, just as was the exposure which small manufacturers – many of them little more than one-man-bands like Tojeiro – were receiving through their participation in motorsport, even if it was, by and large, exposure at a somewhat parochial level. The idea came to Lister in that early summer of 1953 that a car bearing the family name would be a grand idea. Much of the fog of mystique associated with chassis design and racing car construction had been burned through by the insights granted through competition. It was already clear that the key to consistent performance was the chassis rather than the engine. An engine, you can always change; a chassis, you have to put up with.

His father Horace was less enthusiastic, but relented after a token wrangle. He was due to retire soon anyway – better that the project be undertaken under his benevolent eye than not, he thought. The task was therefore to scratch build a sports-racing prototype which, if successful – big 'if' – might serve as a small-scale production project. Don Moore would provide an engine, Brian would design the chassis and body and Archie would drive it. To be fair to them, all three had established a decent track record in a short space of time. The car had in fact already been laid out by the time parental permission was forthcoming in the late summer of 1953; although it was never presented as a *fait accompli*, merely kept rather quiet. For Horace Lister it was a leap in the dark. He gave Brian £1500 and six months. It turned out to be a little more and a little longer, but was to be the forebear of a creation that one contributor to this book, who has every reason to say otherwise, quite unprompted, called a 'national treasure'.

Dick Barton, at this time, had been removed from the scene for National Service. He was not to return for two years, and was to catch up with events in the spring of 1955. Brian Lister did much of the work on the chassis himself, while Don Moore cast about for a suitable engine to develop. The initial choice of an MG unit was perfect for him, as they were his speciality.

Brian was to benefit hugely from the resources which George Lister were able to offer. Apart from those components which had to be bought in, such as brakes, dampers and steering, all the major parts were made in house at the works at Abbey Road. Even at this time, most small manufacturers were dependent upon access to other people's machine shops, carrying out only design and assembly. It was to be a feature of the Lister effort that the constant surveillance of the entire operation allowed a high degree of quality control which an extensive use of sub-contractors would not have permitted.

Chapter 5

'It'll go like a bullet!'

A racing car is a chimera. Often the dream of one rather than many, it is a purpose-built hybrid created for one purpose and one only, rather in the manner of a quarter horse, greyhound or polo pony. By the time the driver is involved, the project is usually nigh fully developed and is offered on a take it or leave it basis. Lister approached the task rather differently.

From the start, Brian Lister had a straightforward attitude to the problem of making a racing car. 'Make it low and make it go' might sum it up adequately. In order to make it low, he designed a chassis that, viewed in plan, was an asymmetric stretched kite shape to be built of 3 in. bore tube, made from drawn T35 steel, of 16 gauge wall thickness. He reckoned that 0.062 in. was thick enough not to distort when fitted with brackets, thin enough not to pay excessive weight penalties and easy enough to work. He confesses readily that he is a practical engineer, not a stress specialist able to calculate loadings on complex space-frames. Some other manufacturers already making such structures probably knew less about them than they should, but may have been reluctant to admit it. Anyway, he only had £1500, six months, and a lot more to pay for than the chassis frame. It was a first effort.

But what a first effort! The triple virtues of lightness, simplicity and strength were reinforced by a fourth – safety. All the mating surfaces of the hexagonal chassis were fully machined to fit and tack-welded in a jig before being webbed and electrically welded for extra sturdiness. This is in stark contrast to the efforts of certain other builders, both at the time and later. The tradition of consistent series production of short-run objects from the Lister works was a real bonus here. Lister was not operating out of a garage – he was operating out of a fully-fledged multi-skilled engineering company. At conception, though, the first Lister car was not generally imagined to be anything more than a slightly speculative one-off, but it was properly made. How well made was to be proven in a relatively short time.

The suspension was an area where Lister had some well-developed views also. At the front he opted for parallel equal wishbones of his own design and manufacture, in order to be able to easily pinpoint the roll centre. MG kingpins and stub axles were used, being freely available, of good and consistent quality and relatively cheap. Helical springs, enclosing Woodhead Monroe struts, completed the moving parts, the whole being attached to an upright rectangular fabricated frame reinforced by more T35 tubing. An inverted left-hand drive Morris Minor steering rack was attached at the extreme front of the car.

Brakes, by Girling, were twin leading-shoe units, 9 in. x 1.25 in. Alfin alloy drums were employed, and the pedal assembly, fully drilled and lightened, operated master cylinders which were split between front and rear. To allow for the possibility that someone other than Archie would drive the car, the pedal gear was fully adjustable.

At the rear, established practice was also followed. Lister's desire to be able to predict axle behaviour led him to the extra expense of a de Dion type layout. The final drive was a Salisbury differential unit mounted on a simple tubular extension of the rear chassis member. Inboard brakes were fitted to the cheeks of the differential unit. Springs and dampers were attached to the chassis in fabricated box structures. The de Dion was located longitudinally by twin pairs of parallel radius rods and laterally by a sliding block within a fabricated upright.

Lister had observed the success that pre-war Mercedes Grand Prix cars had had using such a layout, and felt reasonably comfortable in their company. He could have saved a huge amount of money by using a proprietary live axle, or even an independent layout, but he realized that he was better off with a system which was known to work. After all, if the car wasn't successful or promising then the money would dry up very quickly indeed. Good handling, he reckoned, started with keeping the rear wheels upright. Lister's first chassis had a 90 in. wheelbase and a track of 49.75 in.

There was not a huge choice of engines available for the new chassis, at least, not for anything like a reasonable price. The original concept had envisaged using a Bristol engine, as the example set by Cliff Davis in LOY 500 had proved an encouragement to all concerned. This was the car which Davis had commissioned from Tojeiro after the MG-engined JOY 500 had become uncompetitive. Being pressed hard by Archie in Lister's Tojeiro at Snetterton in late 1952 may or may not have suggested to Davis that some upgrading was needed.

Anyway, money was potentially tight, so initially an MG engine was favoured. The XPAG series was in wide use at club level. Don Moore drove an MG; and so did Archie, as Don knew to his cost. In fact, when the first power unit was put together, Don went back to source, using a very second-hand Morris 10 block to offer 1466 cc, fettled by the addition of a tuned top-end and special exhaust of Moore's own design.

Lister sketched out a bodyshell which owed much to current thinking and which was all about simplicity. Constructed in light 20 gauge aluminium alloy, and supported by a simple version of a superleggera steel tube cage it was to resemble both the new Healey Hundred and, vaguely, the barchetta style of the Davis Cooper-MG. There was also a slight touch of Allard to the otherwise slab-sided body, and a neatly-radiused rear-end, culminating in low-mounted brake lights. The fewer compound curves, Brian calculated, the lower the cost. At the front of the body, which could be entirely rotated forward, was a gaping maw, accommodating radiator and oil cooler. The driver's door was a simple, drop-down affair.

Brian took the sketches to Wakefields of Byfleet who, in exchange for £275, executed it with their habitual neatness, and it was painted British Racing Green by a local firm in Cambridge – Sitton and Mothersole. It was an effective, if dull, colour scheme, livened up by the application of a thin canary yellow stripe fore and aft, which seemed suitably racy.

A simple Perspex screen and a lightly-padded seat completed the appointments. While the body was being made, Archie took the vehicle in chassis form up to Snetterton for a test. All went well for about four laps, with the car handling extremely well, and then, without warning, it spun off into the infield. Scott Brown was less concerned about himself than about Lister's pride and joy. Surveying the frame, he noted that an engine bearer had snapped. Archie was not particularly mechanically-minded, nor did he probably appreciate the role that component failure can play. After all, he had driven 'Emma' for over 90,000 miles without taking the head off. He immediately assumed that he must have made an unforgivable error. Coyly, he suggested that the bearer might be the cause of the problem. His embarrassment was great when it was realized later that a half-shaft had seized, locking the differential and catapulting the car off the track, about which not even the great Nuvolari himself could have done anything. The seizure had been caused by insufficient clearance for the short half-shaft in the hub carrier, and the shaft was flexing and picking up on the inside diameter of the carrier.

The car was road registered in the spring of 1954 as MER 303. 'It'll go like a bullet!' It received the chassis number BHL 1.

To save and raise money, Lister borrowed the company Fordson lorry to use as a transporter. He made up a pair of hardboard and alloy panels to fix to each side to form a cover for the parent company logo and sold advertising spaces on them. Dunlop took one, KLG another, the Philidas locking nut company one more, and Don Moore was given the last. That was the starboard side. On port, BP, Mintex and SU took three of the spaces, the fourth being rather redundantly labelled 'Lister Chassis'.

Once the équipe was as ready as it was going to be, the first entry was made at the Eastern Counties Car Club at their adopted local circuit Snetterton on 3 April 1954. The results were, on the face of it, astounding. There were two races, a five-lapper (totalling 13.5 miles) for all comers, and a handicap event over the same distance, using the results of the first race. Archie, wearing a daubed-on number 3, stormed in 56 seconds ahead of a rueful Don Moore in the first race, and 61 seconds ahead of him, on a scratch basis, in the handicap – Archie having been given a weighting of 45 seconds. There were, though, only four cars in each event. Moore, of course, was giving away 500 cc of capacity, while Archie was giving away only 200 lb. in weight, so lithe was the Lister chassis. The 200 lb. was important, enabling Moore to outdrag Archie for about 100 yards, but once up and running, the Lister showed its mettle in the corners and the extra grunt of Don's engine on the straight.

This was a great start. Brian Lister had already entered the car and driver combination for the important British Empire Trophy race on 10 April, the next weekend. On the day after the Snetterton meeting, the Lister MG struggled in the Weathersfield US Airforce base sprint, apparently because of fuel starvation, but managed a third in the 1101–1500 cc class. It also got thumped rather hard in the paddock. The fuel system was checked over, blown through and pronounced fit; so the new team made the journey up to Oulton Park in Cheshire. Up to then, car and driver had driven a total of 27 miles of competitive circuit events. Despite this, confidence was high. On the way up to Cheshire on the Wednesday night, the team's first business trip, Jose was impressed by the way Archie, using only his left hand, managed to take a match from its box, light a cigarette and pass it to someone while driving at 70 mph. It was one of Archie's little vanities that he didn't use a lighter. The first practice session on Thursday, by any standards, went well. Archie qualified the car third in class, racing in his first national competition. The car was unaltered save for two conical covers to the headlamps, which was the cause of much ribald comment in the pits. They probably helped, though. The British Empire Trophy was a far cry from a few laps on a disused aerodrome; it was 71 miles long and the competition was severe. It was a blue riband event.

The 8-mm film taken by Jose Lister of the post-practice period is both revealing and poignant. Archie is asked for an autograph, which is something of a first. Seen climbing out of the Lister, numbered 48, he turns away to conceal his arm, his habitual quick grin perhaps a little fixed. Attention is on him and, it would seem, his first experience of the adulation he was later to receive is perhaps a little uncomfortable. One is struck by the difference between the slight diffidence displayed in the paddock and the total authority with which he drove the car.

Much worse than this was to come. Archie's extraordinary performance in practice had come to the attention of several of the other participants. One of them was Sid Greene, patron of the Essex-based Gilby engineering concern. The Gilby Maserati A6GCS, driven by Roy Salvadori with great style and skill, had done rather well, particularly at Castle Combe the previous weekend, where it had delivered fastest lap. Archie had not been at that meeting, as he was giving the Lister MG its second outing. Unlike some, Greene immediately spotted Archie's asymmetry. Archie's flamboyant driving style was almost guaranteed to draw attention to him.

Greene was himself one-armed. He had lost his left arm at the shoulder in an accident. He was a fine driver and enjoyed the sport from the point of view of an entrant and occasional participant in hillclimbs and sprints. Having no hand at all, Greene used to brace the steering wheel with his thigh while changing gear, which made for some interesting possibilities on the track, but, as Salvadori said, you got used to it. Whether Greene felt that Archie's competition licence was unmerited by his disability, in the light of Greene's own limited permit, we cannot be sure, but he complained to the Stewards nonetheless. Startled by his revelations, they went, in polite disbelief, to inspect Archie.

In order to be allowed to compete at club level with his new MG, Archie had applied for his own licence in late 1950, by post, as was the custom. When it came to the section which requested that the applicant volunteered any details of disabilities, he had written in his crabby left-handed script, 'fingers missing – right hand'. To be sure, it was an approximation of the truth, compounded by the omission of any mention of his feet, which were also without their full complement of digits, or his legs, which were without their full complement of bones.

Without further ado, once the stewards had had a closer look, his competition licence was summarily withdrawn. This event has been written up, by Archie's fans at least, as a heartless 'Star Chamber' decision. It is, however, only fair to say that the Stewards of the Competitions Committee had other priorities. While Archie had impressed all by his practice times, his style of driving was lurid, to say the least, and no one was to know whether or not he was making a virtue of necessity by driving so entertainingly, or whether he was an accident waiting to happen. It was not a risk that they felt that they could afford to take. They were in a situation from which they could not emerge with any credit whatever they did. The matter of Archie's handicaps having been brought to their attention, they had to address it. Had they permitted him to carry on, they risked culpability if something untoward had happened. After all, they bore a responsibility for more than this single race. There was also concern that the sport should not be seen as an activity for anyone but the fittest. They were, in short, in a corner. 'Scott Brown – the Ace they tried to ban' was the heading of an article written about him in 1958, which was not, in its sentiment, really an accurate reflection of the truth.

There was a right of appeal but, significantly, it was not to be led by Archie, who maintained a deadpan, if slightly tense, mien throughout the whole affair. If he felt himself to be the victim of discrimination, he said nothing. It was potentially a disaster, though. Conversely, it was merely another obstacle placed in the way of someone who had no real option but to press on regardless, one day at a time. Archie's young life had been beset by such difficulties, small and large, ranging from an inability to tie knots, which is why he wore ties so seldom, to difficulties in sports, most of which he overcame to a greater or lesser degree, and to his relationships with new acquaintances. He had learned, basically, to build a wall of disappointment around himself, which, if breached, was a cause for celebration rather than mere acceptance. This time, though, the experience hit him hard and he was facing the prospect of losing his career before it had really started. Despite Jay's efforts to instil in her son a sense of realism about his future, he was used to success and disliked contemplating failure.

Archie became almost clinically depressed. He spent more time in London, and his friends from outside his small world of racing rallied round in support, and thus it was that he was steered gently away from the path of pickled self-pity which had undone Bill so comprehensively. It is clear, though, that he had much in common with his father, at least emotionally, which goes some way to explain their gradual and slightly wary reconciliation.

Cliff Davis had introduced Archie to some of his friends, who when in London quite often hung about at the Little Club, a slightly seedy establishment in Knightsbridge, when they were not rubbing shoulders with the great and the good at the Steering Wheel Club in Brick Street. One of Davis's friends was David Blakely, who was pursuing, with no great difficulty, the manageress of the Little Club, Ruth Ellis. He and Archie became good friends, the more so as Blakely started to develop his own car, grandly named the Emperor, which was a Standard-powered special rather along the lines of a Lister, at least conceptually. He had the assistance of an ex-Aston Martin mechanic to help him, but Blakely was no engineer. It never did any good, but Archie and the raffish if spoilt Blakely got on well.

Archie was, however, even if a little blurred for a while, nothing if not realistic. Lister needed a driver for the car. Desmond Scannell, Secretary of the British Racing Driver's Club had produced the flamboyant Ken Wharton, who was currently minus a mount, and a one race deal had been struck. Wharton had driven the Lister MG to eighth place in the Empire Trophy heats, just missing the final. Oil pressure difficulties had slowed him drastically on the last lap of the heat, besides which, as an alternative driver, he was obliged to start from the back of the grid, not having practised.

Wharton, though, was a high profile character in the sport with an agenda of his own. He had already accomplished much as a professional driver, and ventures of this kind were not quite his style in a long-term sense. Archie had the bright idea that Jack Sears, then more or less unknown, might prove a good substitute and suggested him to Lister. The willingness with which Archie made this suggestion reveals the stoicism with which he accepted the hurdles in his life. It had turned him into a first-rate diplomat and problem-solver. Sears entered three races after getting to know the car at Snetterton, the first being at Brands Hatch nine days after Oulton Park. It was the Half-Litre Car Club meet and he came an honourable second. A fortnight later, at the Bugatti Owners' Club gathering at Prescott, in Gloucestershire, he managed 3rd in class.

The car did him better service at its home circuit, Snetterton, at the West Essex Car Club race meeting on 5 June. Sears won the 1500 cc race outright and came second in the resultant handicap.

While Sears had been familiarizing himself with the Lister MG, Archie's lobby had been hard at work. The minutes of the RAC committee do not reveal the precise details of the capitulation – suffice to say that the combined efforts of Gregor Grant, Earl Howe, Dr Benjafield and not a few of the drivers, including Stirling Moss and Anthony Crook, had quietly persuaded the committee that a second opinion on Archie's fitness to control a car, which was the central issue, was justified. They had, in fact already written to him offering a restricted sprint and hill climb licence, allowing him to drive alone on the track, which he had somewhat loftily refused. It wasn't that he disliked such events, merely that he felt, despite his earlier dissimulation over his handicap, that he merited more. The Stewards were eventually minded to agree, particularly after Dr Benjafield cleverly arranged that they all shake Archie by the hand to test his strength. He had little to lose so squeezed as hard as he could. This was a major ordeal for the unsuspecting committeemen, however much it may have amused Benjafield. Archie was strong enough to dice a rare steak with a fork and do two dozen single-handed press-ups. The committee met at the RAC's Pall Mall HQ for an all-day session covering this and other matters and Archie was notified by Earl Howe of the result by telegram, worded with great economy – 'Licence restored, Howe.' It missed him until the next morning, though, as he was elsewhere – not at all where he should have been and far from sober, having assumed the worst. Oddly, the committee had made no mention of Archie's legs and feet; it never became a matter of public knowledge that he lacked shins, for example, as the speed with which he moved led people to assume that he was merely shorter than average. If Benjafield knew, he didn't let on, and the issue of Archie's hand was the one upon which all the attention was focused, which was just as well. The possibility of a full competition licence being issued to someone so dreadfully stricken as Archie was, would have been, even in those enlightened days, a remote one.

The episode over the competition licence had needled Archie, though, and he was to throw himself into competition wholeheartedly from then on, but never so hard as when the Gilby Engineering Maserati was on the grid. The duels between Archie and Salvadori were to become things of legend. Archie bore no real malice over the affair, certainly not to Roy, he merely sought to push his point home as politely and professionally as possible. The pair's professional rivalry was to prevent them becoming truly close friends, but a sturdy mutual respect grew up between them. Salvadori put it this way about ten years after Archie's death:

> He was a tough … it was a wonderful sort of arrangement, he didn't want any quarter and he wasn't getting any. You had to fight with Archie the whole time to wear him down, very much more so than with other drivers. He was terribly with it – he was there all the time – he would fight back, he would never give up, but would fight back all the time. I cannot ever remember having any advantage because of his disability, and I must call it a disability. He had such magnificent car control – you would imagine, with this stump of an arm, that he would have to be very correct with a car. It was absolutely the opposite. He would have the thing drifting, sliding, continuously correcting where you would need three arms to control the steering wheel … You were led into the trap of thinking that he really couldn't control the car, but he did, he really did.

On Archie's sportsmanship and professionalism, Salvadori had this to say:

> One had to admire Archie, he was such a nice person … a nice person to win … If Jack Brabham wins today, everybody is delighted – you know, people reckon Jack. It was the same with Archie. If you are going to be beaten, then I would rather it was Archie than a long list of drivers that I could but won't name …. To be beaten by Archie you were going to have a nice person come up afterwards and say what a wonderful dice we had … he would never let you think it was his driving ability – he would say 'my car was quicker' – the nice things that a nice driver would say to make a second position feel, you know, a little more comfortable.

The Scott Brown 'fan club', which is to this day considerable, have probably been unfair to Greene over the affair of the licence, as they were later to be unfair to Masten Gregory or indeed anyone else who beat their favourite. More objective observers have noted that the whole issue was merely tawdry gamesmanship of a very low order indeed. The simple truth was that Greene, himself denied a full competition licence by virtue of the fact that he had lost an arm, felt that Archie should be denied one too. He viewed Archie as being similarly handicapped to himself; and the parallel was superficially persuasive. However, Greene had not always been one-armed, whereas Archie had always been one-handed. Archie did not of course consider himself to be remotely handicapped, merely different, a semantic inexactitude with which he had battled from the cradle. Greene had had to come to terms with a loss. The approach to dealing with loss is not the same as the approach to dealing with being different, as Douglas Bader was later to point out to Archie in the course of their relationship when they co-operated for the benefit of charity. It is even possible that there was never any serious risk of Archie losing his licence at all. Earl Howe, not a natural bureaucrat, had after all confided to Bill Scott Brown over dinner on the Friday night that the protest started off as a ruse by Greene to get a drive, and that the whole thing was little more than a crude ambush which got rather out of hand. Whatever the truth of it, and the records are lost bar the basic minutes, it had been a dreadful fright which had tested Archie's resolve almost to destruction.

Thus, on 7 June, after the two worst months of his adult life, he too came second at the Half-Litre Car Club meet at Brands Hatch, just as Sears had done. Honour was satisfied, and experience gained. He tigered round the 20-lap race, but failed to beat Peter Gammon in a Lotus-MG. He did set fastest lap, though, and set a 1500 cc lap record of 67.3 mph which was to stand for most of the season.

He was to have trouble with Gammon for the rest of the season. He came second to the Lotus driver the next weekend at the MCMC meeting at Oulton Park, again at Snetterton at the AMOC meet and yet again back at Oulton Park for the Half-Litre Car Club race.

All these seconds were simply not good enough. The reliability and stability of both chassis and driver had been well proven, but more poke was needed. The Lister-MG had proved much, not least that it was a well-constructed machine possessed of almost neutral and viceless handling which would probably accept a powerplant of a more exciting nature. It had been conceived as a chassis capable of taking up to two litres initially. No-one was to know that eventually it, or something very like it, would carry engines of up to $5\frac{1}{2}$ litres, pushing out 450 bhp and more.

Everyone was content that the car worked very well conceptually, and was capable of further development. So, the search began for an engine which would permit the chassis to reach out towards its potential. No-one had to look very far, in fact.

As for Archie himself, he took the view that the licence episode was done and dusted and that he was now free to make more progress. The driving style which had started to entertain the spectators so much was still in its infancy. The more powerful the cars were to become, the more spectacular was his handling of them. Whether or not he actually needed to drive them by the scruff of the neck or whether he was merely showing off, no-one was ever sure. Classically, the tail-out, drifting style which he developed and made his own should have a negative effect on lap times, compared to the clipped economy of Fangio or Brooks, who both used the racing line to its limits, but stayed pointing straight ahead as much as they could. Certainly, Archie took up a lot of road, but was never considered to be anything but the safest of opponents by his peers, whether driving sports cars or, later, Formula 1.

Broadly, he subscribed to the view that brakes slow a car down so that they should be used as little as possible on a circuit. There is a case for this; ask any rally driver. There is no doubt in anyone's mind, however, that Archie enjoyed driving as much for the flamboyance it allowed him to display as for winning itself. He only made the mistake of showing off once; he was on the last lap at Snetterton in 'Emma' and broke his concentration to wave to his photographer friend, the late George Phillips. He spun off, hitting the bank, and finished third. Afterwards, Phillips explained in a few choice words the virtue of winning a race as slowly as possible and not showing off. Although he was to become much more serious about winning as his career developed and the stakes rose, he was basically in it for the fun of it. Here, he differed radically from his yardstick, Moss, and to a lesser extent from many other drivers on the circuit. His competition with them was almost as much a matter of style as it was of victory. He pursued his pleasures after the races, however, with the same determination as most, and with much more than many.

The Archie style, though, was now established, at least in terms of sports car racing. Formula 1 was something else, as he was to discover ruefully. His philosophy was simple – it is easier to corner a car with your foot hard down than it is to take the slow in, fast out approach. His sense of balance was quite uncanny; he seemed to be able to feel, literally through the seat of his pants, one cheek to another, as it were when a car was going out of balance and correct it before it started to go. It was and is a rare skill, and totally unassociated directly with his handicap. Some take the view that nature compensates and this may be so; others have remarked that Archie was not handicapped in any way for racing, rather the contrary – his build was an advantage. Short, immensely strong, with the sort of balance that enabled him to sit still on a bicycle for minutes on end, he might have been purpose-built for the job. This is a very tempting conclusion at which to arrive but it was one which few shared during Archie's brief life.

Of the concern which some drivers may have felt, that Archie was not entirely safe, as reflected by the impression which he gave of not quite being in control, Stirling Moss had this to say:

> As far as I was concerned I always found him a tough driver. Not dirty. He
> would be a man to beat in the same way that Jack Sears was a man to beat,
> Roy Salvadori was a man to beat .... When practice times came out, one of
> the men you'd look at first was Archie and you would expect Archie to be
> the quickest ... therefore you would consider him to be a definite threat in
> a race. This is the highest honour you can bestow upon a man when you
> say, 'Christ, I wonder what old Archie's doing.' I did not at any time feel
> worried if I was alongside him in a corner. He was a clean driver and he
> worked hard.

Salvadori in 1968, on the same subject, is a little more detailed:

> Well, I would have thought that anyone shying away from Archie would
> have been a bit of a freak himself. As I said, when you knew this man, he
> was just a bloody fine driver and that was the end of it. You didn't consider
> him as anything other than a super driver, a very good team mate and
> somebody nice to drive against. After all ... let's put the boot on the other
> foot. I was dicing with Archie at 150–160 mph. I wouldn't have wanted to
> be anywhere near Archie if I had any doubts about his capability because
> he could have involved me, and I used to drive very hard against Archie.
> When I could nip in to corners, braking late, I would do it to him, and he
> would do it to me – you can imagine what would have been in my mind if
> I hadn't thought he was in perfect control, because that could have
> involved me. Every driver who drove against him had complete confidence
> in his ability to handle a car because we were the ones who would have
> been involved and we would have complained, not the spectators, if he
> couldn't have coped with the situation.

Archie, like his peers, had mastered the technique of 'drifting' a car,
and it's a fanciful thought that he perhaps first developed this on the
dusty half-made roads of Paisley and Castlehead in ASB 38. It would
be nice to think so.

The received wisdom concerning cornering is that you brake before
them and accelerate out of them. That is fine for the road. On the
track, to slide into a corner, the car pointing the way it will need to be
for the next straight, can, done properly, save precious fractions of seconds per lap, more if the car is in the lead, as it obviously takes up
more road. Of course, the method by which a road car is driven well
and safely bears as much relationship to the way in which a racing car
is driven competitively as it does to pole-vaulting or knitting.

The use of a hard dab on the brakes approaching the corner, while
under power as the wheel is turned, is the essence of the power-
induced final oversteer which Archie turned into his trademark. The
dab on the brakes unsticks the driven wheels from the road, and the
use of a de Dion rear end, which kept the driving wheels upright,

assisted the driver greatly in governing the degree of slide of the driven wheels. More throttle, less grip. Less grip and the rear of the car breaks away centrifugally to orientate it into its next chosen path, at which point the driver recovers from the slide, straightens out the wheels and applies power in the normal manner. In this way, as we can see from the two maps which Archie himself later produced for *Motor Racing* magazine, the car seems to move sideways into the corner, steered on the throttle, ready for the next straight, or the next corner. He is not exaggerating the attitude of the car, as those who saw him race, or who have seen film of him, will testify. The result of all the manoeuvring is that as the car comes out of the corner, it is set up for the straight. Such styles are difficult to replicate now, as tyres are wider, with softer sidewalls and cars are designed to generate huge downforce over the driven wheels – in a sideways drift, at an angle to the intended direction of the car, downforce is lost, with predictably catastrophic results. Downforce was still a thing of the future in the mid-1950s.

The tyres used by sports racing cars 40 years ago were tall, narrow and cross-plied, with a high natural rubber content, as well as inner tubes. The sidewalls were immensely rigid, offering huge resistance to sidethrust, and a smaller proportion of the 'footprint' of the tyre was in contact with the road than it would be today. This sounds risky, and it is. To hold a car in a deliberate slide depended upon the ability to generate an early controlled breakaway, by the dab on the brakes, as well as the sense of balance to control the traction of the driven wheels via, not the steering, but the throttle.

Both Archie and Salvadori were masters at it, which made their duels all the more exciting, given that they both drove in the same fashion, with miniscule adjustments to the wheel being made constantly to reposition, and thus anticipate, the attitude of the car. Naturally, the more powerful the car the greater the control that such a type of driver can exert upon it, provided that the technique remains consistent. As we shall see, in Archie's case, the increase in power/weight ratio which the Listers were to enjoy over their life ensured that Archie was able to refine his technique in the same exponential way. Given his sense of balance, as well as his absurd strength, he was well able to keep up with both Brian Lister's chassis and brake improvements, as well as whatever extra grunt Don Moore could produce for the power plant. He had proved his ability well in the MG-powered car – he was to refine that ability towards the level of art with his next conveyance.

Tiger

THE Bristol car company had, since 1952, been selling engines to all comers after their bilateral arrangement with Frazer Nash had foundered. The engine was, in effect – ahem – a spoil of war, being largely a copy of the BMW 2-litre unit as installed in the famous 328 sports. The story goes that H. R. Aldington of AFN, the pre-war BMW agents and Frazer Nash BMW manufacturer, walked into the wrecked BMW works in 1945 and catalogued all the parts and drawings necessary for manufacture to take place in Britain. An RAF Stirling bomber, loaded with the necessary material, flew it all to Filton shortly afterwards.

Archie knew this engine well; he had borrowed his father's 327 on several occasions, the last time when Bill had embarked upon his drying-out cruise to Cape Town. Don Moore, as a master craftsman in the field of tuning, knew it better – he actually understood how it worked.

The Bristol 2-litre BS4 engine, 66 mm bore by 96 mm stroke, giving 1971 cc, had become a favourite workhorse of the specialist manufacturers; it had already appeared in a Cooper chassis in 1952, a combination which had helped to get Mike Hawthorn started. Its success in Cliff Davis's Tojeiro-Bristol, LOY 500, had already triggered the Hurlock family to push the AC Ace, progenitor of the Cobra, into production. It was a sound, reliable, tuneable unit with almost all of its bugs ironed out.

It was also very, very tall. Not only was it possessed of a long stroke; it used an overhead valve layout operated by crossover pushrods – it looked like a twin cam, but it wasn't. On top of this, literally, it used three 32 mm downdraught carbs complete with chubby pancake filters; it was $2\frac{1}{2}$ ft. high. There was another price to pay for these carburettors; the space on the side of the faithful transporter, previously occupied by the logo of the SU company had to be left blank; the

Bristol unit used Solex devices, and neither Bristol nor Solex were buying.

The use of this engine necessitated a slight reworking of the basic BHL 1 layout. The modification of the bodywork design was a minor obstacle; Wakefields delivered a second body very similar to the first, save a high streamlined blister to accommodate the air filters under the bonnet. It was painted the same green, but the yellow stripe was widened from 4 in. to 15 in., which had the effect of rather camouflaging the hump in the bonnet.

An 11 in. brake alternative was used and track was marginally increased to 50.5 in. front and 50 in. rear. Dunlop 4½J centrelock wires replaced the Rubery Owen discs of the MG-engined car. Tyres were 550x16. BHL 1 had been designed to accommodate engines of up to 2 litres, so here was BHL 2's chance to prove it. It was to do so in a quite startling manner.

Don Moore took advantage of the bolt-on parts offered by the Bristol works to uprate the engine, as well as carrying out his usual polishing, porting, jetting and balancing. Bristol offered a proprietary conversion to provide a precise gear-drive, as opposed to the standard but slightly inexact chain drive, to the cam. This allowed a higher rev limit and more precision in the valve timing, which, when coupled with the Moore tuning, gave the engine exceptional breathing and top-end power – something in the region of 155 bhp at 5750 rpm. The bottom end was much stronger than the MG since it had five main bearings, as opposed to three, supporting the crank more evenly along its length. The car was, altogether, an entirely different animal from the MG-engined one, but BHL 1 was still entered from time to time for the rest of the 1954 season. This second Lister was registered MVE 303. Consistent to a fault, Archie spun off while testing.

On 17 July 1954, first time out with the new car, Archie came first in the 2-litre class and fifth in the unlimited class at the RAC International at Silverstone. He was beaten by three works Aston Martins and a D-Type Jaguar. The Astons, driven by Peter Collins, Roy Salvadori and Carroll Shelby, used engines of 3 litres, the Jaguar D-Type being 3.4 litres. He also entered the MG-powered car in the 1500 cc race and came seventh, despite trying very hard, suggesting that the move to Bristol power was a sensible one. The prototype car had been very strong, but just too heavy for its engine.

It was the first televised race that Horace Lister, or many others, for that matter, had seen. As a businessman he was captivated by the publicity. His investment had long since increased from the initial £1500 – more than doubled – in fact, but he was starting, in retirement, to see the true benefit. National coverage for free. Clearly, this had been a sensible investment. It has certainly been paying off ever since.

Before the class win at Silverstone, the team opened up the transporter to find a small parcel awaiting them, a gift from Horace and Nell Lister. Inside was a toy black cat, wrapped in a Cambridge blue scarf. It was to become the team's, and more particularly Archie's talisman. From that moment on, he carried it everywhere when he drove a Lister car. He was only to forget it once.

A straw in the wind for the rest of the season had been the success enjoyed by Roy Salvadori in the Gilby Engineering Maserati A6GCS, XEV 601. Salvadori and Scott Brown fought some ferocious battles, to be echoed when Salvadori drove again for Aston Martin against Archie in the 1957 season. Had the Lister team realized the problems which Greene and Salvadori were putting up with, Listers might have reconsidered their next power source.

One race that Archie was forced to miss was the 25 September BARC International at Goodwood. Despite the restitution of his competition licence, there was still some doubt whether his entries would be accepted by the BARC. At this stage they were minded to refuse him. For that event he left MVE 303 in the capable hands of Stirling Moss, who came a close second to Salvadori in the Maserati. Very close – 3/5ths of a second is about as close as you could get. Stirling set fastest lap, though, at 83.7 mph.

Archie was quietly delighted with this result. He had won against Salvadori at Snetterton the previous month, so for Salvadori to beat Moss while Moss was driving Archie's car was very good news indeed. Whatever their professional rivalry from then on, Archie was always to be grateful to Roy for that victory. After the humiliation of Oulton Park it was vindication of the most convincing kind, and bolstered his morale greatly. It puffed his ego not at all. He was watching the race with Iain McWilliam and Eileen Price, who were to be married the next weekend – Archie was to be Iain's best man. It was a job he took seriously; not only was Iain his closest and oldest friend, but he had introduced the couple. Eileen and her circle of friends, mainly in the theatre as she was an actress, had been massively supportive of Archie at the time of the licence episode, and he was never to forget their generosity.

The season finished on a high note back at Snetterton at the Eastern Counties Car Club race on 16 October. Archie and MVE 303 won the 1501–2500 cc sports car race and achieved fastest lap in the handicap. Undeterred by the end of the season, he campaigned his new Ford Zephyr, NJJ 414, flamboyantly painted in Lister livery, in driving tests and a rally organized by the Cambridge University Auto Club.

High Performance Cars, the seasonal summary annual published by *Autosport* magazine ranked him third for his performance in the Lister-MG in the up to 1500 cc class for 1954. No team could really ask for more. The équipe decided to mothball the Lister-MG at the end of the season, because of its apparent uncompetitiveness, but it was to be torn down and born again before long.

Archie had encountered difficulties with his right arm at this level of competition. From then on, he religiously soaked his vestigial hand in surgical spirit, and carefully wrapped it in tape and gauze in order to avoid the raw and often bloody abrasions which constant pressure on the wheel was causing. That aspect of suffering for his art was never to get any better. The more powerful the car, the more it hurt; it was, however, a price which he paid more than willingly.

His style developed again with the more powerful Lister-Bristol. The responsiveness of the engine, coupled with the higher power/weight ratio and relatively massive torque, permitted him even more excesses of style. He was becoming more consistent, one of the glittering prizes of competition driving; learning from his mistakes, which were not frequent, but tended to be as spectacular as his successes. He damaged the Lister-Bristol a few times, and Lister took the opportunities offered in repairing the car to gradually modify it to its final form, which was a far cry from the rather slabby body with which it had started life. The Lister-Bristol was, stage by stage, becoming an extremely elegant piece of kit.

The car aroused much curiosity. Alan Brown, who had won the 1954 Empire Trophy race in his Cooper-Bristol, asked Brian if he could try the car out. Perhaps he might buy one himself. At Goodwood, in October, he was approaching Woodcote corner and, about 100 yards before it, gave the wheel a twist to generate a slide. The car promptly went off to the right, and gouged its way into the infield, throwing up a rooster tail of earth and debris, and mud was packed into the wheels and arches. The car was possessed of entirely neutral handling, whereas Brown had expected understeer.

The crash which Archie had at Brands Hatch, which could have been terminal, was eloquent testimony to the general unawareness of his handicaps, despite the furore which they had caused for insiders. He slid the Lister up a bank and overturned it. A marshal approached, fearing the worst and was initially relieved that the driver was crawling out. Archie had gashed his forehead quite deeply and a slice had been taken out of his stump; both bled profusely. The marshal, faced with a man with a bloodied face and what appeared to be a cruelly amputated hand, promptly fainted. Archie, who may have thought that the poor man was pretending, attempted to kick him back to consciousness – not through any sense of malice, mind you, merely disbelief.

Lister had learned much, too. For his first effort at a car entirely of his own design to have gone so well was a cause for great pride, but Brian was and is not a man to rest on laurels, either his or his driver's. As the MG and Bristol-powered works cars were raced, they were constantly modified – from the conical protruberances of the early cars, to the downward-pointing air scoop on the MG, to the final

A rare photograph of an aeroplane which was not as rare as it should have been. It is believed to have been taken by Bill Scott Brown in April 1916 shortly before he was downed, and shows a Vickers FB5 'Gunbus' of No. 11 Squadron in flight. Scott Brown was certainly reprimanded in the spring of 1916 for taking such pictures. The serial number indicates that it is not Bill's plane, but it is recognizable as an FB5 from the skids at the nose, the squared-off gondola and the Lewis gun. Most of the Squadron had FB9s by the time Bill was shot down. (Imperial War Museum)

Bill Scott Brown (extreme right) and Bill Phelan as POWs in Germany. Their two companions are, by their uniforms, French infantrymen. (Moira Scott Brown)

Above left Jay Scott Brown. A picture taken during the Great War. (G. McLachlan)

Above July 1930. Archie (right) and his cousin Gordon McLachlan on the dunes, Ayrshire. (G. McLachlan)

Left A family group at Paisley, 1936. Bill and Jay extreme left and right, Archie and Gordon in front. (G. McLachlan)

Above right July 1939. Archie and an early girlfriend at Hallsands, Devon. (G. McLachlan)

Above far right July 1939. The same holiday. The car is a Rover. (G. McLachlan)

Right Archie, shortly before wrapping ASB 38 around the gateposts. (G. McLachlan)

Left July 1939. More conventionally boyish pursuits. No angel, this. (G. McLachlan)

Below Jay with ASB 38. As Archie grew, the body had to be removed to accommodate him.

Right 1947. Brian Lister, still in RAF uniform, working hard with the Downbeats. Impossible to drum with any conviction and wear a dinner jacket at the same time anyway. (Brian Lister)

Below right Brian Lister with his lightened Morgan 4/4. (Guy Griffiths)

You can tell by its wheels that it is a Cooper. Brian with Jose and his Cooper-MG.

The feral and temperamental Tojeiro-JAP 'Asteroid' at Histon where it was garaged.

This started off its life as an MG TD. Bottisham 1951 was the first time Brian clapped eyes on Archie in competition. Shortly afterwards, Archie was offered the 'Asteroid' to drive. (R. P. Bowyer)

Some members of the Cambridge '50 Car Club pictured outside the Cambridge Playhouse in early 1951. Archie's MG, 'Emma', still looks fairly normal, and had yet to reach the severely abused condition in which it ended its competitive career. Ahead of it is Brian's Cooper-MG. Shortly after this picture was taken, Archie managed to scrape off the front wings on a bridge buttress. (Brian Lister)

Archie developing his style in the Tojeiro at Thruxton. (A. Hollister)

View of the first Lister chassis. (Bruce)

December 1953. The first test of the Lister-MG chassis at Snetterton circuit, before it received its Wakefield body. This was the occasion when the half-shaft seized, propelling Archie and the Lister into the countryside. Brian is wearing the light cap, Don Moore is attending to the engine and Archie is in the seat, waiting for the off.

The completed car, less screen, at Histon. Clearly, Archie views this as a significant occasion. It was.

Archie was never much of a rallying fan unless he did all the driving. As an honorary member of the Cambridge University Auto Club, he was eligible for the Intervarsity Rally. Here, the event is over and he seems quite relieved.

This is a well-known picture. Archie, looking relaxed, having retrieved his licence, in the 1954 manifestation of the Lister-Bristol in the paddock at Castle Combe, 28 August 1954. Behind him is the Equipe's Fordson transporter. The bodywork, apart from the bonnet, is similar to the Lister-MG.

Roy Salvadori chatting to Archie and Brian Lister before the off. Salvadori won the race in his Gilby Maserati A6GCS; Archie was second. It was one of many ferocious duels which the two would contest. They were to develop a sturdy mutual respect.

Engine diagnosis. Don Moore inspecting the Bristol engine. Note its height. (J. H. Horsman)

Above Archie, Brian and Don undertaking their duties at the Motor Agents' Association Ball in Cambridge at the end of the 1954 season. The car was to mutate over the winter into its final form. (Bruce)

Below left Archie as best man to his best friend, Iain McWilliam, September 1954. (Portman Press Bureau Ltd)

Below right Archie chatting in the paddock just before the off at Silverstone on 7 May 1955.

Archie with Lord Brabazon at the RAC Club in 1955. The painting, by Cavendish Morton, is of Archie winning the 1955 Empire Trophy Race at Oulton Park. It still stands in the members bar at the RAC's HQ in Pall Mall. (Autocar)

The 1955 Lucas-designed 'Dan Dare' Lister-Bristol. The design was faithfully adhered to, although all the cars differed from each other in minor ways. This one was to go to Noel Cunningham-Reid. (Bruce)

Above left Alan Moore, slightly out of line in Ormsby Issard-Davies's Lister-Bristol in 1955.

Below left Roy Salvadori, in a Lister-Bristol, causing the marshalling team to sprint for cover at Castle Combe on 1 October 1955. *(Pike and Rew)*

Above Archie taking the long way round at Brands Hatch on 1 August 1955. He is driving Noel Cunningham-Reid's Lister-Bristol, while his own is fettled. In one manoeuvre, he has overtaken Cliff Davis's Tojeiro-Bristol, a C-Type Jaguar and an Aston Martin DB3S, and is challenging a Lotus-Bristol. *(Charles Dunn)*

Right . . . Seconds later, at Bottom Bend, Archie is in second place, the Lotus having held the lead, but not for much longer. *(Autocar)*

Below Not everyone had Archie's deft touch. Jack Sears was lucky to limp away from this one at Silverstone.

SPEED WITH SAFETY

Lockheed

REGD. TRADE MARK

Hydraulic Brakes

Archie heads for his first Formula 1 victory on Boxing Day 1955. The car is a Connaught B-Type. He set fastest lap in the process. It was not yet the top of the tree, being a relatively minor event, but for someone who had lost their racing licence only 18 months before it was encouraging. Archie was to lead the Connaught team at home for 1956. (Geoffrey Goddard)

It does not say so, but this Lockheed advert in November 1955 clearly shows Archie in his Empire Trophy Lister-Bristol.

manifestation of the Bristol car, with no headlights at all, merely a gracefully faired-in front end, with a longer nose intake. It was in this guise that the Lister-Bristol works car was to end its days before being metamorphosed into the greatest Lister of all. By the end of the Lister Bristol era, though, the vehicle was a proper racer, with no serious pretensions to road use. It was fettled and modified through the winter of 1954–55 to emerge as an entirely different car. As much as 40 lb. of weight was shaved off the chassis and a ZF limited-slip differential was installed. This device was not cheap, nor was it entirely trouble-free, but it transformed the handling, along with a more robust roll bar at the front. As well as losing its headlights, which were an unnecessary luxury (costly and needing frequent replacement) MVE 303 had a large area of its rear deck replaced by a canvas tonneau cover, rather like Brian's old Tojeiro, which preserved the airflow characteristics but saved more precious pounds. Brian had secured the services of Thomas Lucas, a Cambridge University engineer, to design bodies for customer cars, and many of the improvements were suggested by him.

Don Moore reworked the porting on the three-port Bristol head a little and experimented with different valve springs and valve timings. He probably squeezed as much out of the three-port Bristol unit as anybody ever had. The six-port engine, with improved breathing, would have been a major improvement, but the architecture of the Bristol unit really militated against its continued application. Given the need for a generally low line of the car, the tall engine made that objective difficult. It simply could not be canted over enough to hide its height, besides which Brian and Don were already considering a new power source which, apart from being a contemporary piece of engineering (rather than essentially pre-war), had already apparently proven itself under competition conditions.

Archie spent the winter chewing his nails, waiting for the off. He was a man easily bored, particularly when there was no racing to be done, and one for whom inactivity of any kind was hard to bear. He chucked himself into his social life that winter, his enthusiasm for which nearly wrecked his career.

Always a little bit of an opportunist where women were concerned, Archie overdid it in November 1954. When offering a lone female a lift to London from Cambridge, he was loading her suitcase into the rear seat of his Ford when he slipped a disc. Wincing but undeterred, he drove her to London, but upon his return Peter Riley took him straight to Addenbrookes Hospital, where he was subjected to the humiliation of being stripped naked and wrapped in a plaster cast after the physiotherapists had done their work. Obviously, Archie disliked plaster casts, having found out rather more about them than he wished when young. He found the ordeal of being manhandled, as it were, by a pair of nurses even more irritating. The air was blue as Archie hung suspended in traction, having wet plaster smeared all over him. 'I'll get you buggers!' was apparently one of his more articulate remarks. He was later to recount that he had 'got' one of them, at least. He generally liked nurses, actually, as they tended to be less discomfited by his structure than some.

Archie was a frequent visitor to Addenbrookes, both as out-patient and entertainer, but attended the physiotherapy department as seldom as possible, except on his own terms. His plaster cast did not stop him from leaping into 'Emma' and haring up to Glasgow for the annual Dobie's dinner dance at Christmas.

Upon his arrival he was greeted with an enthusiastic if slightly vinegary welcome. The sales figures were good, even excellent, but was it really necessary to throw riverboat parties on the Cam and spend *that much* on comestibles?

The incident had nearly got him into serious trouble. The barman hired for the evening had been one of the few available that side of May week and Archie soon discovered why. The man was a drunk. Worse, he was a mischievous drunk. Even worse, he spoke hardly any English, being from Poland, so Archie had great difficulty explaining his fury when the guests started falling overboard as their spiked drinks started to overcome them.

Archie loathed drunks. He had every right to do so, given his experience of having one at home for so much of his life. Bill, though, was coming up fast, certain in the knowledge that the risk of ridiculing his son was not one which he could afford to take. He had been through hell to stop drinking, and resolved to stay teetotal for ever. As the two became closer, observers noted a distinct element of role reversal – almost as if the son was becoming the father and vice versa. Archie, ever aware of the ease with which it is possible to fall off the wagon, even took to checking the contents of mustard jars if he was eating with Bill, just in case the mustard was French – it might have wine in it.

Chapter 7

1955 – 'A man to beat'

FOR 1955, customer cars started to become available. Archie's success in 1954, four wins and a host of places, had potential clients beating a path to Abbey Road. Chassis were supplied in kit form to avoid purchase tax, with a choice of Wakefield bodies – either a barchetta body or a more aggressive design by Thomas Lucas with a front very similar to the works car, and two inward leaning fins at the rear. There were also horizontal strakes over the front wheelarches à la Mercedes 300 SL. Very Dan Dare and very effective, too. The first client car, BHL 3, was so bodied for Ormsby Issard-Davies. It was registered VPP 9.

The chassis of these vehicles were similar to the revised works car. The same structure was employed, with the addition of 12 in. Dunlop disc brakes and the same lightening procedure. The Lucas cars used a metal rear deck, though.

All in all, four Lucas-bodied cars were completed by the works – for Issard-Davies, Bill Black/Jack Sears, John Green and Noel Cunningham-Reid. They were chassis BHL 3, 4, 5 and 6. The rest were of the barchetta type until 1956 when a new style came in. A client could, of course, put his own body on. The Murkett brothers, of whom more later, ordered chassis BHL 8, into which they fitted a Rover P4 engine, which seemed like a good idea at the time, and even achieved a class win on one occasion. The cast-iron overhead-inlet, side-exhaust engine, though, was not up to much in competition terms. It caused a measure of ploughing at the front end – the car being reluctant to go where the engine wanted to. This car later had a Jaguar XK unit fitted and now resides in a German museum. It thus had the dubious distinction of being the only barchetta-bodied Lister with a Jaguar engine. It now wears a later body. That its frame was possibly not strong enough to support the weight and output of the engine is clear but this potential weakness was seldom, if ever, put to the test. Perhaps that is the reason why it is in a museum rather than on the circuit.

Archie's season began with his customary effort at the Cambridge

University Auto Club speed trials, held that year at Tempsford on 6 March. Driving Peter Riley's Peugeot 203, he came second in his class. If this seems tame stuff when compared to events like the British Empire Trophy, then it must be borne in mind that most drivers at a good club level, even at National or International level, regularly took part in low-key events. The enormous variance between the vehicles involved sat oddly with no-one. This was not, after all, the age of the specialist driver; rather it was the age of the complete enthusiast. Even then, some drivers eschewed club racing as soon as they possibly could, when works drives beckoned. As the technology of racing developed, though, with the resultant specializations which that development brought with it, it was to become less and less possible for drivers to spread themselves so thinly. Also, as casualties mounted, simple shortages of talent manifested themselves. Archie's generation of drivers were the last of the generalists – one weekend a saloon car trial or a sprint, the next a Formula 1 event or a World Championship sports car race. Owners and entrants were under more and more pressure to secure driving talent, and had started to pay up for it. In return, drivers were expected to concentrate their talents first in the direction of their paymasters, and later their sponsors.

The first competitive outing of the revamped Lister-Bristol was at the SMRC (Snetterton Motor Racing Club) meeting at Snetterton on 26 March. In the 1500–2000 cc class Archie set fastest lap and came first. In the Formule Libre race which followed, he came second to Roy Salvadori, who drove the Gilby Engineering Maserati 250F F1 car to an easy victory. Salvadori and Greene had, in the winter of 1954, decided that the Maserati A6GCS was no longer competitive. They were later to regret their decision to insert the engine and transmission from this car into a modified Cooper-Bristol Mk 1 chassis. Maurice Gomm bodied it, but it was an embarrassing though pretty failure and the équipe looked to Roy's ex-works Aston Martin DB3S to deliver results in sports car racing from then on.

The next weekend was the British Empire Trophy at Oulton Park. This was probably Archie's most important race so far. Having been humiliatingly excluded the previous year in the Lister-MG, he had everything to go for and, arguably, everything to lose. He was somewhat tense at Blossom's Hotel in Chester, where the teams stayed – despite qualifying on pole position for his heat – and on the morning of the race suffered his usual butterflies, nausea and constipation. It drizzled on race day, and Archie behaved with great maturity in the first heat, not pushing the issue too much with Reg Parnell, who was driving the Aston DB3S used by Salvadori at Silverstone the previous July, with its new 2.5-litre engine. As the rain looked threatening, Archie, in the lead, eased off and allowed Parnell to nip past and win the heat by 17 seconds. Lister had been concerned that Archie might ruin the car trying to win and had signalled caution. Archie was not always to be so co-operative, particularly when racing against the David Brown équipe and the tactic spoke volumes about his burgeoning maturity.

The field for the final was perhaps a little awe-inspiring. As well as the Aston Team entries, George Abecassis was there with his HWM Jaguar, Duncan Hamilton in a D-Type Jaguar, Ken McAlpine in a Connaught as well as assorted Mercedes, Healeys and Ferraris. It was not an easy race; the track was soaked and draining poorly.

Archie made an extraordinary start; by the end of lap one he was clear of Parnell by 200 yards. After 13 laps, Archie lay second on handicap, behind McAlpine. He had been rather concerned at the handicap weightings. Then, he went for it. He was still second to McAlpine with ten to go and 30 seconds to make up. He pulled out the stops and drove at least at ten tenths for six laps. On lap 21, he was dicing with the Connaught for the lead. He took McAlpine on the 22nd lap and pulled away, extending his lead to take the flag at an average speed of just over 73.5 mph. At the end, he was 25 seconds ahead of McAlpine and 40 seconds in front of Parnell. It was a total triumph, provoking screams of delight from the Lister pit, particularly from Marion Armour, his friend from Kilmacolm. Archie allowed only a little of his deadpan facade to crumble; he treated triumph and disaster in a properly Kiplingesque manner. Brian was exultant – Jose less so; she knew all along that Archie would win. Not only had Archie driven a brilliant race, he had help. The Lister pit was No. 9, her lucky number; the Listers' bedroom at Blossom's was 54 and Archie's race number was 36. The omens were insufficiently powerful to stop her tearing her new trousers as she leaped off the pit counter to congratulate the winner, however. The Lister win was hugely popular with the crowd, and Archie was surrounded by a sea of frantic well-wishers.

It was a big win financially, too. The Lister works grossed £750 in starting and prize money, of which Archie's share was about £170. From then on Lister and Scott Brown established a formula which they more or less adhered to for the whole of Archie's time with them. Broadly, Archie would take between ten and 25 per cent of organizer's and commercial backer's starting money, and around 50 per cent of the prize money. Any bonus payments from sponsors or organizers in excess of prizes, for the fastest lap, or the quickest practice, for example, would be treated like the starting money. For the Empire Trophy the team was given starting money by the BRDC, Shell, Dunlop, Lodge, Lucas and Ferodo. It was becoming quite a decent living, compared to selling tobacco. Here were people actually paying him to do the thing he loved most.

The party at Blossom's that night was predictably something of a riot. There was a formal dinner for Archie, with Gerald Lascelles on one side of him and Marion Armour on the other. Archie spoke after dinner, but not before trotting down to the end of the U-shaped table to check that Bill was OK. Whether he was concerned about Bill's mustard or the service he was receiving is uncertain. He seemed satisfied, though, and proceeded to send the boozy dinner into paroxysms. Jose was asked to say a few words as well, and in inviting her to do so, John Eason-Gibson grabbed the chance to administer a modest ticking off for filming the race from a restricted area.

All there who had seen him after the last Empire Trophy, sat back with a certain quiet satisfaction. Their protégé and hero seemed well in control; all the efforts that had gone into his rehabilitation the previous year were justified. Those who had gone out on a limb had had their efforts repaid with interest. They were, of course, many. Most of the Clixie club became incoherent and bore Archie off to a sort of away game gaudy. It was what *they* wanted, even if it was probably the last thing on their hero's mind.

Gregor Grant, one of Archie's most vociferous supporters after the licence incident, was fiercely exultant. 'Archie Scott-Brown [sic] ... has quickly jumped to the forefront of Britain's motor racing conductors,' he wrote in the leading article in *Autosport*, of which he was Editor.

After Oulton Park it got better, if that is possible, as the last barriers to Archie's entries in national events were lifted. Archie was admitted to the ranks of the BRDC (member No. 707) and, from then on, was seldom seen without the club sweater. The next weekend the team was down at Goodwood for the BARC International race meeting. His entry had, this time round, been confirmed with alacrity. Archie set fastest lap and won the 2000 cc sports car race. If the news of the death of his friend Blakely the previous night, shot three times by Ruth Ellis outside a North London pub, distracted him at all from the task in hand, he concealed his distress very well. If there were any other drivers hoping for a Lister works drive, then their hopes were to wither for the rest of that season.

On 16 April, he was closer to ethnically home territory at the Winfield Joint Committee national race meeting at Charterhall in Berwickshire. This time he won the sports car race for up to 2700 cc sports cars, setting fastest lap, and repeated this in the unlimited sports car race. This, like many of the victories in the Lister-Bristol, was a remarkable achievement against a grid of much more powerful cars, complete with experienced drivers. Unlimited meant just that. Any car over 2700 cc qualified as an unlimited entry – the Lister-Bristol was three quarters of a litre shy of that.

A fortnight later, on 30 April, he won the West Hants and Dorset Car Club event for 1501–2750 cc cars at Ibsley, near Ringwood.

On 28 May he was back at Snetterton for the West Essex Car Club meeting. He won the sports car race for cars up to 2000 cc, once again setting fastest lap, and winning the unlimited sports car race and was placed second in the Formule Libre Curtis Trophy event as well. The sight of Archie in a 2-litre sports car coming second to Salvadori in a proper Grand Prix car as well as beating a Cooper-Bristol and a Connaught A-type was the cause of much appreciative comment. Archie was never in danger of losing his second place in the rather strung-out ten-lapper, although he was not really threatening Salvadori's lead either. There were limits, after all.

The next day he won the Wrotham Cup for unlimited sports cars at Brands Hatch at the BRSCC meeting.

The day after that he was up to Crystal Palace, where he won the Norbury Trophy for unlimited sports cars. Two unlimited capacity victories on the trot was remarkable, even unheard-of, given that the Lister was giving away more than a litre routinely, and up to 1½ litres in many cases, particularly against Jaguar-engined cars.

Three weeks later, on 25 June, he returned to Snetterton, where he came second in the 100-Mile unlimited race, his colleagues in customer Lister-Bristols winning with him the team prize.

On 10 July he was back at Brands Hatch for the BRSCC meeting, where he won the race for sports cars over 1900 cc.

On 13 July Ruth Ellis was hanged, an event which gave Archie grim and rather untypical satisfaction. Archie was on record as having been very much in the pro-hanging lobby on this occasion, unlike much of the country, whose friend Blakely was not. Archie was outraged at Ellis's action, which suggests that he did not know much of her complicated and tawdry life, or her relationship with Blakely. Perhaps he felt that Blakely's own death sentence for the minor misdemeanour of having a 'loose zipper' was, to say the least, unjustified.

Archie returned to Crystal Palace on 30 July for a second place in the unlimited sports car race, and two days later, he was back down to Brands Hatch to win the Kingsdown Trophy for cars over 1900 cc. He set fastest lap while he was at it.

He went back up to Charterhall for the 6 August Winfield Joint Committee meeting. He won the 2700 cc event and came third in the unlimited race. His effort in the *Daily Record* Trophy event also gave notice that he was a man to beat. He lay third for 11 laps, behind two Maserati 250Fs, but ahead of another Maserati and a Connaught B-Type. On lap 12 the front suspension of the Lister gave out, a symptom of its extremely hard-worked condition.

On 20 August came the BARC International 9-Hours race at Goodwood. Archie was partnering Les Leston in a Connaught 1½-litre sports car entered by Peter Bell and they survived the distance to win the 1500 cc class. More remarkably, they came sixth overall, against first line cars such as DB3S Astons, D-Type Jaguars and HWM Jaguars. Aston Martin won the race for the third year in a row.

Archie's friend from St Andrews, Desmond Titterington, was partnering Ninian Sanderson in an Ecurie Ecosse D-Type and came second. A nice touch was the success of two Lister-Bristols; David Hampshire and Peter Scott-Russell came ninth overall and won the 2-litre class in John Green's entry, HCH 736, and the works decided to support Ormsby Issard-Davies's car, driven by Allan Moore and Bill Holt; they came third in the 2-litre class and 13th overall. Archie's own Lister-Bristol was still being repaired after its suspension failure at Charterhall, which is why he was able to enter the Goodwood event for Bell. His success here was to be significant.

It had been planned that Archie and the Lister-Bristol should enter the TT race at Dundrod on 17 September. Archie had been turned down the previous year, a knee-jerk reaction to the licence problem, and he was nervous that it should happen again. Lister made discreet enquiries and was mortified to learn that Archie's forebodings were well-founded. The Ulster Automobile Club refused his entry on medical grounds. The BRSCC official magazine, *Motor Racing* was incandescent; so were many others. *Motor Racing* pointed out that given the junior nature of the UAC vs the RAC, whose Tourist Trophy the race was, was this not a case of the tail wagging the dog? It was further pointed out that no member of the medical board had ever clapped eyes on Archie, and who the hell were they to argue with Dr Benjafield, the founder of the BRDC? The article concluded:

> … Of course he is safe, the RAC's doctors say so and moreover his record proves it. In this country we deplore discrimination and restriction. We do not readily limit freedom and when a national organization has made a ruling it should be honoured by subsidiary organizations.
>
> The BRDC should take a lively interest in this, their founder has been snubbed and a member unjustly treated. Let action be swift and let there be no doubt as to who sets the standards for motor racing in the British Isles.
>
> The UAC has thought fit to 'cock a snook' at the RAC. To avoid suffering further indignities the RAC should strive to bring the TT race to this country.

Punchy stuff for 1955, this. Quite correct, too. The tone of this editorial merely reflects the esteem in which Archie was held by then. He certainly deserved to be. The sense of outrage which permeated the redder-blooded elements of the sporting media at this, and other snubs which Archie received characterized both a fine sense of jingoism as well as a deeply held indignation at the lack of fair play so often found in others and this is an attitude which still persists today when the subject of Archie comes up. As we come to see later, many of the assumptions concerning 'Continental Race Organizers', that breed of people who in the British subconscious of the 1950s existed on a plane somewhere between estate agent and child molester, are just plain wrong. More often than not it was the insurance companies not the race organizers who gave to Archie's entries such a negative response. The Ulster AC's attitude was therefore perplexing in the extreme. It did them no good anyway, as the RAC followed *Motor Racing*'s advice; 1955 was the last year that the TT was run at Dundrod. It was a pity Archie missed it, tragedy though it was, with three drivers losing their lives; he would have seen his friend Titterington soar in public esteem driving a D-Type works car with Mike Hawthorn. They were not classified but were technically fourth behind a trio of works Mercedes 300 SLRs.

The Lister-Bristol, having had a hard season, started to look and sound a little moth-eaten by the autumn. It had two successive head gasket failures, at which point it became quite clear that the faithful Bristol unit was probably rather more tired than the driver. There were no plans to rebuild it comprehensively as there was something quite exciting on the blocks back at Cambridge. Lister and Moore resolved to make do and mend for the rest of the season, a strategy which worked until 3 September at Aintree, when the Bristol engine finally put a conrod through its engine block and comprehensively destroyed itself. The team, for financial reasons, were forced to devote themselves to their next season's project.

At Snetterton and Brands Hatch on 25 September and 9 October, Louis Manduca was on hand to offer Archie his ex-Gillie Tyrer Jaguar C-Type, RAU 450. On both occasions Archie won the unlimited category, setting fastest lap at Brands, but he confessed that he found the burly Jaguar a bit of a handful after the lithe Lister-Bristol. He enjoyed it very much as a road car, though, driving it all over the country as his personal transport, taking a childish pleasure in terrifying hitch-hikers, one of whom, an American serviceman, preferred to alight in the middle of nowhere rather than continue as a passenger when Archie gave him a lift on the way to Scotland. Archie bought his own XK 120, complete with C-Type engine, quite soon after that.

It was a useful coincidence that Archie had time on his hands late in the season. That year, his victory in the British Empire Trophy had been over Ken McAlpine in a Connaught in the final, and he had already driven a 1500 cc car with Les Leston in the Goodwood 9-Hours. At the end of 1955 he had been invited by Connaught down to Goodwood to 'have a go' in their Formula 1 car. Archie was soon to learn that this machine was an entirely different species from the Goodwood 9-Hours car. Firstly, he stalled it. Then, after a prolonged push start, he set off and had the car completely sideways at the first hint of a bend in the road. He later wrote:

... On all the cars I had driven up to this time, it was quite permissible and possible to put one's foot down hard in any gear more or less at any time. This you cannot do in a Formula 1 car. The power is such that it is essential to get the car facing in the right direction and then apply the throttle gently if firmly. I think that this is why the lap speeds of the smaller and less powerful cars are so near to the racing cars. It is very much easier to corner with one's foot hard on the floorboards than it is to have to exercise throttle control ...

The crucial feature which the Connaught B-Type enjoyed, and which made it possible for Archie to even attempt to drive it, was a preselector gearbox. The essence of the device was its self-change capability; the driver moved the gearshift, up and down on a single plane like an automatic, into the ratio he would need next, and actually changed gear via a foot pedal. This allowed Archie the luxury of using both arms to steer most of the time, whereas most racing cars used a conventional gear lever to the right of the driver with a clutch pedal. It eased pressure on his stump, as he had to brace the wheel with it much less often, given that his strong left hand was free all the time.

After sorting out the vehicle's attitude to the satisfaction of all present – which included breaking Hawthorn's all-out circuit record, set two-and-a-half years before in a 4½-litre Thinwall Special (not bad, first time out) – he was offered a seat in the Formula 1 team, at least domestically. In order to satisfy the curiosity of the Connaught personnel, Archie was requested to demonstrate his strength in the lounge bar of the Fleece Inn, near Goodwood. His response to this tactless, good-natured but vital request was perfect; he dropped and gave them twenty press-ups, one-handed, right there and then. They were impressed. Archie dealt with his asymmetry so well that even Jose Lister had caused hilarity once, when she had fetched Archie's helmet and kit from the car. She could only find one glove and spent several moments rummaging around as she searched for the other one.

There was always the possibility that overseas events would be forthcoming, but the skittishness that insurers felt, in the light of the fearsome accident at Le Mans in 1955 which resulted in the deaths of over 80 spectators, always made this a slightly remote contingency, whatever the reaction of the fans and the media. Initially, then, this was to be a one-race-at-a-time deal, but Archie would, in effect, lead the team when they competed at home. It was a particular pleasure for Archie to be reunited with his old friend Titterington, and for the two of them to be on the same side for once.

The Connaught concern, however, had a serious structural problem; lack of cash. Possibly the best engineered of all single-seat racers at the time apart from Vanwall, the équipe was being supported by the efforts of Ken McAlpine, who had invested over £40,000 in 1955 alone. In fact, had it not been for Brooks's victory at Syracuse, and the consequent willingness of race organizers to put up serious starting money, the team would have folded under its own weight at the end of 1955. The financial condition of Connaught was no secret. Brooks himself preferred to opt for BRM, a decision he was later to allude to as something rather worse than life-threatening.

The parlous and stretched state of Connaught as a business had a second, more pressing consequence. Whilst the firm had the expertise to develop their four-cylinder $2^{1}/_{2}$-litre engine, based around a pre-war Alta design (originally the work of Geoffrey Taylor) there was no money to do it. Certain improvements had been made, notably the use of huge valves to improve the breathing, but the pressures required to operate them imposed further problems. Ultimately, the lubrication system's capacity was found wanting. Piston failure, even with conservative rev limits, was to be a consistent problem. Another was that whilst the engineers had managed to develop the motor to the limits of reliability on a shoestring; beefing up the drive train to match was an exercise beyond the resources of the company.

All this was compounded by a generally low level of race entry, which meant that the overall testing of the cars under competitive conditions was generally inadequate. Finally, the cash shortage meant that the team could not pay the going rate for top-flight drivers. By the end of 1955 Connaught was a hand-to-mouth operation, limping along in the commercial equivalent of the poverty trap. Being total professionals, though, they could and would not indulge in any cost-cutting which might compromise quality or safety; which honourably compounded their difficulties even further. They particularly suffered by not being able to attract top names as other, richer, teams snapped them up. Archie was not particularly minded to exploit financially the clear lack of quick drivers in the racing firmament, it was merely that the prospect of competitive single-seater racing was a compelling one. He was becoming well-known for trying anything, and money was not the issue – which was a relief to Kenneth McAlpine, Rodney Clarke and Mike Oliver. They would come to appreciate both Archie's mechanical sympathy, however uninformed it was, and the value for money which he offered.

Archie's Formula 1 career started auspiciously well at the Boxing Day 1955 meeting at Brands Hatch. The prize was the Air India Trophy. Driving the ex-Les Leston Connaught B2, with which Archie's old colleague had come ninth in the Syracuse Grand Prix, Archie made a poor start, second to Paul Emery, but soon reeled him in and streaked home in first place on the 15-lap race, setting fastest lap – a remarkable achievement. As a debut, it was probably unique. Apart from the fact that he had never driven a Formula 1 car in competition before, he only had time for half a morning's practice. As we see again later, Archie needed less familiarization time than any other top driver, either with the car or the circuit. He paid a price, though. Marion recalled:

> He was very touchy before and after a race, and perhaps this was why he got his reputation for being rather critical of any service he received at either hotel or restaurant. I know he never complained when I was with him. He was always very tight-lipped and nervous before a race. If he was changing to an entirely new car he would be nervously sick in the mornings. He had a good appetite but a queasy stomach, in fact he had a rather weak stomach anyway.

Certainly we can be sure that Archie preferred competitive driving, whatever its stresses, to selling tobacco. Dobie's thought so too – they sacked him. They had little choice, as they were lurching towards eventual receivership and liquidation. Their venture to introduce Four Square as a cigarette had been met with some consumer resistance, which is business shorthand for financial catastrophe, one of several which finished them off. Their products were very popular in East Anglia, though, as Archie's sales figures for those he didn't smoke himself had shown. He was broke again, or at least facing the prospect. This fact had been noted by several members of the 163 Club and it was decided, by a few of them who could afford it, that what they really needed was a garage, given that they all loved cars so much. They were in part driven to this baroque expedient by a desire to keep up with Archie. As they followed him around the circuits, they were more and more dismayed to see him engrossed in conversation with drivers like Moss, Hawthorn and Salvadori. So, this was perhaps an attempt to keep his attention.

Archie, Peter Riley, Malcolm Boston and Peter Hughes found, funded and acquired a lease on a site on the Huntingdon Road out of Cambridge, which they christened the Autodel Garage, for Automotive Developments. Malcolm Boston had a silver blue Porsche 356, and they acquired a service agency on the strength of it, being too finely stretched to rise to a distributorship from AFN the UK concessionaires. Archie became the co-tenant and de facto manager. Whether they seriously thought, at such a tender age, that they could make it work is a question the answer to which is lost in the mists of time, but Archie was now a garagiste rather than a rep., which seemed rather more respectable given the line of work towards which he was gravitating. Many of the luminaries of 1950s racing had such businesses – Mike Hawthorn, Ivor Bueb, Roy Salvadori, Cliff Davis and many others. The plan was straightforward; they would build the business, capitalizing upon Archie's growing success as a driver, and attract distributorships on the basis of it. For Archie, the transformation was a blessed relief. Although he hid his feelings well, he disliked intensely being a travelling salesman, and alternating between a Grand Prix

Connaught and a tired rep's car bordered on the humiliating.

Archie and Riley bought a pair of Ford Zephyrs, identical in white with red roofs. They were both improved by the addition of a tuning kit from Alexander conversions – an Autodel activity – and on the strength of it Riley embarked upon his racing career (barely over as I write). He later drove for the Austin-Healey works team. Archie's colour scheme for the new car met with rather more approval from his mother than the previous one had; green with a yellow stripe was fine for a racing car, but on the road ...

Jay and Archie had found a new house at 17 Portugal Place, a pretty walk-through precinct not far from Magdalen Bridge, and had engaged a butler to go with it. Well, not really a butler. Jay employed the services of Bill and Alma Gillingham, two retired college servants, who lived around the corner in New Park Street. Bill Gillingham's main job was to polish Archie's silverware, while Alma 'did' for Jay and Archie in the domestic sense. Bill Gillingham was very much on Jay's side in the matter of Archie's chosen career and railed at him in a thoroughly un-Jeeveslike manner about his predilection for rushing around risking his neck for a load of tin cups. Archie's response to this is not on record. Bill Gillingham was also a little confused at the lack of a hyphen in his employers' surname. Friends who telephoned were often mystified at the greeting: 'Scott and Brown here.'

It is probably to Archie's credit that he was a rotten motor trader. He wasn't even a qualified mechanic. It didn't seem to matter, the Autodel concern lost money hand over fist, despite the prominent display of his name, artfully hyphenated, over the door. A major obstacle to success was that he was also a terrible businessman, another characteristic inherited from Bill. It is often said that selling to a salesman is easy – they respond to the stimuli of the sales pitch rather like one of Pavlov's dogs. It was certainly true in Archie's case. He evolved a strategy of ruthlessly overstocking everything, of buying equipment he would never need, but which looked good to him, with consequently disastrous effects on the cashflow of the business, and its ability to pay the bills from the petrol company. It was never to become a proper business, and remained an indulgence. Bill could bring little to the party. He popped up on race days, of course, but could be of little help in a practical way. Perhaps he realized that his own track record in business was not one for his son to emulate; not that Archie didn't try.

If Jay Scott Brown, who presided over the now oddly-named 163 clubhouse at their new house in Portugal Place suspected that her only son had gone entirely bonkers, she said little. She quite understood why Archie enjoyed racing; inside a racing car, he sat inside a carapace of indifference to his everyday problems. It never made her want to attend the events, though. She seldom did, actually. In the early days she was content only to keep house for her son – with the aid of the

Gillinghams – to hear blow-by-blow, corner-by-corner accounts from Archie's greatest fans, the diehard members of the society, was sufficient. In truth it was probably too much. She hated Archie's racing; she found it dangerous, pointless and frightening. His decision to enter the motor trade in whatever guise, triggered responses in her which took her straight back to the 1930s. They had not been happy memories at all and she was never to let up in her quiet crusade to stop her son racing. His response bordered on the cruel. He was heard on more than one occasion to tell her that when he died it would be in a racing car, and that was that. She further understood quite well that, although Archie never thought he would be rich, he could certainly make his mark in an arena where Bill had only ever amounted to a Brooklands footnote. The prospect horrified her.

Her attitude to the 163 club was a little schizophrenic; she was always there to play both lady bountiful and surrogate mother to a collection of ill-cared-for students, at whatever cost (they presumed a lot), but seldom adopted an attitude which was less than politely spiky. The more famous her son became, the more she loathed it (given what he did for a living) but the more she supported his success. There was nothing paradoxical in this, of course, merely the naturally mixed emotions of the loving mother of a successful racing driver. That Jay's natural demeanour was perhaps a little distant concerned his friends not at all; it annoyed Archie sometimes, though. His total lack of side struck sparks from Jay on occasions, but Archie possibly failed to appreciate that Jay resented Archie's exclusion from Pembroke College ten years before. That most of Archie's admirers were themselves Cambridge students possibly sat ill with her, but she showed it seldom.

He avoided contradicting her whenever possible but was to confide to friends that he should probably move out and find a house of his own. This is something he never did, but that he had started to think about at the time of the crisis over his licence in 1954, an event which had worried Jay not at all. His infuriation at the comments which she made about his friends drove him almost to distraction at times, but he was a sensitive enough man to realize that it was not necessarily his friends she was sniffing at, but his occupation and the lifestyle which went with it.

Moving out was always going to be difficult. Had he ever done so he would have come face to face with all those little problems which assistance would solve – who would tie his ties and laces and fry him his beloved omelettes? He knew who he had in mind, but she hadn't accepted his often voiced proposals yet. He proposed to Marion so often that no-one was sure whether it was serious or not any more. Clearly, staying at home made a virtue out of necessity, despite his mother's aversion to his career and however much it cramped his style in other ways.

Jay lived for Archie. Her mixed feelings towards his friends and lifestyle, not to mention his improving relationship with Bill, made for some good arguments, generally about the same old topics. She had the predictable mixed feelings about girlfriends and was particularly sniffy towards Marion Armour who she felt, possibly correctly, was messing her son about more than she needed to and very much more than was good for him. She was not to know that Marion was having problems selling the idea of her relationship with Archie, innocent though it was, to her family.

Failure with Marion, for whatever reason, spurred Archie on to greater heights with others, though. He pursued women with an assiduous single-mindedness that is usually the stuff of fiction. It seemed that women adored him. He was extremely handsome, generous, funny and great company. Other men, though, would tactfully steer their dates away from him. Sex was one area where he could be a truly ferocious opponent, and several peers have given heartfelt testimony to this. The impression is handed down that men who were quite relaxed about being hung out to dry on the circuit were perhaps a little more circumspect about him when it came to relaxing after the race. For Archie, this was not just an itch to be scratched; he craved company, too.

Moss, who competed with Archie only on the circuit, put it this way:

> He was always competitive, not only in cars, but with women as well. Although he was deformed it didn't stop him with his racing and it didn't stop him as a personality. I liked Archie and I would have liked to go out on the town with Archie, but I wouldn't like to have competed with him as far as girls are concerned … Why the hell invite trouble by inviting along a guy you know is an attractive sort of person?

So, 1955 had gone well. Archie had a new business, a new house, several new girlfriends and, thanks to racing, some money in his pocket. He was to swap the Ford for an XK120, much more in keeping, and looked forward to a 1956 which held great promise. The new Lister was almost ready, and looked as if it would pick up where the Lister-Bristol had left off. Coupled with Formula 1, which had proved much, Archie had every reason to think that 1956 would usher in the big time. He was half right.

Chapter 8

Lister-Maserati, Connaught and Formula 2

IT WAS MORE TROUBLE THAN IT WAS WORTH.
– Dick Barton

THE abandonment of the barchetta style of body design as expressed in the MG and Bristol-powered works vehicles had been hinted at by the futuristic appearance of the Lucas-designed cars. It was merely a start. The long-stroke Bristol unit was showing its age a little, and both Archie and Brian Lister had been fascinated by the Maserati A6GCS engine as used in Salvadori's XEV 601 – the left-hooker which he had piloted with such verve during 1955. This engine was a blood relative of the 2.5-litre Grand Prix engine which powered the bench-mark Grand Prix car, the immortal 250F, and there was no reason to have anything other than the highest expectation of it. This was to be sadly misplaced, as it turned out.

In fact, the Gilby Engineering team had had a miserable time with the engine on their Maserati sports car, despite the ministrations of their Italian mechanic, Daniel. Salvadori remembers it as a dreadful lump, unpredictable and low on power. Whatever trouble they had, all of it being a well-concealed secret, they got off lightly when their experience is compared to that of Brian, Archie and Don Moore.

The Lister-MG had been gathering dust in a lock-up since it had been honourably retired. Its registration and chassis were recycled, the new car thus being the second to bear the MER 303 number. The chassis was left more or less unchanged, with the exception of the use of Girling discs front and rear à la works Lister-Bristol. A few chassis members were removed or replaced by lighter ones. All up weight was thus marginally lower than the Lister-Bristol and the output of the Maserati unit, reputedly 173 bhp, promised a power/weight ratio of a truly impressive level. In fact, Lister had acquired the engine and transmission early in 1955 in exchange for £1500, and the parts lay about at Abbey Road for much of that 1955 season as gradually, in between racing dates, the old Lister-MG chassis was modified to accept it. It was given its disc brakes and built up as a running chassis by the summer of 1955 before being given its new Wakefield-built body.

The choice of bodywork was decided by the twin imperatives of low frontal area and stability. Some weight-saving had been achieved by the use of disc brakes, as opposed to the heavy drums of the old car. Scuttle height was dropped to 27 in., marginally lower than the tops of the front and rear wings, which humped over the wheels rather in the manner of the Goldie Gardner MG, EX 179. The nose was a simple continuation of the curvature of the front wings. At the rear the tail was short, pert and tucked under, building into a very small headrest. Archie had concurred, with apparent enthusiasm, with the view that, in the event of an accident, he would dive under the passenger side tonneau panel to avoid injury. Well, he was the driver.... He was proud of his reflexes, which were at times akin to those of a rabid mongoose, but as a strategy to stay undamaged, this seems at best slightly flawed.

Thus, frontal area was reduced by almost a quarter from that of the barchetta body. So, it was lower, lighter and with less wind resistance. Drop in the Maserati engine, its short stroke and sidedraught carburation contributing much to the lower bodyline, and the results should have been electrifying. Even the beautiful and expensive wire wheels wore earless hubs to reduce unsprung weight.

In the cockpit, instrumentation was minimal, most of the space being taken up by ducting which began at the windscreen and went to the left of the driver, along the centreline to cool the inboard rear brakes, and to the right looping back into the engine bay to supply the cold air box for the triple Weber DCOE carburettors.

Lister was soon to regret the choice of the Maserati unit, both from a competitive and a financial point of view. It seemed at times that the wretched device was not made of metal at all, so quickly did it wear itself out. A combination of poor preparation, indifferent after-sales spares quality and a generally low level of engineering integrity all combined to give Brian Lister, Don Moore and most of all Archie, a miserable time. These engines operated under ludicrous internal pressures in the first place, necessary because of the differences in expansion coefficients between the steel crank, the iron cylinder liners and the alloy block. The engine, like its Grand Prix cousin, used fully machined mating surfaces for the most part, with little use of main gaskets; so effective cooling, of both oil and water was crucial, as was the task of keeping these fluids separate.

The overall quality of the engine from an engineering viewpoint was frightful. Camshafts were almost unhardened, followers likewise, workmanship very skimpy and customer attitude a tutting indifference. When the exasperated team at Abbey Road ordered a new set of pistons, for example, they came with little ends and piston rings, but the piston crowns were merely raw blobs of aluminium, completely unfinished. Conrods were not weight-matched. Liners were just tubes of seemingly random length, and camshafts were not case-hardened. The transmission, though, was superb. The genius of Valerio Colotti had been brought into the Maserati factory in 1952. This young man was to become the Thomas Tompion of gearbox manufacture in Italy – it was said of him that he could scratch build a gearbox in a few weeks. Certainly, the great gear manufacturer in Britain, David Brown, was to later benefit, at the cost of some embarrassment, by his use of a Colotti-designed Maserati transaxle in one of his own Aston Martin cars.

The first hint of what was to come was dropped when Archie and the team set off for Snetterton for a development shakedown. The car looked perfect – Sitton and Mothersole, the painters, had excelled themselves, and the swooping coachwork was resplendent in the familiar green and yellow. The engine howled away through Moore's custom-made exhaust in a thoroughly convincing manner. Archie went on ahead, delighted with his new conveyance, blipping the throttle to top C just for the fun of it. The little car shot off, followed by Lister, Moore and Dick Barton in the trusty Morris Minor.

Archie made it as far as Barton Mills, just outside Mildenhall. When the rest of the équipe caught up with him, he was prodding thoughtfully at the engine, but totally unable to start it. 'It just stopped,' he said. It transpired that the oil pump filter was clogged with solder, effectively halving the oil flow to the cams, one of which had run its bearings dry and snapped. It was to be typical of the level of factory preparation of this engine, and the after sales service was even worse.

'It was more trouble than it was worth,' said Dick Barton later.

One of the difficulties was that the A6 engine was a multi-purpose road-race unit and was probably overtuned beyond the limits of reliability, in stark contrast to the Bristol unit which was evolved slowly and methodically. The point was, you could choose your own compression ratio and crown profile. Basically, it was a case of building your own, and here's one we did earlier. Maserati were in dire financial trouble at the time, a fact reflected in the quality of service and customer care. As a firm, they were almost an indulgence of their owners, the car-obsessed Orsi brothers. They were two years away from receivership.

The A6 engine was originally the work of Antonio Bellentani and Alberto Massimino in 1952. They designed it as an exactly 'square' engine, 75 mm x 75 mm. When the great Colombo arrived at the Maserati works, it was revised to oversquare with twin ignition and revised valve angles. However, as the $2\frac{1}{2}$-litre Formula 1 engine – the 250F – started to take up scarce resources, the development of the 2-litre power plant was rather shoved on the back burner. As a result of this, by the time the 2-litre engine arrived at Abbey Road, there were several versions of it extant. The A6, the A6G and the A6SSG were all discrete variants upon a common theme. The 88 bhp per litre output of the GCS engine was the main reason for selecting it; coupled with the low line, dry sump and very light weight (a function of the alloy block). It was a justifiable error. That the works were already having bother with the 250F engine, as it wept oil from the head and the timing case at high revs was a straw in the wind, but not one which Lister or Moore could be expected to know about. For Archie, there was a small improvement over the Lister-Bristol, though, as the Don Moore exhaust ran along the nearside of the car. With such tightly wrapped bodywork as this, there was a major advantage in driver cooling. Salvadori, driving the left-hand drive A6, routinely roasted his feet.

Don Moore – upon the advice of Alf Francis, who was Stirling Moss's mechanic – experimented with exotic brews of lubricants, particularly 'Corsair' oil, and the car did give some moments of unalloyed pleasure when it was on song. Archie achieved several fastest laps, but only four outright victories in the car. Of these, three were class wins and one was a victory in the unlimited capacity race at Brands Hatch on 6 August. The class wins were at BRDC Silverstone on 5 May, BARC Aintree on 23 June and BRSCC Oulton Park on 18 August. In truth, though, he was having more success driving a DKW.

Despite the trouble they were to have with the car, Archie was inordinately fond of it. He regularly used to drop by the Moore workshop just to listen to it running, so much did he enjoy the sound of a highly-tuned short-stroke twin-cam engine. It handled superbly, of course, a feature of the car which Archie did full justice to whenever the opportunity arose, which was sadly seldom. The car reappeared at the time of writing, owned by Syd Silverman, the American collector and enthusiast, after a total restoration. Ironically, the engine – not the original troublesome lump – is fine. Silverman owns several Listers, all of which, admits Brian Lister, are probably rather better than new.

There was never any plan to sell Lister-Maseratis to the public, although the flat-iron body was offered to Lister-Bristol clients, its lines rather inevitably spoiled by a huge haystack on the bonnet to accommodate the tall engine. There were loose plans for an Alta-engined car, but the bush telegraph worked well enough between Send and Cambridge, via Archie, that the notion was best dropped quickly. Connaught had developed the Alta unit as far as it would go, but it was still not quite up to its task.

The first event of the 1956 calendar was not a sports car race at all, but the Monte Carlo Rally. One good turn deserves another, and Jack Sears invited Archie to share the driving in his works Austin A50, with Ken Best as navigator. The trio started at Glasgow. Salvadori was there, too, rather wary of being press-ganged into a Ford Anglia along with his friends John Young and John Coombs.

Archie did not enjoy the event one bit. He disliked driving on the opposite side of the road, and cowered in the back under a travelling rug during Sears's spells at the wheel, imagining every delay to be an accident. However, he did his bit at the wheel with his usual flair, drifting the heavy car from bend to bend on their route southward, and they arrived at Monte Carlo just about bang on time. Many who drove Archie as a passenger have commented upon his truly dreadful attitude to the driving of others. He was not unique in this – many racing car drivers are the same, most famously Jim Clark, but Archie developed his dislike to the levels of phobia. He was even known to wear his racing helmet in the passenger seat of road cars. He made one exception, though. He had helped teach Jose Lister to drive fast but, not unnaturally, she was a little shy of having Archie as a passenger. His solution to her nervousness was simple. After a race from which he would usually have driven himself home, he tossed the keys to her, claiming fatigue. He then stretched out on the back seat and made a great show of going to sleep. Whatever agonies he endured in the back, it was a great morale-booster for the driver as she drove him home.

The Monte Carlo trio had, of course, qualified for the mountain time trial, an event which Roy Salvadori famously and neatly avoided, and nothing would do but they had to compete, despite Archie's reluctance. They lost a wheel while Sears was driving, and lost their brakes while Archie was in control. The car ended up in a ditch, and Archie, relieved, assumed that that was it. Sears, more enthusiastic, co-opted some spectators, righted the car, and limped, brakeless into Monte Carlo. They finished sixth in class. Archie never even considered entering the Rally again.

Archie sat slumped in a café reliving the horrors of the event, dwelling particularly upon the role of the hapless passenger in the time trials with a few fellow-sufferers, one of whom was Lance Macklin. Over a few sharpeners, Macklin suggested that Archie might like to try his hand at the Sebring 12-Hour Race which was coming up in March, just before the beginning of the UK season. Macklin was an experienced exponent of the Austin-Healey 100S, (Sebring) and had indeed narrowly escaped with his life in such a car at the catastrophic 1955 Le Mans race when Pierre Levegh's Mercedes had launched itself up the rear deck of Macklin's Healey before breaking up and ploughing into the crowd. That Macklin was still racing at all was remarkable enough, but that he wanted Archie to compete with him was a special vote of confidence, although one delivered with the Surrey driver's customary insouciant charm. Archie agreed to the proposal with understandable alacrity, and spent the intervening period worrying about the eventual outcome. A new circuit in another country meant a new medical.

The Healeys had swarmed all over Sebring the previous year, with first to third in class and a sixth overall with seven finishers out of nine entries. The car which Archie and Macklin were to drive, OON 440, had already had an illustrious career, having completed both the 1954 and 1955 Mille Miglia events. It was extensively modified for the race, to deliver 145 bhp and 175 lb/ft of torque, which was not bad for something with distinctly hackney carriage origins. The car weighed in at just less than 1800 lb.

Archie and Macklin arrived at Sebring three days before the start so that Archie could acclimatize to both circuit and car. The circuit was on an airfield and, therefore, instantly recognizable to him, even down to the cement-filled oil drums which marked it out. No sport for wimps, this. The Healey 100S was just his type of car; bags of torque, a wide power band, neutral handling. He had been justifiably nervous about the medical rules – the Dundrod episode had left its mark, but he was waved through almost without a second glance. He had another problem, though – he had forgotten his wallet and couldn't even buy a round of drinks. With the help of Geoffrey Healey he was able to draw funds from Ship and Shore Motors, the local dealer in Palm Beach to be repaid in sterling to Austin's back in England. This was always happening; the draconian exchange control laws in Britain at the time were a notorious handicap, despite being easily circumvented by this loan scheme, a variant of which was used by many people at one time or another.

The Healey went well for almost eight out of the 12 hours, and Archie enjoyed himself immensely, drifting the little car in his usual style and entertaining the knowledgeable and critical crowd hugely. The Healey was and is a ferociously quick car, light, torquey and powerful. The engine, though, at $2\frac{1}{2}$ litres and four cylinders, was possessed of little of the smoothness of a six-cylinder. In order to pare down weight, the original cast iron exhaust manifolds were replaced by a rather hastily-prepared fabricated alternative. One of the exhaust downpipes eventually blew off because of the pounding vibration, which exposed the starter motor to a blowtorch of flame from the truncated manifold just above it. Not surprisingly, this caused the starter motor windings to melt and short out, with the attendant result that they were welded solid. The car was unable to restart after the stop to fix the exhaust, even with a hefty push, and the pair reluctantly retired. The same malady affected the other works car driven by Jackson-Moore and Forbes-Robinson. Ship and Shore's standard car came 11th.

Archie arrived back in the UK with barely enough time to become reacquainted with the Formula 1 Connaught for the Easter Monday Goodwood meeting on 2 April. The highlight of the day was to be the 32-lap Glover Trophy Formula 1 race, with some quite serious competition, notably Stirling Moss and Mike Hawthorn, driving Maserati and BRM cars respectively. Archie tried particularly hard in practice, and managed second on the grid to Moss, although he uncharacteristically over-revved the tired and fragile engine. He had been operating to a 6250 rpm limit, theoretically within the limits of safety, but just exceeded it. At the start, Hawthorn sped away, to be overtaken at the end of lap one by Archie and then Moss. The battle which ensued has gone down in history as one of the most splendid motor races of the year, if not the decade. Archie held Moss off for 15 more laps before his brakes started to fade and he was unable to out-brake Stirling. The Maserati got past and Archie, almost brakeless, set off in pursuit. One lap later, oil loss through a leaking cam cover caused the crankshaft to pick up on it bearings and snap, loudly, at 130 mph. The transmission was wrecked and it locked solid. The Connaught spun several times in its own length at Woodcote and came to rest in a huge cloud of dust. Archie just sat there expression-less for a few moments, and then slowly clambered out to rapturous applause. Gradually, he 'came back' and patiently waited for the end of the race. Moss pulled over and stopped on his victory lap and Archie hopped on to the tail of the Maserati. He sat, Gordon Richards-style, using the fuel filler as a pommel while Moss drove him back to the paddock. His habitual grin returned as he circulated past the 60,000 people who had seen the race. Bill had been one of them. He was stag-gered by Archie's competitive spirit, and like any man who has seen his son lead the best of the best in the world, was close to tears.

Motor Sport, in 'Matters of Moment' in their May 1956 issue, were moved to write:

THE SKILL OF ARCHIE SCOTT-BROWN (sic)
Those who were at Goodwood on the occasion of the BARC Easter Meeting were able to witness the great duel between Archie Scott-Brown in a works Connaught and Stirling Moss in a works Maserati. On this epic occasion Scott-Brown displayed outstanding skill and judgment, and it is apparent that he ranks with Hawthorn, Moss, Brooks and Collins as one of Britain's drivers of Grand Prix calibre. He led Moss for half the Richmond Formula 1 Race, until erratic brakes forced him to slow, and a lap later the engine of his Connaught – which was known to be "tired" before the race, the best engines having been put in the Syracuse entries – broke up and he spun off. Even then this astonishing driver came to no harm and displayed no emotion; in action he had given a remarkable demonstration of driving, controlling his car from impossible-looking slides and giving Moss much to think about! This ability is all the more creditable because Scott-Brown has only been racing for three seasons and in sports cars, his first race in a G.P. car being at Brands Hatch in the rain on Boxing Day, so that Goodwood marked his first real debut in this exacting sphere of the Sport. True, he over-revved his engine in practice, which may have precipitated its "blow-up" in the race, but he wasn't alone in this, for Moss made the Maserati suffer likewise, as our report in this issue will show.

In recording our appreciation of Scott-Brown's driving we would add our admiration for Connaught, who had three cars at Goodwood and entered two for Syracuse, whereas B.R.M. had only two cars running on Easter Monday, neither B.R.M. nor Vanwall being ready for the Sicilian race.

A fortnight later came the British Empire Trophy back at Oulton Park. Expectations were high – an excusable touch of hubris given that the full horror of the Maserati's unreliability had not yet been fully appreciated. Archie came second in the 1500–2700 cc heat, setting the fastest lap in the process, but the Lister-Maserati boiled over in the main race.

On 21 April the BARC 200-Mile race took place at Aintree, and Archie led the Connaught effort. Originally the Junior Car Club 200, it changed its name as that organisation evolved into the BARC. The Vanwalls of Moss and Schell did not make it for the race, as their cars were not ready, so the opposition consisted of five Maserati 250Fs, Moss reverting to his own car to replace the Vanwall, two BRM 25s, driven by Mike Hawthorn and Tony Brooks, two other Connaught B-Types, driven by Titterington and Parnell, and Paul Emery in the similarly Alta-powered Emeryson special.

The omens were encouraging as Archie set fastest time in practice, 2.2 seconds quicker than Hawthorn, who was two tenths quicker than Titterington. Moss and Salvadori, both in Maserati 250s, shared the second row. After a struggle with Hawthorn, Archie led the race by six seconds from Brooks. Then, on lap 13, the overstressed engine let go a piston and Archie's race was over, the conrod having ventilated the block – a re-run of Goodwood.

The Lister-Maserati failed again at the BARC Goodwood meeting at the end of April, and Archie went up to Silverstone for the BRDC International rather warily. At this meeting he contested three events, the most important of which was the Formula 1 *Daily Express* Trophy race. The opposition was of the best quality. Juan Fangio and Peter Collins were there in a pair of Lancia-Ferraris. Moss and Schell drove the Vanwalls which had not been ready at Aintree. Hawthorn reappeared in the BRM 25, and Salvadori in the Gilby Maserati. Against these entries Connaught pulled out all the stops, entering (for the works) cars for Archie, Titterington, Piero Scotti (an amateur) and Mike Oliver. There were five other private entries, including one from Rob Walker, as well as an assortment of four Type-A Lea-Francis powered cars.

Archie managed seventh on the grid, the fastest of the Connaughts. The pace was predictably furious and it told quickly. Oliver, as quick as any of his day, cartwheeled at Woodcote corner, but walked away from it. As the field fragmented, Moss took the lead, with Archie hanging on grimly in second, with his friend Titterington third. The British 1–2–3 was augmented by a new lap record shared between Moss and, before his brakes went again, Hawthorn. Even Scotti, a rank amateur, managed seventh. It was his last event, as he decided to revert to being a drinks manufacturer.

Archie crawled home ninth in the unlimited sports car race, winning the 1500–2700 cc class; but by way of compensation he romped home first in class (up to 1100 cc) in the saloon car event which he and his team won. The other members of the trio, Hughes and Utley, acquitted themselves with distinction in their tiny 896 cc DKWs, entered by the AFN company – with which Archie had a tenuous connection, Bill having been a Frazer Nash agent – and the three of them took the team prize. One report read:

> Quite amazing was the progress of Archie Scott-Brown [sic] in the little ... DKW, who appeared to be scarcely slowing down at all for the corners and hurtled merrily around, hustling Consuls, Magnettes and Malavasi's Alfa Romeo out of the way with blasts on the horn.

It was not quite Formula 1, but victory was victory just the same, even if the race was a little tongue-in-cheek compared to the big stuff.

The West Essex Car Club Meeting took place on 19 May at Snetterton. Again, the Lister-Maserati failed, but not before Archie won the heat for the 'Double Twelve Trophy'. He set fastest lap in the final before the Maserati engine expired noisily in a cloud of steam; it was not terminal, merely a fractured pipe. He entered Jack Sears's Jaguar XK120 for the Jaguar handicap, and set fastest lap, but spun off.

The next day at Brands Hatch was a little more encouraging; he came second in the repaired Lister in the sports and racing car handicap, setting fastest lap again.

He didn't have any more success in the Lister until 23 June at Aintree. He came fourth in the unlimited class and first in the 2-litre class. In contrast, he came third in the 1500 cc race, driving Ron Frost's Lotus XI for the first time, which he liked a lot. He was familiar with the mechanical layout employed, as the car used a centre change MG gearbox, and delighted in its light weight. The Formula 1 race at this venue was the Aintree 100. Opposition included Tony Brooks in the BRM and Bruce Halford, Horace Gould and Jack Brabham each entering their own Maserati 250Fs. Apart from Bob Gerard in a Cooper 23 and Paul Emery in his Emeryson special, the rest were Connaughts, all of which were Type-As, including Salvadori's, borrowed from Tommy Atkins. Archie led for eight laps after passing Gould (who later won) before the Alta engine started spewing oil everywhere from the crankcase breathers. Ever aware of both fire and the fact that Connaught were in no position to build an infinite number of engines, he stopped, hopped out and abandoned the car to its fate. It did not in fact explode, but the engine was history.

The Lister was not entered for the East Anglia Motor Club sprint at Snetterton on 8 July; the équipe was still waiting for an assortment of spare parts from Maserati. Archie did rather well in the Murkett brothers' D-Type Jaguar, though, winning the racing car class. He also won the over 3000 cc production class in an XK 140. Still, winning was winning. Despite his enthusiasm for the sheer appeal and aural qualities of the Maserati engine, he was beginning to have severe doubts about it as a competitive unit.

The major event of Archie's calendar had to be the British Grand Prix at Silverstone. Connaught entered three cars, for Archie, Jack Fairman and Desmond Titterington. Four Lancia-Ferraris, 11 Maserati 250Fs (four of which were works cars), three Vanwalls, three BRMs and Paul Emery made up the bulk of the field. Archie jousted round in the top half dozen or so, sandwiched between the two Lancia-Ferraris of de Portago and Castelloti before, just by way of a change, the Connaught lost a wheel on lap 16 through stub axle failure. Titterington, ironically driving the car originally designated for Fairman, lost a piston on lap 74. Fairman brought the third Connaught home fourth.

A week later on 22 July, Archie entered the Lotus XI again (this time at Snetterton) and came second, but set a new class record. In the Formula 1 event he set a new absolute circuit lap record in the Vanwall Trophy, but the poor Connaught expired when an oil pipe failed on lap six, but had led the race until then.

He sparkled again, well within the mechanical limitations of both the Lister and Connaught cars, at Brands Hatch on 6 August, setting fastest lap in part one of the Formule Libre event in the Connaught and winning the unlimited sports car race in the Lister – now restored to full, if fragile, health; thanks, finally, to the service department at Maserati. The lap record he set in the Formula 1 Connaught served as an absolute Brands Hatch record for the rest of the season, until he broke it again. He retired in the final because of a reappearance of lubrication problems in the Connaught.

The weakness of the Alta-type engine was tiresome for Connaught, but not considered to be terminal. It was certainly powerful enough, after all, and if treated with sympathy it was capable (despite its pre-war roots) of delivering the goods, but only on occasion. Connaught, like many others, were looking forward to the V8 'Godiva' engine from Coventry Climax, mooted to be about as powerful – 240 bhp – as the Taylor design, but much more rugged. That it was not to appear was to prove the last straw for the Surrey firm.

On 18 August, Archie and John Horridge, who was driving the Ecurie Bullfrog Lister-Bristol, managed a 1–2 at a BRSCC meeting at Oulton Park in the 2-litre class, but Archie only came fifth in the unlimited race as a whole. After the excesses of the Lister-Bristol the previous season, during which no less than six of the works victories had been in the unlimited capacity class, against machines with up to almost twice the engine size, the Abbey Road effort was becoming a little limp.

Despite the lowering gloom at Cambridge, Connaught were delighted and entered him for the Italian Grand Prix on 2 September. The Send team had entered four cars – for Archie, Les Leston, Archie's partner in the 1955 Goodwood 9-Hours, Ron Flockhart and Jack Fairman. Lister could not and would not stand in Archie's way – the unreliable Lister-Maserati was hardly a compelling alternative to the Italian Grand Prix, after all – and it transpired that the Connaught entry had been made on the understanding that the organisers would, in all probability, turn down Archie's entry anyway. They didn't at first, so Archie set off with the Connaught team to Monza.

It started well. In initial practice, Archie set fastest time to achieve pole position ahead of Fangio – this on a circuit which he had never even driven on before. To be fair, nor had many people, as it had been extensively modified. This was a trick he was to repeat at the Nürburgring the next year.

It would perhaps be churlish to suggest that the organizers were wary of the Connaught concern since the unknown dental student, Tony Brooks, had trounced the Italian opposition the year before at Syracuse. Nonetheless, they banned Archie. One of the committee, a medical adviser, had not been present when the initial approval was given, and either because he needed to assert his authority and importance upon the process, or because he really thought that Archie was unsafe, he insisted upon preventing him from starting. The same jack-in-office had just revoked the permit of one Mantovani who had rather optimistically reapplied for an entry after a period of convalescence from a crash which had cost him a leg. There was an echo of Oulton Park 1954 in all this, insofar as it was an acquired disability on the part of another driver which really drew attention to Archie. The media in Britain were predictably belittling about all things Italian for a few issues, and the Tifosi were angry too. Their joint view was that you don't ban the man who has just made fastest lap and beaten Fangio. A few primordial shrugs followed the trackside British protest, led by Eason-Gibson of the RAC, and Archie finally went into the lists as reserve driver to save his face for the record book, but he was not allowed to compete, and his practice time was declared void.

The three other drivers were permitted to enter, with the result that Flockhart came third, with Fairman fifth. Archie's fury at being thwarted can only be guessed at, as he went into deadpan mode and hid it well, but after the disaster of the season with the Maserati engine his opinion of the descendants of Romulus can hardly have been buoyed overmuch. Moss won the race in his Maserati 250F at 129 mph, setting fastest lap in the process. There had, though, been a Lister success that day. John Horridge had won his class (up to 2700 cc), at Snetterton in the Ecurie Bullfrog Lister-Bristol – although this good news was hardly enough to make up for such humiliation.

Mary Rose Jones, née Harper, the childhood friend from Paisley who had helped bathe the baby Archie and cut out the lint dressings for his legs – for which she was rewarded by having her bike pinched – lived in Milan, in the Piazza Giulio Cesare. She and her husband played host to Archie whenever he came to Milan, but, like many childhood friends, preferred not to watch him race. Bill was there, too, and Archie hid his depression well. After the race, the team went out to dinner with Mary Rose, her husband and Bill. Bill drank only water, and watched his son carefully. Archie generated enough spark to be the life and soul, as usual, but both Bill and Mary Rose could tell that he was in a very lowered state. His pole position had been taken by Fangio, who had finished second, and a Connaught had been placed both third and fifth to deliver a grand result for the team. It could all have happened for him as it had happened to Brooks at Syracuse. The Connaught already had proved its speed against Moss's Maserati at Goodwood, and Archie would have had a serious chance of winning. He stubbed out his resentment like a half-smoked fag and went to the coast to catch some sun before returning.

Connaught tried out Stuart Lewis-Evans (who was almost as tiny as Archie and fresh from Formula 3) at Brands on 14 October, and Archie, ever mindful of his seniority in the team, went for it. It was a BRSCC event of 15 laps and Archie won it from Lewis-Evans and set both new outright and Formula 1 lap records in the process, breaking the old record which he had set on 6 August. Clearly, Archie's skills had not after all been blunted by his relative lack of success that season. This was, by way of compensation for Monza, beginning to feel a little less of a disaster.

Archie's success at single-seater racing did not, in retrospect, necessarily send the right signals to Brian Lister, even though the Scot led the Connaught team at home and achieved notable success, unreliability of the hardware notwithstanding. Lister was working, along with several others through the 1956 season, on a car which could be competitive within the Formula 2 regulations to apply from 1 January 1957, which called for 1500 cc unsupercharged cars running on 100 octane fuel – no alcohol allowed for car or driver.

The result was an interesting vehicle, especially when considered against the other products which were to vie for the same honours, and it has been much neglected by historians, having been written off as a white elephant. The assumption has been made that it never even ran under power and was very much a display vehicle. It ran once, in fact, at Snetterton and not even then in anger, but on test in the hands of Don Moore and Archie. Over the years it was assumed that the project had been abandoned through lack of interest. That it was abandoned is true, but for other reasons.

Naturally, Listers were not the only concern looking at the formula, but Brian went about it his way. He had never built an open wheel single-seater before, but he had learned through the success enjoyed by the sports cars that this lack of experience should not particularly deter him.

The car was built around a proper space frame, as opposed to the elongated kite shape of the sports cars. The structure was fabricated from 1 in. T45 tube, of 18-gauge wall thickness, braced by $^3/_4$ in. tube of the same grade. As with all Listers, the tubes were fully machined to fit and welded electrically. The basic structure weighed in at 30 lb. A front bulkhead of $^3/_{16}$ Duralumin plate, placed between engine and clutch housing, added extra torsional stiffness. It was attached by Silentbloc bushes.

The front suspension was a slight departure for Lister. Unequal length wishbones were used for the first time, although the upper was only $^1/_2$ in. shorter than the lower. They were fabricated from 16 gauge $^3/_4$ in. T45. The springing, Girling struts inside helical coils, was broadly similar to the sports cars, but rose joints were used all round for the first time.

At the rear, predictably, a de Dion layout was used. The final drive casing was made from very light 20-gauge sheet. A channel was let into it to allow movement of the sliding peg location mechanism. Location to the space frame was by a pair of 20-gauge tube steel radius arms, also rose jointed. Brakes were Girling discs, 9 in. at the front, $8^3/_4$ in. rear.

Power was provided by the Climax FWB single-cam engine, with a bore and stroke of 76.2 x 80 mm, displacing 1460 cc, with a convenient centre-change MG gearbox. Like everybody else, Lister was waiting for the Climax FPF twin-cam engine promised for 1957. It was never to be fitted to this car. The FPF was the result of a nervous reassessment which was taking place at Coventry Climax of their $2^1/_2$-litre 'Godiva' V8, which appeared, if press reports were to be believed, to be somewhat less powerful than the latest wares from Modena. As things turned out, the 'Godiva' engine probably would have been a total triumph, throwing Ferrari's ears to the crowd, but such was the hyperbole employed by the press offices of the other manufacturers that Coventry Climax were persuaded that the cobbler should stick to his last – a great pity since Ferrari really had nothing new at all except an enthusiastic press department. The FPF engine, then, was basically a 'Godiva' sawn in half lengthwise and bored out a little. In the end, it would grow to $2^1/_2$ litres itself, which was ironic, and too late for Connaught.

The power:weight ratio of the new Lister-Climax was over 300 bhp per ton. With the new FPF engine, reportedly, that would have increased to closer to 400 bhp. The car was only seven pounds heavier than the T41 Cooper which was on the blocks down at Surbiton. By way of comparison, the Lister-Bristol which Archie had campaigned so successfully had a power:weight ratio of 240 bhp/ton. With the twin-cam Climax engine fitted, one would have been hard put to sort out Formula 2 from Formula 1 – which was, of course, the whole point.

Brian was at a competitive disadvantage, though. The opposition down at Surbiton had already made huge advances in the design and construction of racing cars, particularly those with the engine behind the driver. The T41 was basically an adaptation of the well-known bobtail car which had been actively campaigned in the 1956 season. In short, they had already done the work. Lister had been forced to start from scratch.

Looking back, it is easy to be persuaded that the mid-engined Formula 3 and 2 cars which were emerging so successfully were a clear and obvious harbinger of things to come – but at the time it did not necessarily seem so. This was the most important time of change in racing, with marques such as Vanwall, Connaught and Maserati still resolutely favouring the front powered layout. Indeed, 1957 was to be the year that Fangio was to win his last championship – in a Maserati 250F. The issue was not to be sorted out fully until the 1959 season, in fact, as smaller capacity mid-engined cars started to sweep the board. At the end of 1956, the Cooper school of design was merely one way to go.

Archie was not particularly in one camp or the other. He was on record as being a rear-engined Porsche fan, and had been most disappointed at Autodel's inability to achieve a dealership. His problem with other racing cars was their right-hand gearchange rather than their structural geometry.

One thing – the car was pretty, at least in its original form. The use of a front-engine layout, though, necessitated a propshaft running under the driver's seat, leaving the driver rather shoved up into the airstream. Attempts were made to fair the driver in with a higher tail and scuttle, but the results were less attractive. Given the delicious look of the flat-iron sports cars, and what was to come for 1957, this revised version of the vehicle was a slight aberration, but it was designed to go rather than look good. It certainly ran well under test at Snetterton in August of 1956, driven by both Archie and Don Moore. Straight from the works, its 20-gauge Wakefield alloy body as yet unpainted, it performed well and showed great promise. It was provisionally entered for the potentially lucrative International Gold Cup Meeting at Oulton Park on 22 September, an event at which all but five cars were Coventry Climax powered. Pre-empting the new 1957 regulations, the *Daily Herald*, which could just about afford it, was putting up £1000 for first place, which Salvadori neatly scooped up.

The Lister-Climax was not to appear, not being fully ready, but Archie entered a works Elva-Climax, KDY 68, which came nowhere up against the Cooper 39s, 41s and Lotus 11s. The Elva was to provide Archie with at least one embarrassing moment. Unlike the cars he had driven before, it had not been built around him, and like many race cars it used a detachable steering wheel, which the Listers did not. He succeeded in removing it more than once, as a result of his habit, ingrained by now, of pulling up on the wheel to steady it while changing gear.

Brian Lister was not the only one who felt that the Bristol engine was perhaps becoming a little long in the tooth for sports car racing. Austin Nurse, the garagiste from Birmingham, had bought BHL 5, the last Lucas-bodied Lister-Bristol, which was registered HCH 736. He comprehensively destroyed it at Silverstone. To replace it, he bought another car from the same owner, John Green, and attempted to buy a works Jaguar engine to install. Jaguar, or rather F. R. W. England, refused, despite the best efforts on Nurse's behalf of Norman Dewis, Jaguar's senior test driver. Norman Hillwood was to have rather more luck.

Hillwood, an antique dealer and jeweller from North London, had been building and competing hill climb and sprint cars since 1952. When he approached Listers to buy a chassis for the purpose of putting in a wet-sump Jaguar C-Type unit, Brian was, to put it mildly, rather less than keen. His chassis had basically been engineered to accept engines of up to 2 litres, but here was a man offering up a 3.5-litre lump weighing in at 700 lb. He felt that it was a poor conception. Hillwood, though, had artfully written to Sir William Lyons at Coventry and had been obliged with a spare C-Type unit, by now obsolete at the works. Brian had already sold Hillwood the chassis and, fearful that the job of offering up the engine might be compromised if anyone else did it, somewhat grumpily set to to put the vehicle together with the usual Abbey Road thoroughness. He made some small adjustments, including making up a beefier de Dion tube at the back, and gave Hillwood back his rolling chassis. The delighted new owner ordered a body, somewhere between D-Type and Aston, from Maurice Gomm, and Lister rather thought he'd seen the back of it.

Brian had had a rough year; not necessarily lightened, except on a personal level, by Archie's foray into Formula 1. Had 1956 been more enjoyable, he might have been more immediately constructive about the Hillwood project. His Maserati-powered venture had proved to be ruinously expensive for an article that, although singularly beautiful and having generated a bit of start money, seldom brought home the bacon. Given his success at the top end, Archie was being uncharacteristically reluctant about the Formula 2 enterprise and, to cap it all, the customers were having more success with 1955 model Lister-Bristols than he was with his own car. Scott Brown had had more success *out* of Lister cars than he'd had in them. There was also the faint risk that the Scot's attention would wander, which would entirely change the focus of the racing enterprise. Lister and Archie, though, had a first-class working relationship and trusted each other completely. There was no real risk of Archie going elsewhere, and the serious blandishments from assorted third parties were not to be waved under his nose until the next year. Nonetheless, the sheer cost of racing was mounting up. Scratch-building one-off cars was fine provided they paid their way, but the third manifestation of the Lister marque was doing anything but that, despite the use of a basically recycled chassis. Don Moore lost count of the times he rebuilt the Maserati engine and the depressingly slow and offhand service received from Modena infuriated all concerned. Morale at Abbey Road had dipped. It seemed that the Lister-Maserati might have terminally limited both prospects and credibility. Publicity works both ways, after all. Brian had already begun investigating other engine options, most particularly Climax, but the choice was severely limited. It was, in short, not going according to the script, but help was on the way, initially from a very unexpected source indeed. All the frustrations of the Maserati period were to be paid back with interest quite soon, for the cavalry was just over the horizon.

On 13 October 1956, Sir William Lyons made the following announcement:

JAGUAR TO SUSPEND RACING

Jaguar Cars Ltd, after very serious consideration, announce their withdrawal from the field of international racing and other competitive events and state that no official entries or works teams will be entered for events on the 1957 calendar.

The information gained as a result of the highly successful racing programme which the Company has undertaken in the past five years has been of the utmost value, and much of the knowledge derived from racing experience has been applied to the development of the Company's products. Nevertheless, an annual racing programme imposes a very heavy burden on the Technical and Research Branch of the Engineering Division which is already fully extended in implementing plans for the further development of Jaguar Cars.

Although withdrawal from direct participation in racing in the immediate future will afford much needed relief to the Technical and Research Branch, development work on competition cars will not be entirely discontinued, but whether the Company will resume its racing activities in 1958, or whether such resumption will be further deferred, must depend on circumstances.

Lyons's statement did not preclude returning to racing, but it was important to concentrate the efforts of the works on selling cars, and monitoring the effect upon sales of the success seen so far. There was much going on at Brown's Lane, Coventry, of which competition was merely one part. The door was left ajar. Certainly, the racing programme had paid its way. Using more or less production engines, the XK120s, C-Types and latterly the D-Types had shown the way in endurance racing, the prize for which is to be able to sell road cars, which Jaguar were starting to do in laudable numbers. The firm was to reinvest much of the benefit from racing into its new sports model, already under development at Brown's Lane, which was to rightly become immortal – in effect, a civilized D-Type with clever rear suspension and rather more room. It was to be a long time before it was for sale, but Jaguar wisely allowed privateers to spend their own money for a while, rather than going to the expense of a full works-supported programme. They had won everything worth winning, and Lyons knew full well that the only place to go from number one is down.

Above The Lister-Maserati under construction at Abbey Road during the winter of 1955–6. It was a beautiful car, but not destined to achieve greatness. (Autocar)

Below A close-up of the elegant, but temperamental Maserati engine, problems with which were to dog the Lister works for 1956. (Autocar)

Bottom A profile shot of the Lister-Maserati, now painted and ready to go. Shortly after this picture was taken, the engine snapped a camshaft and, with occasional moments of pleasure, it was downhill from then on. A great pity, but nonetheless it gave Archie the chance to do other things that year. (Cambridge Evening News Ltd)

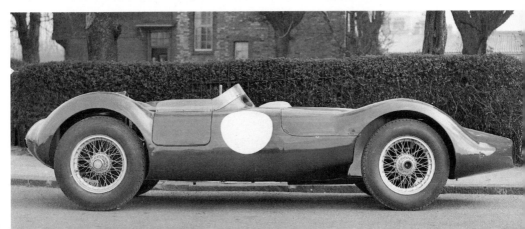

Left Despite its problems, Archie adored the Lister-Maserati. Here he is trying his best. Note how he rests the stump of his arm on the wheel. More often than not, he would pull up on the wheel in order to brace himself while he changed gear. (Geoffrey Goddard)

Below left The Bristol-engined car did not wear the 'flat-iron' body with the same ease as the Lister-Maserati. Here is Gil Baird in BHL 14, registered JCH 888, on his way to victory at Mallory Park on 22 June 1957. (Autosport)

Bottom left A study in concentration as Archie slides the works Elva-Climax at Brands Hatch on 14 October 1956. He loved this car, feeling it to be inherently safe. The body being made of glass fibre, it was also light. (Charles Dunn)

Right Concentration shifts to Petula Clark, who presents Archie with his award after victory in the Elva at Brands Hatch. (Temple Press Ltd)

Below A Formula 1 driver merits a new car. Here, Archie, as ever beset by requests for autographs, obliges outside the Norwich garage where he has just taken delivery of an XK120 coupé. It is fitted with a C-Type engine. (Eastern Daily Press)

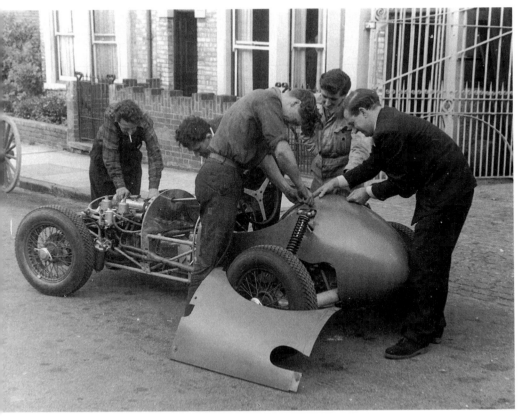

Fitting the bodywork to the first Lister-Climax prior to its tests at Snetterton. Much work went into it before it reached its finished state. (Autocar)

Archie trying hard in the AFN-owned DKW at the CUAC opener to the 1956 season at Great Dunmow. (John Horsman)

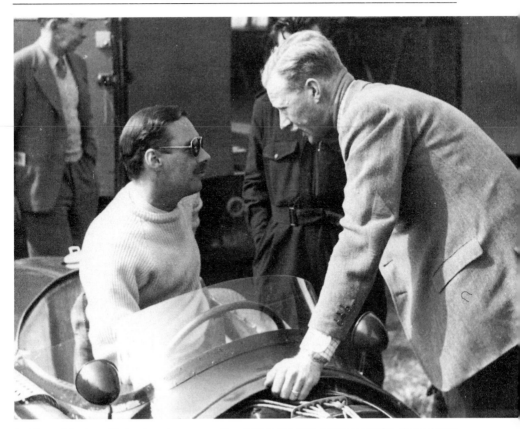

Archie and Rodney Clarke deep in conversation before the Glover Trophy at Goodwood over Easter 1956. (John Horsman)

Pushing the Connaught to the starting grid before the British Grand Prix at Silverstone in July 1956. (John Horsman)

Archie's Formula 1 career started 1956 well. Here his Connaught is leading Stirling Moss's Maserati 250F in the Glover Trophy on 2 April 1956 at Goodwood. Archie led until half-way, when the crankshaft broke. (Charles Dunn)

Archie hitches a ride with Stirling after the maestro has won the race. He clearly likes the applause.

Drivers briefing before the British Grand Prix. From the left: Desmond Titterington, Fangio, Eugenio Castellotti, Tony Brooks, obscured by Archie, and Roy Salvadori with his arm on Tony Brooks's shoulder. (Patrick Benjafield)

Archie getting comfortable before the British Grand Prix at Silverstone on 14 July 1956. Archie retired from the race on lap 16 when a hub broke. (Charles Dunn)

Top The car that begat the Lister-Jaguar. Norman Hillwood in his Lister-Jaguar special, 673 LMK, equipped with a wet-sump version of the XK C-Type engine. Hillwood found the car so reliable it bored him. (Richmond Pike)

Above The car that would shortly become MVE 303 parked in Abbey Road in the winter of 1956–7 stripped for inspection after its return from Wakefields of Byfleet. Note how far back the Jaguar engine is placed. (Autocar)

Below Building up the bodywork at the Abbey Road works early in 1957. The clearly derivative shark's fin stabiliser was quickly discarded. (Brian Lister)

Now that it all fits, the car has been denuded once again. Note at the rear the completed and painted panels. Note also the modified rear panel, not yet completed, with the rear fin deleted. It is nearly finished now, all bar the bulkheads. (Brian Lister)

The finished product, fresh from the painters. The air intakes have been modified now and the fairing looks much happier. (Brian Lister)

Left A shot of the cockpit. Note how the switchgear had all been placed at the left of the dash panel; Archie's physiology prevented any other layout. Down to the right, out of sight in this shot, a bulb horn was placed, which Archie could punch to give 'audible warning of approach' as if that was necessary. The starter motor can be seen in front of the gearlever, which shows how far back the engine was placed. Archie's height, a shade over five feet, allowed Lister much latitude. It all helped to fine-tune weight distribution. (Brian Lister)

Below left A shot taken on the banks of the River Cam, showing the shrink-wrapped nature of the body. Lister was able to place engine, driver and final drive within a relatively short 89-in. wheelbase. (Brian Lister)

Right The Autodel Garage is still there on the Huntingdon Road out of Cambridge (now known as the A14). Here, Archie works on his Ford Zephyr. Note the Connaught badge on the front wing of the car. (John Bull)

Below A touch of lurid cornering at the CUAC Driving tests at Witchford aerodrome in March 1957. Archie won this first event of the 1957 calendar from Jack Sears, Marcus Chambers, Peter Riley and Tom Threlfall. (John Horsman)

Top Archie trundling out of the paddock for the 1957 British Empire Trophy race. His race numbers add up to 9, as they had in his 1955 entry, although he always maintained that 13, the date of his birth, was luckier for him. People born on the 13th, particularly Fridays, often maintain this. (T. C. March)

Above The start of the final of the Empire Trophy race. Archie gets away in fourth place, but won by a margin of 12 seconds from Salvadori, here in the lead. (Peter Elinskas)

Left Archie in the paddock with one of the prizes after the Empire Trophy – the Fairfield Memorial Trophy – and looking a little older than 29. (Peter Elinskas)

Archie, just about to lap Alan Moore at Goodwood on Easter Monday 1957. Moore is driving Archie's old car, the Lister-Maserati. Archie went on to win. (Autocar)

Archie and MVE 303 at the school fête, summer 1957, in Cambridge. This was the occasion when he made a long detour to Old Addenbrooke's hospital as a morale booster for a sick child. (Cambridge Evening News)

Archie thumbing his nose at Patrick Benjafield during the saloon car race at Silverstone on 17 August 1957, shortly after his return from the Swedish race. (Patrick Benjafield)

Archie's own sketch, done for Motor Racing magazine, of his idea of his course around Silverstone in the Lister-Jaguar. Extravagant though it may look, film of our man driving rather tends to confirm it.

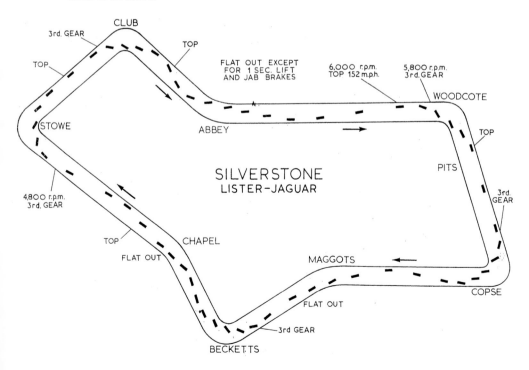

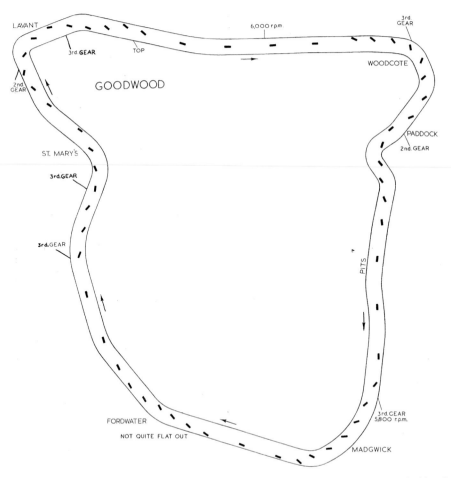

LAVANT

6,000 r.p.m.

3rd. GEAR

3rd. GEAR   TOP

WOODCOTE

2nd. GEAR

GOODWOOD

PADDOCK

2nd. GEAR

ST. MARY'S

3rd.GEAR

3rd.GEAR

PITS

FORDWATER

3rd.GEAR
5,800 r.p.m.

NOT QUITE FLAT OUT

MADGWICK

Scott Brown's assessment of his line around Goodwood, to a different scale, is even hairier. As the article in question says: 'His illustrations, studied in detail, tell more than any written description of his methods could ever impart.'

Stirling Moss, oblivious of the distress of his passenger, trying out the Lister during the practice session for the Unlimited Sports Car Race at Crystal Palace on 10 June 1957. Apart from a couple of road testers, Stirling was the only other driver, apart from Archie, ever to drive this car. When driven in road cars Archie often wore his helmet, which can hardly have boosted the confidence of the driver. (A. R. Smith)

Archie looking faintly sinister before the off at the race preceding the British Grand Prix at Aintree, 20 July 1957. Given the weather, his goggles were, to say the least, unseasonal. Roy's gardening gloves are merely to wipe his visor. Nothing is awry – Reg Parnell, in the duffel coat behind Roy Salvadori, was the Aston Martin Racing Manager, and is merely wearing his habitual expression while leaning forward to overhear. The rain is just starting.

On the start line at Aintree. Note the hastily modified Lister-Jaguar. The full-width screen is fitted with small studs to accept a rudimentary hood, the car has had headlamps crudely installed on rather obvious pods, and there is a windscreen wiper. The car remained in this form for the rest of its life. (Bernard Cahier)

Chapter 9

Archie's missile

THE LISTER-JAGUAR IS A NATIONAL TREASURE
– Walter Hayes, President, Aston Martin Lagonda

THE decision at Jaguar to withdraw from competition activity as a works team, at least on a temporary basis, had much more effect than just freeing up a few works engines for privateers to enter. The fuel and oil backers of the Jaguar team had been Shell, who were now without any serious representation on the UK club and unlimited capacity circuit. If this seems a small thing now, it was not then. The home market for fuel and oil (not to mention tyres and brake pads) had established itself as a worthwhile area for offering what we would now call sponsorship. There was fierce competition for motorists' loyalty, and sports cars were correctly held to be closer to road cars in function and appeal than single-seaters. In the UK the racing efforts of Shell, and their rivals British Petroleum, were managed by Shell-Mex & BP, a marketing cartel which was 60 per cent owned by Shell and 40 per cent by BP. The racing manager of the joint venture was Bryan Turle.

Jaguar had decided that the game was not worth the candle any more, as the purely business objective of the racing programme – increasing car sales – had been met. This left Shell with a severely limited marketing window and it was a hiatus which they were most keen to fill. The Aston Martin team was sponsored by Esso, as was Ecurie Ecosse, and the view at Shell-Mex House was that the gap left by Jaguar's departure would best be filled by a British manufacturer. Listers were already with BP as a fuel sponsor, so the full attention of the Shell-Mex & BP operation was brought to bear on the matter. Fair is fair, and BP's starting money sponsorship would be doubled. Evan Price at Fort Dunlop, with whom Archie also had a tyre testing contract, was also all for it. Lister never really had a chance to say no.

The approach was made in October 1956, actually just before the decision by Sir William Lyons was announced, which suggests a fair degree of collusion in the ambush. Brian Turle suggested the idea at his annual pre-Motor Show meeting with Lister at Shell-Mex House in the Strand. Much was assumed, mainly by BP. If Lister would build a suitable chassis, a full race works D-Type engine would be provided for them at cost price, or about a third of what the Maserati engine had cost. Brian did not give his answer immediately, but pondered during his drive back to Cambridge. Lister already had a suitable chassis conceptually, but it needed to be a little beefier, given the power and, more particularly, the weight of the XK unit. As the possibilities offered by Shell-Mex & BP (and therefore, by default, Jaguar) emerged, Brian Lister reluctantly put his Formula 2 ambitions on the back burner. He was to revive them again in 1957, but the little F2 car was not properly developed, so he assented to the joint approach.

He knew that the Lister chassis had proved itself and that Archie was happier driving sports cars than Formula 2. Brian also calculated that there would be less work to do to adapt the chassis to Jaguar power than there was left to do on the F2 car. Brian talked to Don Moore about it. Moore made a prescient remark: 'You know, you might get Briggs Cunningham interested in a car like that.'

Lister started to feel a frisson of anticipation go through him. Suddenly, there seemed little doubt that this was the way forward. If the car did well, he would be able to sell them in large numbers and this was surely a better advertisement for the engineering business than low-profile F2 racing. He called Turle, and work began (initially on the back of the proverbial cigarette packet) to build a suitable vehicle. Hillwood's machine had at least allowed Brian the chance to think about such an installation, so he was not caught completely by surprise. Back he went to first principles.

The requirements for the new chassis were slightly more complicated than before. The weight, power and torque of the D-Type engine, not to mention its shape (albeit marginally lower than the standard XK engine, by virtue of its dry sump) set certain parameters which had to be followed scrupulously.

Another important factor, of course, was the existence and frequent appearance of the D-Type itself. The new Lister had to be at least as good as the works product, and in that particular Brian had several salient advantages. First, the D-Type had been built to contest Le Mans which, above all else, required it to be reliable for 24 hours of non-stop racing. Consequently it was a substantial machine and relatively heavy for its size. Second, given the constraints of cost, simplicity and the fact that it was a production car rather than a money-no object racer like the Mercedes 300SLR, there were few radical concepts employed in its construction. It had a conventional live axle, for example, which was simple and reliable, but which paid weight and handling penalties unacceptable in the world of fast circuit racing of relatively short duration. Much of what made the D-Type a remarkable piece of kit could be traced to the genius of Malcolm Sayer, the aerodynamicist who penned the body and structure, rather than to any particularly advanced thinking behind the running gear.

The basic Lister chassis layout was kept, as was the material of its construction (T35 3 in. tube), but now the wall thickness was increased to 14 gauge from 16 gauge before, which strengthened it considerably. It was a design formula that worked, so there was little point in changing it. The only concern was the weight distribution, as the XK unit, being iron-blocked, weighed in at almost twice that of the Maserati A6GCS. There was an advantage here. Archie's physiology was to allow Lister to 'cheat' a little with the position of the engine.

The front suspension reverted to equal length wishbones, as on the Maserati-engined car (but not as the Formula 2 car). Again, Girling struts inside coils were used, attached to a fabricated bridge structure at the front of the frame.

At the rear, hub and driveshaft were now one large machined unit. It had to be beefy to absorb the huge torque of the Jaguar engine. It was also simple, and easy to make on a decent centre lathe; such tooling with which Lister's works were more than adequately equipped.

Along its length, the frame supported Duralumin bulkheads, which in their turn braced the tubes upon which the body was hung. Neither the outer panelling nor these bulkheads were actually load-bearing, as the chassis absorbed all the loads, the body being easily removed by the simple expedient of undoing Dzus fasteners. The whole body could be removed in a few minutes.

Then, there was *that engine*. A Jaguar D-Type radiator, made by Marstons, was fitted in the nose, canted backwards 20 degrees to preserve the low nose which was becoming such a Lister trademark. The motor itself was a 3.4-litre dry-sump full works D-Type unit, bench tested at the factory to produce 250 bhp. The unit was itself canted 15 degrees to port, again to lower frontal area. It was placed as far back in the chassis as was practicable, an exercise which was eased by the shortness of Archie's legs. A six-into-three-into-two exhaust (fabricated by Moore along the same principles as he had used on both Bristol and Maserati engines) ran along the nearside of the car outside the body, but recessed flush with it, ending just forward of the rear wheel. The layout of this system, based upon the experience that Moore had had as far back as pre-war MGs, was to add 6–7 bhp to the XK output. Careful porting, polishing and scrupulous balancing (not that much was necessary) added a few more. By the time Moore had finished, the unit was probably putting out in the region of 265 bhp gross. Moore's exhaust system made sure that each cylinder had equal back pressure; the exhaust path of each one was exactly the same, just like its inlet pipe. In this it differed slightly from the D-Type layout.

Lister found to his pleasure that he got on well with F. R. W. England, the Jaguar racing manager. 'Lofty' was well-known for his dislike of bull and found Lister and his organization reassuringly free of that commodity. Theirs was to become a first-rate working relationship.

The power was transmitted through a production Jaguar D-Type four-speed transmission, with an all-synchromesh layout. The gear ratios chosen were 7.61:1, 5.82:1, 4.52:1 and 1:1 with a final drive of 3.54:1. This axle ratio offered a top speed of just over 140 mph, with 60 coming up in 4.6 seconds, 80 in 8 seconds, 100 in 11.2, and 120 in 15.2. All on 10 miles per gallon. Salisbury's offered final ratios as diverse as 2.93:1 and 4.78:1. The former would allow a terminal maximum of close to 200 mph, and the latter would require an engine with a higher rev. limit if the ton was to be exceeded by much. Naturally, the final drive ratios were juggled, depending upon the circuit.

Now, some of this had been done before. Tojeiro, Cooper and HWM, as well as a host of privateers before Hillwood, had all built sports car chassis to accommodate the XK engine. Some of them were successful, others less so. Few were as beautiful. An excellent account of the results can be found in Doug Nye's book – *Powered by Jaguar* (Motor Racing Publications, 1980) – but, as Nye says, the Listers were quite simply the best. It is hard not to agree. The comparatively brief period of chassis development confirms the fundamental soundness of the core design. The neutral handling made them quite friendly. The body design, the best of Lister's work, made them slippery, even if it was at the expense of the brake and driver cooling. The heart of the beast, though, was that wonderful engine, which must surely rank among the all-time greats, whether as power plant or simply as sculpture. From XK120 to Scorpion tank, this landmark piece of engineering has few vices and fewer critics.

The development of the Jaguar XK engine to its ultimate competition form has been extensively documented elsewhere, but a brief assessment is worthwhile, given its role in the construction of the most famous Listers of all. From the conception of the device during the war, to the last Le Mans victories in the 1950s, the gradual progression of the XK engine to possibly the finest general purpose large capacity unit ever made is an inspiring story.

William Lyons had an artist's eye. He felt that the core product of the Jaguar company's post-war success would be an elegant engine in an elegant body, built to a price. He had already proved that he could produce an elegant body – the SS100 has gone down in history as the definitive 30s sports car (a little sharp, perhaps, the bonnet a shade obvious and not as good as it looked, but that is the essence of sports car design on a budget). As for the engine, the Jaguar concern had always used someone else's engines, generally Standard's. Lyons now wanted to make his own – to make the great leap from assembly to total manufacture.

Thus the engine would certainly have two camshafts. It would be clean in appearance. That appearance should attract the interest of all red-blooded buyers save the most uninformed. Even the merest tyro would have a hard time resisting the allure of an engine architecture inspired by Miller, Bugatti, Alfa Romeo and Peugeot. It would be about three litres, because you need a crankshaft of sufficient beef to provide reliability if you are going to take on Rolls-Royce, Armstrong-Siddeley and Daimler for your share of the carriage trade image built to an austerity price.

It has been written elsewhere that William Lyons was no fool. Even he, though, was to underestimate the success of his formula when it came to sports cars. The XK 120 was a previously unheard-of success. To a weary public in 1948 the future was revealed. The Earls Court Motor Show car was bronze, lithe, capable of 120 mph, convertible and less than £1000. The competition was aghast, the public exultant. Customers fell upon it like starving orphans. They still do, actually. The SS 100, the XK120 and its somewhat removed descendant the E-Type probably still define the sports car to the satisfaction of most.

To be sure, the XK 120 was, and is, a remarkable car even if you draw a discreet veil over those bits which did not and do not bear close scrutiny. This was a road car which offered racing car performance; and for the customer of the late 1940s it was the closest thing to being able to have your own Spitfire.

Development was quick, responding equally fast to snags and opportunities in a way which simply could not be done today. The competition potential was obvious from the start, as the engineering had already hit the ground running. Ron 'Soapy' Sutton's record-breaking run on the Jabbeke autoroute in Belgium in May 1949 served to whet the appetite for more.

Of course, the public was entirely correct as it often is. The XK engine was to provide the backbone of Jaguar engineering until the dawn of the XJ40 series in the late '80s. It has operated in various states of tune in capacities from 2.4 to 4.2 litres – private tuners have taken it up to as much as 4.5 litres. As conceived, though, it was a 3.4-litre unit, eventually to be reluctantly enlarged to 3.8.

The issue of increasing the output without sacrificing reliability was addressed logically and speedily. The benchmark unit of 3.4 litres was of a longish stroke and lowish compression, allowing for flexibility and high torque on low-octane fuel. It was, let us not forget, designed to power a large saloon car and offer reliability – this, of all its virtues offered the most potential for development. The huge seven-bearing Laystall crank was the unit's strongest feature – the same attributes which offered smooth running at touring speeds also offered formidable bottom-end strength for racing, particularly when artfully dry-sumped with a separate oil tank to offset the long stroke and resultant height of the unit. In fact, over its factory racing life, the output of the core design was more than doubled, from 160 bhp to 340 bhp; although, of course, the latter was extracted with an alloy engine block and fuel injection.

Most of the changes over the life of the XK engine took place at the top end of it. The head was always of alloy, to save weight and dissipate heat. A process of gradually increasing valve size, camshaft height and compression meant that by 1954, the C-Type unit, running on three Weber carburettors as opposed to the earlier 2 in. SU devices, was producing a reliable 220 bhp. A final change to the exhaust valve angle and the development of a very high-lift cam produced the famous wide-angle '35–40' head, a design purely for racing. It was this 3.4-litre engine, beWebered and dry-sumped – a full works unit – that Jaguar supplied to Listers at something just under cost price, to make Archie's new missile.

There was some debate over the bodywork of the new Lister. All agreed that it should be of 20-gauge alloy and that it would only serve the purpose of keeping the rain off the precious engine, chassis and driver. There was nothing structural about it. The first effort produced a rather unsubtle and clearly derivative fin stabilizer at the headrest (somewhere between the one on Norman Hillwood's car and that of a basking shark) which was quickly deleted. What Lister finally came up with has possibly never been bettered. At first glance it was the beautiful Lister-Maserati on steroids. Certainly, much of the former delicacy was present, despite the car's meatier hindquarters. It was a pure projectile, and although its later appellation was 'Britain's fastest sports car', in this configuration it was just a racer. The note from the engine was several octaves lower than the Maserati-powered car had produced, more basso profundo than top tenor.

There was no excess bodywork at all. Archie sat so low in the car that his presence added nothing to frontal area. Behind the front Dunlop bolt-on wheels, the bodywork was recessed as much as possible. Shrink-wrapped around the frame, this body was Brian Lister's finest effort. It was also his most successful car. Scott Brown was all over it like a rash. Nobody ever drove it in competition but Archie. It had been built for him, and in all probability, nobody else could drive it, at least not in any degree of comfort. It was what the Lister-Maserati could, or should, have been.

Rumours persist to this day that it still survives, tucked away in a barn or lock-up, a subject to which we can revert later. The car was given the identity of the works Lister-Bristol, with BHL 2 as a chassis number, and MVE 303 as a registration. The Bristol-engined car had long been broken up, and elements of it had been recycled elsewhere or disposed of. It was always Lister strategy to dispose of redundant spares (particularly structural ones which might later fail) by scrapping them. In the originality-conscious 1990s, this is a point well worth bearing in mind. That more Listers are around than ever came out of the Abbey Road works is now a matter of public record and an issue addressed in the Appendix. To put it in succinct perspective, something over four dozen cars were made, on rather less than that many chassis numbers, of which only 60-odd survive.

It is not surprising that so many 'replicas' exist. The Lister-Jaguar rapidly became, for a period of three years, the benchmark of circuit racing cars. It was better designed, developed and manufactured than any of its peers and, in its first manifestation, it was driven by a man to whom even the greatest have deferred. It was and is a very special device indeed, and rather easy to make. Anyone with a decent electric welding plant, a good universal milling machine and a centre lathe can have a go. Several, it seems, have done just that.

Chapter 10

The Flying
Scotsman

THE PARADOX OF COURAGE IS THAT A MAN MUST BE A LITTLE
CARELESS OF HIS LIFE EVEN IN ORDER TO KEEP IT.
– G.K. Chesterton: All Things Considered

A PHENOMENAL PILOT WITH UNCANNY CAR CONTROL.
– Juan Manuel Fangio

LISTER'S eased back into competition on the last day of March
1957. Appropriately enough, it was at Snetterton that the Lister-
Jaguar entered, anything but blushing, on to the racing stage. The
practice times which Archie put in were almost up to his Connaught
Formula 1 efforts and he was accordingly awarded pole position. The
crowd settled down for a spectacular display, given that Archie was
sharing the front of the grid with Dick Protheroe in the ex-John Ogier
Tojeiro, also equipped with a D-Type engine. The rest of the front
row consisted of Peter Whitehead in an Aston Martin DB3S and a D-
Type Jaguar driven by Peter Blond. Henry Taylor, driving the
Murkett's D-Type was one row back. On paper, Lister's new car
looked hard to beat. Mind you, so had the Lister-Maserati. Archie
seemed confident, so much as he ever did, chewing gum furiously in
the cockpit as the flag dropped.

The Lister hared off the line, immediately opening a gap, but the
clutch jammed out on lap 1. Six laps later, the mechanism was freed,
with some crudity of method and language, and off he went again.
The public was treated to the controlled drifts and slides which were
now almost the patent trademark of Archie the entertainer. He was, of
course, unplaced, but set fastest lap, to be unbeaten all day. Dick
Protheroe won the race easily after Taylor and Whitehead collided.

This was an irritating and embarrassing teething problem, particularly as it happened at friendly Snetterton. But the following weekend,
6 April, was the BRDC British Empire Trophy at Oulton Park, where
the track was friendly even if the authorities hadn't always been.
Archie had only managed second in heat in 1956 in the fragile Lister-

Maserati, and this was the first proper event that MVE 303 had contested. All eyes were on him; not just the 50-odd thousand spectators, but BP and Jaguar as well. This was the first full works-supported effort that Jaguar had attempted with another manufacturer and much face was at stake.

It was as close to perfect as anyone could have wished. Archie qualified three seconds ahead of Noel Cunningham Reid's Aston Martin and beat Salvadori's similar car to win the Empire Trophy for the second time. Allan Moore came fourth in the 1200–2000 cc heat in the Lister-Maserati, which was now owned by that dedicated Lister customer, Ormsby Issard-Davies. Lofty England, normally a paragon of phlegmatic calm, could hardly contain his glee.

One problem did emerge; the brakes – they had to work inordinately hard. They had been designed for the Triumph TR3, not a 150 mph monster like this. There was no servo assistance either, which was Archie's preference – he liked the direct feel that unservoed brakes gave, on the rare occasions when he used them – it was basic to his driving style. The price paid, though, was boiling brake fluid and a lot of heat which had nowhere to go. There was always concern about the impact of the heat generated by the inboard rear brakes on the differential seals, a common problem with such a layout, even now. It didn't worry the driver overmuch, though. He adored the car. It was the perfect antidote to the 1956 season, with neutral handling, a 420 bhp/ton power/dry weight ratio and a 48/52% front/rear weight distribution, giving it amazing traction through the $6\frac{1}{2}$ in. rear tyres. He was able to fling it about in a manner which the crowds and the press found irresistible. As for the brakes, he would live with them, using them as seldom as he could. A sharp jab from time to time on a briefly-trailing throttle was Archie's style. Bill Heynes at Jaguar gave Girling a very hard time indeed for failing to supply the larger callipers with which they had equipped Aston Martin. Lister got hold of some later in the season, but meanwhile Brian Lister and Don Moore ruefully watched their Formula 2 ambitions gurgle away as Archie and the new car steamrollered all before them that season.

The Lister was parked in the Murkett's showroom for a week, surrounded by its haul from Oulton Park – the Empire Trophy, the Siam Trophy and the Fairfield Memorial Trophy – so that local fans could see the beast at rest. It didn't do any harm to the Murketts' business, either, or to the Lister order book. It was one of the few rests that the car or its driver was to have that season.

With an interval of nearly 40 years, it is hard to believe how popular Archie was. He enjoyed a relationship with the racing public and, more importantly, his peers, that virtually no British driver, before or since, has even approached. He was not grand in any way, gave of his time freely, lived modestly and would drive anything. His contractual relationship with Lister was a bilateral arrangement made between them without the use of a formal contract. Archie, though, was to invoke a 'phantom contract' when it suited him (at least once), just as he would take recourse to law when he was described as one-armed – a phrase which became a tabloid cliché. Given his sunny disposition, this was, superficially at least, an odd conceit. However, he could not afford to allow the myth that he was one-armed to gain credence; it could only create obstacles to race entries. Trawling through press photo archives now, one still comes across hastily-scrawled instructions to sub-editors lest they be prone to being carried away: 'Under NO circumstances describe this man as one-armed!' It would seem that the *Scottish Daily Mail* was a particular culprit of journalistic inexactitude.

His relationship with the public was, of course, mainly conducted via the motoring press, who as a rule loved him. Photographers generally captured him from the waist up, in left profile if possible. Nowadays, in the unlikely event of another Archie coming on the scene, no doubt photographs of him at birth would be syndicated worldwide. His disabilities were not, then, common knowledge amongst the rank and file of racegoers; or if they were, they were seldom alluded to except in the broadest terms. His legs, for example, or his height, were hardly ever mentioned, and many fans remained ignorant of the weakness in his lower limbs.

Archie didn't fight shy of the public, though. Nobody in his position could have done, anyway. Later in the season, when asked by a local school to open their summer fête, the children were told of his prospective attendance some days in advance. The inevitable requests for autographs were passed on and Archie duly obliged. On the day, one poor little chap was unable, because of an illness, to attend the event on the lawn and was instead, hospital-bound at Old Addenbrookes hospital. When Lister was told of this by an only slightly supplicant Headmaster, he communicated the news to Archie, who was sitting in the cockpit, surrounded by admiring kids and parents, not to mention teachers. Without further ado, Archie put aside his mild dislike of infants and trundled down Tennis Court Road to the hospital grounds, stopping the behemoth outside the ward window and sat there, happily burbling the engine, so that the little fellow who could not attend could at least see the car, and by default of course, him. The event made the day in the eyes of most concerned, although there were some grumbles at the aural impact of 260 bhp of barely-silenced racing car growling about the premises. This probably did more to make Archie a local hero to those children, if not Addenbrookes hospital, than anything else he ever did. Certainly, he is still remembered for it.

The 1957 season was to be a remarkable one. Given the restrictions placed upon certain overseas entries because of Archie's handicaps, the profile achieved by the one-car team was astonishing. It was really down to consistency and a total lack of hubris on the part of both driver and entrant. Nothing was assumed unless it was proved. A predictability of results emerged through the season. By the end of it, if Archie lost, so did the bookies. He seldom did, though. Overall, he would win 13 races with MVE 303, setting or matching fastest lap on each occasion, and setting four new absolute lap records.

Given the promising start to the season which the Lister-Jaguar had shown, Brian Lister resolved to enter Archie in a major Continental race. The one he chose was the sports car Grand Prix at Spa on 12 May. At first, his application was rejected out of hand, but Lister persisted. The second time the application was successful, but another problem was thrown up. The race was to be run under Appendix C regulations, which called for a full width windscreen, wipers and proper headlights. By the time his appeal had been accepted, there was no time to modify the car. There is a school of thought that suggests that the Belgian organizers deliberately delayed their acceptance until it was too late for Lister to comply. This argument is probably meretricious as most other British entrants already complied with the regulations, Appendix C being the standard Continental specification, whereas MVE 303 had been designed for UK racing.

To Archie, the forced acceptance had been encouraging. This was in large measure offset by the decision by Connaught (announced after the Monaco Grand Prix the weekend after Spa) to discontinue competitive racing at all levels, for reason of financial exhaustion, made worse by the collapse of the 'Godiva' project, the abandonment of which by Coventry Climax left them without an engine to use. The engine makers were as prone as any to believe that the Continental opposition would flatten them. For Archie this was gloomy news, although not really a surprise. The last time he had sat in a Formula 1 car was at Goodwood the previous October. He had made his mark in Formula 1 though, and the acceptance by the Belgians of the sports car entry, despite the confusion over the regulations promised future success. There was only one problem – he was now out of a works Formula 1 drive.

However, as soon as the word was out that an organizer had accepted an entry from Archie, however belatedly, the Murkett brothers of Cambridge, who had been the buyers of one of the earliest Lister chassis ordered, BHL 8, made an entry on behalf of Henry Taylor and Archie to drive their D-Type Jaguar at the Nürburgring 1000 km race on 26 May. The Murketts knew Archie and Lister extremely well and thought much of the Scot's talent as well as his capacity to attract customers to their business. Archie had after all conducted this very car to win the racing car class at the Snetterton sprint the previous July. The

Germans were initially very iffy, but Tony Murkett insisted – no Archie, no entry. The Germans were insistent in return, but found they were pushing on a piece of string – no Archie, no entry; suit yourselves.

If it seemed surprising that Lister himself did not enter this event, the fact that there was no-one else available to partner Archie in the new car goes a long way to explain it. The original purpose of the liaison with Jaguar, and Shell-Mex & BP had been a domestic endeavour, rather than Coventry's desire to subcontract a new generation of D-Types. Outside the UK, Shell and BP were as hostile as any two oil companies ever are; domestically, they couldn't do enough for each other. The Lister-Jaguar, fruit of their union, proved that. It had been built for and around Archie and no-one else, but not to Appendix C. Henry Taylor was well-acquainted with the D-Type, having performed heroically at the Spa race which Archie missed out on. They were a logical pairing, with complementary talents, both skilled in the wet and both possessed of a properly tigerish will to win.

Archie and Taylor arrived in the trusty Ford Zephyr and drove around the huge 14-mile circuit a couple of times in a Ford Taunus, deceitfully rented in Cologne, to get acclimatized, shredding the unfortunate vehicle's tyres in the process. Familiarization was completed in Tony Murkett's Jaguar Mk I saloon. Being such a major event, there was little time for practice, only two laps per driver. Archie had never driven at the Nürburgring at all and spent one lap feeling his way around, and towards the end of the practice session, went for a one-off fast time. He set fastest Jaguar time, in fact, which was just absurd so far as the onlookers were concerned. Quite ridiculous. They were not to know that this sort of thing had happened before and that it was just a re-run of the Connaught practice at Monza the previous September, another example of Archie's ability to 'sight-read' a track.

Ecurie Ecosse were just starting to pack up for the day. David Murray, appalled at Archie's time, insisted that the team unload the cars and all try again, but no-one could come near the time set by the Nürburgring rookie. There was much shuffling of feet, downward stares and mumbling, but Murray wouldn't let it go at that. He stalked over to the works Maserati pit and asked Fangio, who was partnering Moss in a 450, to take Ivor Bueb's D-Type around. Good-naturedly, the Argentinian agreed, but he couldn't better the time either. This pantomime had Taylor and Tony Murkett rolling about with laughter, with Archie rather more poker-faced, but Murray was having a massive sense of humour failure about the whole issue. In the end, he had no choice but to let it go, and Taylor and Scott Brown ended practice as the fastest Jaguars, to Ecosse's embarrassment and Murkett's delight.

The organizers were, in fact, most unhappy at Archie's participation once they had had sight of him but, in view of his ludicrously fast practice times, they had little choice but to let him continue. Not to have done so would have offended the scrupulous sense of fairness of which the Germans seem to be so justifiably proud. Still, there were some adverse comments. That Archie's entry had been accepted at all though was a persuasive precedent. It has often been assumed, not least by this author, that Archie received no European approvals (Sweden excepted) until 1958. The stigma of his disability was clearly diluted in Europe by his own success as early as May 1957. History has thus been unfair to the organizers of Continental events. Xenophobia may have played its part, or a traditional British delight in rooting for the apparent underdog. Either way, it is clear that Archie was an international star in the ascendant rather sooner than it has generally been acknowledged, although it clearly required more than a little stonewalling to provide his opportunities.

The pair agreed that Taylor should drive first, which eliminated the risk that the Le Mans-style sprint start might penalize Archie; and so it was all set. Archie, for his size and structure, was a good (even phenomenal) sprinter, but Henry Taylor was faster, and had had more long-distance driving experience. Taylor was a spectacularly good driver, especially in the wet, as he had shown, at Spa. The strategy was simple enough. Driving to survive the long punishing course, they would stay within reach of the leaders (expected to be the works Maseratis and Aston Martins), look to reliability to give them an edge on the opposition, and go for a good place. Archie was to be saved for the task of fine-tuning their position later in the race. Like many plans, however, it was not to survive its first contact with reality.

In the event, Taylor found the temptation of dicing with a privately entered Maserati too hard to resist, and succeeded in spinning the D-Type off, but not before he had held the lead over the eventual winner, Tony Brooks, for a lap or two. Thus Archie never got to turn a wheel in anger on his Continental debut. It had indeed been a persuasive precedent, though, and yet another hurdle had been overcome. For Taylor, there was another development. Aston Martin had been so impressed with his driving in the wet that he was asked to be a reserve driver for them for Le Mans that year, and on many occasions afterwards. The D-Type was soon afterwards sold to the Border Reivers team, the 'other' Scottish racing équipe and was to be used by the man who had followed Archie into Clifton Hall prep. school, Jim Clark. Clark was later to compete in his Continental debut in this car at Spa in 1958.

Archie was soon back on top. The Whit Monday BRSCC meeting at Crystal Palace on 10 June gave him his fourth Lister-Jaguar victory of the season in the unlimited sports car race – only a ten-lapper – setting, as the spectators were starting to expect by now, fastest lap as well.

Stirling Moss tested the Lister for a few laps around Crystal Palace, Archie gritting his teeth and hanging on grimly in the miniscule passenger seat. Moss was the only driver to ever drive Archie in his own car, and was able to get the measure of it quite well. He was only entering the Norbury Trophy in a Cooper-Porsche that day, so was not to meet the Lister in competition until the next year. He could also see that Aston Martin, faced with the Lister, verily had a problem. Moss was not to drive for the Feltham team that season – virtually all his sports car racing activity in 1957 was to be in Maseratis – but he knew what to expect when he was hired for 1958.

Archie had drifted into national hero status by the middle of the 1957 season. Over a million people would have seen him race by then, and he had seldom been off the cover of the enthusiast's press, whether in a Lister, an Elva or a Connaught, but the children's comic industry was to grant him an even greater accolade soon. The *Lion* (later to be renamed the *Vulcan*) had, since 1952, been running a strip cartoon character which answered to the unlikely title of 'the Jungle Robot', a sort of cross between Mr Spock and a Dalek. Clearly ahead of its time, it or he was possessed of an ice-cool temperament and an enviable facility for problem-solving at short notice. Despite these virtues, the character never generated the following its creators felt was deserved. This creation was mutated at the end of 1957 into 'Robot Archie', and never really looked back – the strip actually ran until 1966, possibly even longer, although records are sketchy, as are memories. This writer will not confess to having read it any later than 1963.

Brian Lister was cautiously reviving his Formula 2 ambitions by now. Having seen the competition at work, he resolved to pick up where he left off with a development of the concept he had abandoned once already. The withdrawal of Connaught from racing suggested that his works driver might now concentrate just a little harder on the issue in hand. The machine he proposed seemed to make eminent sense. Now that the Coventry Climax 1500 cc twin-cam FPF engine was available and, more important, proven, he felt that the prototype could be developed with some real benefit. In fact, it was totally redesigned, from scratch.

It was a more sophisticated car which owed little to either its precursor or its current stablemate. It was almost as light as the 1956 car, but weight distribution was considerably improved by a longer wheelbase, within which the fuel tanks were placed outside the main structure of the body. A slight increase in frontal area would, it was thought, be compensated for by a uniform change in weight distribution as the petrol was used up, as well as a low centre of gravity. The new Climax engine was very powerful for its size, offering 141 bhp at 7000 rpm. So, to improve traction as well as front/rear balance, an integrated gearbox and final drive was employed, the shaft to which was offset to allow the driver to sit lower in the car. The unit was made at Abbey Road from a Bristol gearbox and a Salisbury differential. To permit the offset, the engine was canted over 30 degrees. All sound stuff, and reminiscent of the offset Maseratis which Modena had tried out at Monza in 1956. It was, as an exercise in engineering, Lister's most complex project yet.

Archie didn't like it at all. He felt, laying eyes on the bare frame (now made from square section tube), that it looked like a coffin. He was right, it did – but so do all single-seaters. This was just superstitious nit-picking, a characteristic of many drivers, and one which Archie was to develop to almost a fine art – his list of do's and don'ts almost deserved its own manual.

His main problem lay in the fact that the final drive layout required the propshaft to rotate at crankshaft speed, and it sat right beside him, offset as he was to the right. He was also concerned that it might come adrift at the front, drop, and catapult the car into the air; or come adrift at the back and, flailing about, cut him in half. All concerned were quick to point out that this was highly unlikely, but he remained adamant in his opinion of it and he was never to be at ease on the few times he drove the car. As we have seen, Archie was no engineer, and his simple refusal to come to terms with the layout was a cause of a little debate at Abbey Road. The Lister-Jaguar had a similar layout after all, albeit with a propshaft spinning more slowly. Archie sat low in that machine because of the width of the space between the frame and the propshaft. Eventually, all agreed to differ.

On 4 July a small diversion was offered. Jaguar Cars were working hard on their successor to the XK series of sports cars, the duration of which had been eked out somewhat by the stopgap XK150, which was showing its age a little by now. The new vehicle was conceptually complete, but had not been tested under circuit conditions – a polite way of saying thrashed. It had first been run on 15 May and road tested nine days later by Sir William Lyons and William Heynes. It was code-named the E1A, and was Malcolm Sayer's logical development of the D-Type/XKSS cars. This would soon become the E-Type. It ran at the time with a high output 3-litre alloy-blocked XK engine, and Archie and Ivor Bueb were asked to test the car at Silverstone. Bueb, in partnership with Mike Hawthorn, had won the fateful 1955 Le Mans race in a D-Type, and Archie was currently the leading Jaguar exponent in the country. It was a further vote of confidence in Scott Brown by Coventry, and it served to cement their relationship with Lister's even more firmly. Not that this was a sinecure; they really wanted to know what he thought. The new car had a complex and advanced rear suspension and final drive subframe, totally unlike the D-Type's rather crude live axle. The opinion of Archie, the great drifter, would be quite important to them, given that the firm was already reassessing the possibility of entering competition as a works team. In effect Archie was being provisionally shortlisted as a works driver should that decision be made. What he thought is not on record now, but a comprehensive test was carried out by Mike Hawthorn (on loan from Ferrari) a week later, which concluded that the handling was a little wayward, which was an odd reaction, given that Ferrari were still using cart springs.

Two days after the Silverstone test, Archie entered the Elva Climax for a BRSCC meet at Mallory Park and he came third. The car's steering had been adjusted for his needs by now – the wheel was more difficult to tear off.

It was a frequent feature of racing then that big sports car races were used as 'warm up' events for Grands Prix, and so it was at Aintree on 20 July 1957. This event has subsequently gone down in Lister lore as a great conspiracy, possibly with some justification.

Roy Salvadori was entered in the event to drive Aston Martin DBR1/1, the car which he had driven a scant month earlier at Le Mans. That race was run as unlimited capacity, after the rather limp 1956 event with a 3-litre limit from which the spectators stayed away in droves. Salvadori drove the car to Appendix C specification, though, with a full-width screen, wipers and headlamps. Salvadori had also come second to Archie at the Empire Trophy and at Goodwood driving this car. To say that Astons were dismayed by Lister's success would be an understatement. The cost of their racing programme was clearly threatening to cripple the finances of not only Aston Martin, but the larger David Brown corporation as well – a state of affairs made all the worse by a signally limited level of success, given the scale of their investment. Other than an occasional pipe dream, Lister was not seriously contemplating the manufacture of road cars, whereas this activity was Aston Martin's core business, and the public relations exercise was proving ruinously expensive for Brown. To be bested by such a tiny manufacturer as Lister was an irritant, to say the least. Reg Parnell, despite his huge respect for both Lister and Scott Brown, routinely and bluntly referred to the Cambridge car as a 'fucking special'. It *was* a special, technically, but so reliable was the Jaguar engine that Lister was to spend something pleasingly less than £50 on engine maintenance that season. When asked by the ever-curious Parnell at the end of the season how much the effort had cost Lister, Brian replied airily, 'Oh, about four or five thousand,' at which Parnell almost burst – Aston Martin regularly spent that much on one cylinder head.

In 1957 the *News of the World* was largely the same, qualitatively, as it is now, save that motoring was a bigger element of its content than mammary glands, and the motoring correspondent, Keith Challen, was a highly respected journalist – fair, unbiased and unusually accurate.

Brian Lister, being a careful planner, had written to the BRDC, the BARC and the BRSCC at the beginning of the season in order to clarify the rules for domestic competition for 1957 races. All had replied that UK competition would be run under 1956 regulations – which meant no lights, aero- or wrap-around screens, wipers and so forth were required. This, in short, was why MVE 303 was built the way that it was. The Aintree race was to be run under the auspices of the BARC. Two members of the Competitions Committee of the BARC, both Feltham men, insisted that the race be run under the 1957 Appendix C specification, as most of those taking part were also entering Continental races where the 1957 regulations were in force – the same point which Brian had forgotten when making Archie's application for the 1957 Spa race. To force them to change their cars, it was argued, would put them to needless expense and inconvenience, particularly because entries for Spa, a bare month later, would require reversion to Appendix C.

Trouble was, nobody told Brian Lister. Someone felt that the news should be leaked, though, and telephoned Keith Challen to tell him the details. Challen quickly calculated that whatever the whys and wherefores of the regulatory change, it was grossly unfair to let Lister be disqualified through ignorance of the 'conspiracy', so he phoned Cambridge. There were 12 days to go and MVE 303 had no lights, no wipers and no full-width screen. The car was modified immediately. There was literally no room to fair the lights in without running the risk of fouling the front wheels, so they were put in rather unattractive pods on the front curvature of the wingline. There was a small risk to the aerodynamics of the car, but at least it would get to compete. Accordingly, the équipe arrived for practice fully ready for the fray. Throughout the whole of its career, the car had to suffer the indignities of the tinsnips and dolly as cooling slots were placed in as many locations as could be found, particularly on the rear deck. The use of an Appendix C full-width screen was to exacerbate the problem. The car, designed as a slippery projectile with tiny frontal area, did not take well to the addition of this type of screen, as it interrupted airflow and reduced air pressure in the cockpit. Archie was to have problems as well. Given his low location, the low pressure of the cockpit overheated him as well and left him short on breath. He tired easily, anyway – another, less visible, legacy of his mother's illness while carrying him.

It was not merely the appearance of the car which had changed. Jaguar had been rightly pleased at the results so far for the new hybrid – they had exceeded expectations. The news that Aston Martin had introduced their new all-alloy 3.7-litre engine at Le Mans caused some small concern at Coventry. The engine had acquitted itself well at the Le Mans race and the risk was that, with an estimated 290 bhp available, the Aston would beat the Lister. Lofty England decided that a

3.8-litre D-Type engine should be made available forthwith, to be fitted prior to the Aintree event. It was engine No. E5007–9, and was
bench tested to 290 bhp (about as powerful as could be managed without using fuel injection) in the competition department at Coventry.
Don Moore's exhaust pushed the power towards 310 bhp, so possibly
this engine was the most powerful of the carburated iron-block units
at the time. The engine was prepared initially to have twin ignition,
but the extra complexity involved might compromise reliability, so the
extra spark plug openings were ultimately blanked off. The extra
power of the 3.8 engine, in fact, just about cancelled out the extra drag
from the full-width screen and headlights. In pre-Appendix C form,
the Lister would have been an even more extraordinary vehicle with
the 3.8 engine. In the event, Aston Martin did not use the 3.7 engine,
but kept to their 3-litre unit which, although more of a racing design,
displaced 20 per cent less – which made Salvadori's performance in the
race all the more creditable, given that the boot was now on the other
foot.

In practice, Lister was worried that Aston Martin might substitute
Moss for Salvadori, which would stiffen the opposition and disturb
Archie. This may have been naïve of Brian, for everybody knew
Salvadori would be as quick as he could. Moss was driving for Vanwall
in the main race and Tony Vandervell might not have taken kindly to
his arrangements being compromised. Nevertheless, that was Lister's
view. He advised Archie to go for a good grid, but not to totally humil-
iate Aston Martin in practice, lest they produce Stirling. Archie went
for his place, and got it, and then proceeded to lap faster and faster.
Lister pulled him up and demanded to know what he thought he was
doing, or words to that effect. Scott Brown's reply is revealing. 'Well, I
thought if I could go a bit quicker they'll bring Moss in. Better to win
beating Moss ...' They didn't bring Moss in, and Archie won his place
on the front row.

Moss was Archie's benchmark. When Peter Riley asked him if he
was nervous before a race, Archie's reply was: 'Yes, but only of making
a fool of myself ... of doing it wrong in front of Stirling.' Moss and he
were not the closest of friends, but enjoyed rather more than a nod-
ding acquaintance and a huge mutual respect. That Archie took
Stirling so seriously as a man to beat was not merely the ambition of a
junior clubman raising his sights; he had led Moss, beaten Moss, and
could in many ways be considered as a peer of Moss. Salvadori is convinced that had Archie been driving the Lister-Bristol at Goodwood in
September 1955, Salvadori would not have beaten him. No doubt he
never told Archie this, of course. Nonetheless, Archie respected
Stirling more than any other driver, except perhaps Fangio.

The splendid irony of Aintree 1957 was that under 1956 rules
Archie would not have had a chance. The reason was the weather. It

rained very hard and without a full-width screen, Archie would not, in all probability, have won. As he came up against the back markers to lap them, hotly pursued by the Aston of Salvadori, the spray, mud and racing debris thrown up by the cars ahead totally occluded his view. Accordingly he tore off his goggles and crouched behind his new full-width screen in order to see the rabbit. Naturally, had he been forced to look over the screen rather than through it, he would have had great difficulty seeing where he was going. As it was, his eyes were terribly scoured by the rain and mud. He was unable to see the pit signals properly and nearly eased off a lap too soon, at which he had Salvadori snapping at his heels in inimitable style. He worked it out just in time and pressed on, pedal to the metal, to win by two seconds from Salvadori. His average speed was nearly 79 mph and he shared fastest lap at 2.11.8 with his old rival. Salvadori had wisely worn a visor. From then on Archie always carried a spare pair of goggles.

Archie slumped in the car, cold compresses over his eyes, and after receiving his prize and pocketing £115 in prize money, blundered off to see the doctor. He was well enough to win both the Formule Libre Vanwall Trophy and the sports car race for 2700 cc and over at Snetterton a week later on 27 July. This meeting was the one which effectively ended John Horridge's racing career, as he broke, comprehensively, both his Lister-Bristol and his neck. It didn't stop him buying another one, though. He couldn't exactly shrug off the loss, as he was in plaster, but he bought from Brian Lister the ex-Allan Moore-driven car which had been originally ordered by Ormsby Issard-Davies with a Dan Dare body. When Horridge bought it, it had a flat-iron, Lister-Maserati body. One theory is that the original Issard-Davies body was used to replace the one that Jack Sears wrote off so spectacularly. Lister retained the registration number from the Issard-Davies car, VPP 9, as it was considered at Cambridge that 9 was a lucky number for Archie. Actually he preferred 13, as people born on the 13th often pretend to.

BRM had hung out their shingle at the Aintree meeting, looking for a new driver. Salvadori had quit the team after the Monaco Grand Prix, irritated by the patronizing attitude of Raymond Mays. The major problem with the car seemed to have been the brakes. The car had three of them, two at the front and one at the back, mounted at the transaxle. The problems created by binding, failing, and locking were hard to eradicate. Mays seemed stubborn enough to believe that the system could work (despite poor Mike Hawthorn's experience) whereas the drivers were firmly of the opinion that it would not. The consensus view was that the car was mechanically underdeveloped, had unjustifiably exotic pretensions and was potentially a death trap. Few were more vociferous on the subject than Hawthorn who urged Archie: 'It already tripled my laundry bills – don't go near the bloody thing.'

Salvadori did not need to be consulted, of course, having already voted with his feet. A string of drivers had tried the car and disliked it, but had been persuaded up to Bourne to conduct further tests. Raymond Mays was well known as being a persuasive fellow, but upon their return they were unanimous in their criticism of the car. They told anyone who would listen, but particularly Archie, who was inordinately popular, to forget it.

The temptation for Archie, however, was great. It was, after all, a Formula 1 effort, a class at which he had proved his ability beyond the doubts of all but the most uninformed. Further, like Connaught, the BRM suited Archie's physiology. Again, it was down to the gearchange. Whereas the Connaught's strong point was its use of a preselector, the BRM used a conventional transmission, but with the gear lever placed on the left rather than the right. Any other top-line Formula 1 car would have to be modified in this respect. Archie's error, if it was one, was that he was used to working on a continuous basis with people like Lister and Moore, with whom he had established a portfolio of successes. Lister was also spending his own money; Mays and Peter Berthon were not, as they were funded by the Owen Organization. The amount of money under discussion was possibly suspiciously high, also. Raymond Mays's blandishments and clear ambitions probably sounded reasonably convincing to Archie, though, despite the fact that Mays was not attempting to negotiate from a position that even resembled strength or relevant track record, given what Brooks, Hawthorn, Salvadori and Moss thought of the car. Mays was pressing on contrary to the evidence.

Archie had already had a go in the BRM, a fact unbeknown to many at the time, and described the handling, with his usual technical inexactitude, as 'queer'. The oddest characteristic that the car seemed to possess, and one which was particularly inimical to Archie's style of driving, was an apparent tendency for the front end to break away first, causing a spin if any attempt was made to apply more power to slew round the rear end of the car. Thus, the machine was immune to the throttle control which Archie, and most other drivers, used to manage their cars around corners. This, of course, was precisely the point. The BRM was to become a superb car once engineer Tony Rudd gave it some input, but that time was some way off.

Archie, against the advice of everybody (including Brian), went up to Lincolnshire to try the machine out again at Folkingham aerodrome, the BRM race headquarters. This time round the brakes failed and he went straight on through a corner. He shrugged it off, assuming that the problem could be fixed. He thought very hard before telling Lister what had happened, eventually getting around to it several weeks later. When Mays pestered him again, he prevailed upon Lister to hold him to his 'contract' so that he could sidestep the issue without giving offence to either party, but possibly to extend his options further. The fact that Lister had only a rudimentary indemnity agreement with Archie, an arrangement which had frequently let him drive for other entrants, bothered him hardly at all. Other people did not necessarily know that, and may have assumed a closer formal relationship than they actually had. Brian was happy to participate in the harmless subterfuge, if only to contribute to saving his works driver's life. Archie was rather sorry about the money, though.

Two weeks after Aintree saw the BRSCC meet at Brands, where Archie competed in three cars. He came third in the 1100 cc sports car race, driving the Lotus-Climax and made a good showing with the prototype Elva-AJB in the 1500 cc event. Indeed he set fastest lap before the greedy engine gobbled a valve.

The Kingsdown Trophy, for sports cars over 1900 cc, was a walkover. Archie led from the flag and won it going away. He set fastest lap at 73.2 mph which established a new sports car lap record for the circuit. At 61 seconds, his time was two seconds slower than his fastest lap in the Formula 1 Connaught the previous October at the BRSCC Formula 1 race, but would still have put him on the second row of that particular grid. Archie had won that race at 73.8 mph, to put things into perspective.

David Murray, the Patron of the Ecurie Ecosse team, based at Merchiston Mews, Edinburgh, had a slight problem in his entry for the Swedish Sports Car Grand Prix, to be held on 11 August. Ron Flockhart had been entered to share a D-Type with John Lawrence, but had not fully recovered from a previous injury. Murray had already seen, to his embarrassment, what Archie could do in a D-Type when he had stomped all over the Edinburgh team in practice in Germany. Archie was invited to substitute for Flockhart, and accordingly he shot off to Kristianstad, where the race, which counted towards the World Sports Car Championship, was to be held. He was phlegmatically nodded through the medical. It was a Continental-style road circuit, a type upon which Archie had never competed before. It showed a little bit, too.

Most of the heavy metal was there. Moss was in the Maserati 450 which he had driven at the Nürburgring, shared with Behra. Collins was in a 4.1-litre Ferrari. Aston Martin were absent. The weather was foul. Archie took over the D-Type on lap 62 when it was lying fifth. He raised the position to third before losing a place by spinning off several times. He clawed his way back to third and, with some relief, gave the slightly battered car back to Lawrence. While in his care, it went off again and cracked a pipe, losing its oil. The result was that the duo were classified eighth. It had been a fine result, and triggered Murray to start stalking Archie as a candidate for a seat in an Ecosse car on a regular basis. To achieve this objective, Murray started to make extravagant promises of both overseas championship entries as well as top-flight starting money. Archie's sense of national pride as a Scotsman was invoked, as was any other lever which Murray could think of. But, as the courtship, with its quickly-moving goalposts (well, maybe not six races next year, perhaps four …) dragged on towards the end of the season, Archie was eventually minded to stay where he was and take his chances on international competition. He had every reason to believe now that it was going to get easier, not harder. He was discussing Le Mans with Lister.

Archie returned via Frankfurt and Prestwick for a few days rest in Scotland before heading south to Silverstone for the rigours of the 750 Motor Club six-hour relay on 17 August, where he was piloting an Austin A35. Archie liked these cars rather a lot. When the A35 van was launched, Archie was fascinated to know whether or not it was faster or slower than the saloon. Nothing would do but to find out. Accordingly, Marshalls of Cambridge were inveigled into providing one of each so that Archie could try them out along the road past the Autodel garage. Archie would drive one vehicle, Gus Benstead, an employee of Marshalls the other. Rodney Tibbs, the motoring correspondent of the *Cambridge Daily News*, went along as ballast. Whichever car had one occupant went the quicker, which was not a great surprise to anyone. Still, Archie competed in a car, not a van. In the event, the A35 team came second.

On 1 September, Lister's entered MVE 303 in the SMRC meeting at Snetterton. Archie slid home a relatively easy first in the unlimited sports car race, albeit at the crawling pace of 75 mph. Snetterton was at least a 90 mph circuit in the dry, but it was pouring with rain. In the Formule Libre race which followed, Archie led until the last mile, when a broken oil pipe forced him to retire.

There was another Lister-Jaguar in the lists that day. It was the first time out for the newly reconstituted HCH 736. This registration number originally graced the Lister-Bristol with the Dan Dare body, BHL 5, originally owned by John Green. Austin Nurse, the man who had almost built his own Lister-Jaguar, bought the car from Green and competed with it with some success in 1956, the year of the Lister-Maserati. The car was comprehensively thumped at Silverstone at the 1956 British Grand Prix meeting on 14 July. It was written off, but not before the engine had been saved. The engine went into another ex-Green car, JCH 888, which had some success in the latter part of 1956.

This left Nurse with a log book and a few bits of bent metal. Now that he had another Lister, he sold the wreck's identity to Tom Kyffin, who ran Torquay-based Equipe Devone. Kyffin commissioned a Lister-Jaguar from Abbey Road at the beginning of 1957, but by the time the car was ready he had rather lost interest in being an entrant.

His attention instead had been caught by sailing as a pastime. He was labouring under the delusion that ocean racing was a cheaper hobby than car racing, so had clearly not noted Sir Thomas Lipton's well-known aphorism on the subject, that it was like 'standing under a cold shower, tearing up ten pound notes'. Accordingly the project was taken over by one of the Equipe's members, Dick Walsh, for Kyffin to drive in the meeting. Kyffin never drove it again, as it was reserved for Bruce Halford for the next year. It had a beautiful body, made by Maurice Gomm, which followed the lines of the works car, albeit with slightly neater headlights and a full-width screen. It was to become a legend in Lister circles.

Two weeks later, at Silverstone, Archie was up against Salvadori, Brooks, Cunningham-Reid and his old team mate Stuart Lewis-Evans in a full works team of Aston Martins, a pair of 3-litre DBR1s and another of 3.7-litre DBR2s. Salvadori and Cunningham-Reid drove the DBR2s.

Prior to that, though, there were three other races for Archie to enter. The first was the International Trophy Formula 2 race, where Brian had entered his redesigned Lister Climax F2 car. Archie practiced at 1.54, which was a whole six seconds behind Salvadori on pole, and earned a place on the last line of the grid. He was only a second behind Cunningham-Reid and Leston, in fact, but the car was not running as it should. Despite Archie's dislike of the car, he was a tryer, after all. Oil was flowing out through the crankcase breathers and the pressure was inconsistent. It was decided to abandon the entry, a decision which upset Archie not at all.

Next up was the Elva-AJB for the 1500 cc sports car race. Once again, the Butterworth engine ate a valve.

The Murkett brothers had entered Archie in the saloon car race in their 3.4 Jaguar which gave Archie a fairly terrifying moment. The main opposition was a works-prepared 3.4 driven by Mike Hawthorn with disc brakes and a limited-slip diff. The Murkett car had the special diff., but only standard drum brakes. Archie and Hawthorn were in the lead for most of the event, neck and neck, but Archie suffered total brake failure at Copse corner after overtaking and trying to out-brake the works car. He had overdone it and was way off the racing line. Faced with this he did the only thing he could. He jammed the gearbox into second and held on for dear life. The XK engine wailed up to 8500 rpm, bouncing valves furiously, but stayed intact. Archie managed to halt the car on the trackside. Tony Murkett was greatly relieved at their car remaining in one piece and there seemed, despite the torture inflicted upon it, to be no major engine damage. Archie had set fastest lap with Hawthorn and had also set a new saloon car lap record for the circuit. Then came MVE 303's race.

In a fierce practice session, after which Archie had mentioned that the Lister felt a little 'queer' (Archie's catch-all expression), Salvadori had pipped him for pole position. The two of them fought hard for the lead, swapping it twice by the sixth lap when Salvadori regained it and held Archie off for the rest of the race. Salvadori won at just over 96 mph, Archie was second at 95.6 mph and Cunningham-Reid was third at 95 mph. Brooks was fourth, but only just. Not surprisingly, Aston Martin were delighted to have at last beaten the Lister-Jaguar for the first time that season.

The Lister team trudged back to Cambridge to tear down the car for the last race of the season at Goodwood on 28 September. Don Moore found a bent valve in the engine, and Dick Barton found that the rear springs were coilbound. This had had the effect of slamming the de Dion assembly up against its bump stops at the expense of adhesion. That Archie had even been placed in the race was remarkable enough, let alone achieved second. He shrugged it off. He was a first-rate tester, but lacked completely the technical expertise to diagnose and articulate mechanical problems except in the vaguest terms.

A depressing interlude for Archie was the holding of the liquidation auction at Send (in Surrey) of Connaught Engineering. Despite the efforts of sundry deal-makers to sell the operation to a major manufacturer, the concern was dissolved and knocked down, to survive as the South of England's largest Goggomobil dealer – which was rather a tragic comedown.

With the Lister-Jaguar back together again, complete with new springs and a top-end overhaul, the only serious maintenance which the car received that season, the team headed for the last effort of 1957, the Goodwood Trophy.

As it was the last proper race of the year, the event was more than usually good-natured. Dick Barton took pains to ensure that Archie left both fuel switches in the 'down' position before taking his spot for the Le Mans-type sprint start. Duncan Hamilton observed this exchange and mischievously flicked them up as Archie was crossing the road for the off. Hearing the clicking sound, Archie rechecked the cockpit, and Barton clicked them down again, firmly. Hamilton repeated his trick. Eventually, after another attempt, the D-Type driver gave up and took his place in the line up. Up went the flag and, during the pause, Archie, flicking a sideways glance at Hamilton, shouted for the starter to get on with it just as the flag was dropping. Archie wrong-footed the whole field back to the other side of the track where the cars were, and got away first, a position he was to hold for the whole race. The luckless Hamilton, caught out and never a great sprinter, leapt into his D-Type Jaguar and pressed the throttle rather too hard prior to dropping the clutch. The skid marks described a perfect parabola as Hamilton ended up facing the wrong way, clearing the pits rather rapidly in the process. He was forced to wait while the entire field sped by before he could turn the Jaguar around and set off in pursuit. Archie won going away at 89 mph. It was a suitably amusing end to a season which had seen Archie confirm his place among the very top echelon.

The Woodcote Cup for Formula 2 cars was more problematical. He made a reasonable grid and drove an entertaining six laps in the Lister-Climax, but retired on the seventh. First three places, Salvadori, Brabham and Allison were all also Climax-powered. Clearly, though, the engine disliked being canted over 30 degrees, as the volatile oil pressure showed.

After Goodwood the Lister-Jaguar was lent to *Autosport*'s John Bolster for a road test; he achieved 0–60 in 4.6 seconds on a 3.77:1 diff and 0–100 in 11.2. He estimated that top speed was in the region of 140 mph, which he did not see, but he did confirm that 120 could be reached in 15.2 seconds. *The Autocar* tested the Lister shortly afterwards and reported in a slightly less breathless style that the car would reach 100 mph in 11 seconds and do a standing start quarter mile in 13.

Lister's season may have been over, but Archie's wasn't. Before packing up for the winter he returned to Brands Hatch on 6 October for the BRSCC meeting. He entered two races, driving an Elva-Climax in the 1100 cc sports car race and an Elva-AJB in the 1101–1500 cc event. He won them both, setting a new lap record in the smaller capacity event. Now, he could relax, particularly chuffed that the AJB engine had held together. He had driven a phenomenal season, unmatched before or since, but had also pushed himself very hard. He had competed at every level of the sport, from baby Austins to Formula 1. He had entered over 50 races. He was very, very tired.

Plans to put a variant of the prototype Lister-Jaguar into production had been finalized in the late autumn of 1957. To design a body which would be as effective as Archie's car, whatever the regulations (which, of course, had to cater for Appendix C), was the main task. In arriving at the ultimate design, Brian Lister put all his ingenuity to work. The whole racing community knew of his skill as a body designer, but what he now produced has rightly become immortal.

Much of the overall beauty of the Lister-Maserati and its Jaguar-engined derivative had been unavoidably lost. In truth, on being subjected to the Appendix C specifications, MVE 303 lost most of its minimalist elegance, anyway. Beating those regulations while maintaining the core Lister qualities of small frontal area and modest height became the key objective. Lister had no plans to be caught out again as he had been at Spa and Aintree.

Broadly, the method by which Lister did this was to keep the engine exactly where it was in the chassis and lower the body around it. This of course had the obvious effect of creating a hump over the cam covers. Behind the engine the scuttle dropped away sharply, as did the front shroud at both sides, leaving the XK engine standing proud. The broad shape of the raised area continued down to the air intake. The wings hugged the shape of the wheels fore and aft, being blended smoothly into the high rear deck, but remaining separately defined at the front, where headlights were faired in behind Perspex covers.

The exhaust, the same Don Moore fabrication as before, was no longer outside the car, but hidden behind the nearside of the neatly radiused centre section. The tailpipes exited as before just forward of the nearside rear wheel. Cooling vents were optimistically let into the rear wings to protect the new 12 in. inboard rear brakes from vaporizing the brake fluid and cooking the rear de Dion seals. The screen was a full-width Perspex assembly, studded to accept a rudimentary hood, as the regulations required. Its overall height was 2 in. lower than the 1957 car.

Under the skin there were a few changes, too. The broad outline of the chassis was little changed, save for the addition of two parallel tubes to replace the apices of the kite plan. This allowed the driver to sit lower than before, with more space and take advantage of the lower screen and scuttle. A new final-drive casing of cast Elektron magnesium was made and partially offset to the nearside, demanding unequal length drive shafts. Again, this created a slightly roomier cockpit. Inside the casing was the same Salisbury diff. as before, with the full set of optional ratios which that company offered to be decided by customer choice. Brakes, front and rear, were Girling alloy callipers which grasped solid 12 in. diameter discs.

A giant 38-gallon fuel tank sat behind the driver, occupying the whole width of the car. Beneath it lived the spare wheel, tyre and all. Either side of the spare sat the 8-gallon dry-sump tank (nearside) and the battery (off side).

Inside the car, the appointments, although less than luxurious, were a marked improvement. Two seats, very thinly padded, sat either side of a transmission tunnel which now sported a cover of lightly stuffed leather. Compared to the 1957 car, it was positively sybaritic. Mechanics were to find it a joy to work on compared to some of its peers.

Brian decided to appoint Williams and Pritchard to make the bodies, but before he did, he asked Cavendish Morton to provide a three-quarter view for release to the press. Williams and Pritchard, located in Edmonton, were closer to Cambridge than the previous contractors, Wakefield of Byfleet and more convenient for potential series production. W & P suggested that much weight could be saved by using Elektron panelling for the body as opposed to the conventional aluminium. It was expensive, of course, and hard to work and weld, but might save 40 per cent on the weight of the body. The issue was left to the customers, but Brian elected to use it for the works cars, at least. He was to regret it.

Brian announced his intentions to the press on 15 October 1957, almost a year after Jaguar's announcement had afforded him the opportunity to create the Great Car:

THE 1958 LISTER-JAGUAR

This is artist Cavendish Morton's impression of the 1958 Lister-Jaguar. Basically, the specification is similar to the 1957 works car which has been driven so successfully this season by Archie Scott Brown, the main difference being a 10 per cent reduction in frontal area over the 1957 car, (the height of the car has been reduced by 3 inches) this being achieved partly by the low seating position. The tail, running at the same level as the top of the windscreen, ensures aerodynamic efficiency and has the added advantage of providing extra fuel storage space, (tankage capacity now being 35 gallons). The body conforms to current Appendix C specification. Basic price of the complete car is £2750, plus tax. This car offers the best combined price to performance, power to weight and power to frontal area ratios available anywhere in the world for a sports car.

The 1957 racing season has now ended and out of the 14 races for which they entered, Scott Brown and the Lister-Jaguar won 11, finished second in one, and had minor mechanical trouble in the other two when in the lead, nevertheless setting up the fastest lap in both races. They have also either equalled or broken the existing unlimited sports car lap record during either the racing or at practice on all circuits where they have appeared.

Any other information required about the latest Lister car may be obtained from Brian Lister (Light Engineering) Ltd., Abbey Road, Cambridge, Tel. Cambridge 55601/2. We welcome your enquiries and interest.

Chapter 11

Cunningham

BRIGGS Swift Cunningham had been taught to drive by the family chauffeur. Born in Cincinatti, Ohio, in 1907, Cunningham was fortunate enough not to have to earn a living. His father, a wealthy banker, left him a considerable fortune in trust money so that the young Cunningham was able to amuse himself playing sports, sailing and, eventually learning to drive.

At the age of 23, Cunningham built his first car, a special called a Bu-Merc. As the name suggests it was a hybrid; the chassis and running gear were from a Buick Century, the body from a damaged Mercedes SSK. Miles Collier, a founder member of the Automobile Racing Club of America, drove this car for the first time at the 1940 ARCA meeting at the New York World's Fair. It lost its brakes and crashed. The winner, Frank Griswold, was to repeat his success at the first post-war race at Watkins Glen in 1948, driving an Alfa Romeo 2900. The runner-up was Cunningham, in the Bu-Merc. The organizer was the Sports Car Club of America, the successor to the ARCA.

Never one to hang about, Cunningham had resolved to attempt the Le Mans race for 1950. It was important to use an American car, and the marque he selected was Cadillac. One car, driven by Cunningham and Phil Walters, who raced under the unlikely pseudonym of Ted Tappett, was a gross open affair, possessed of a vaguely aerodynamic nose, engineered by Grumman, the aircraft manufacturer of Long Island. It was deliciously ugly and nicknamed Le Monstre. The second was a rather more conventional coupé, driven by the Collier brothers. The Colliers came tenth, Le Monstre eleventh.

It was an encouraging start, sufficiently so to encourage Cunningham to attempt production of his own marque, which he began to do in 1951, three years before Brian Lister. He took over Tappett-Frick Motors of Long Island and relocated it south. The base he chose was West Palm Beach, Florida. The objective was series production, at least 10 cars in a 12-month period, in order to qualify as a constructor under FIA rules. The main effort in manufacture went into the chassis, which was proprietary. The engines would be (by choice) American – typically Chrysler – although at least one Offenhauser engine was installed in one of the later cars. The bodies were designed by Vignale and built by Bob Blake. Altogether, three dozen were made in the period up to 1955. They were painted in a stylized version of National American Racing colours from before the war, when chassis had been blue, bodies white. The blue was transferred to the body in two parallel stripes, representative of the chassis underneath.

The cars acquitted themselves well at Le Mans – Cunningham himself came fourth in 1952, after what was virtually a solo effort – and the following year John Fitch and Phil Walters came third. In 1954, Bill Spear and Sherwood Johnston managed third, with Cunningham and John Benett fifth. Two events then took place which effectively finished off the enterprise. The first was that the American Internal Revenue Service decreed that since this enterprise was really just a hobby, it was not allowable as a business – post tax income would have to be spent upon it. The second, following on from this, was that Bill Frick decided to depart and return to Long Island.

If Cunningham was to continue racing, he had to build it around a proper business, and having met Sir William Lyons at the Le Mans prizegiving in 1954, when the Jaguar boss suggested a distributorship in the New York area in exchange for a team of racing cars, Cunningham did not have to look very far. Lyons sent a D-Type over to Cunningham's Florida base for a test drive at Sebring. Cunningham, Spear, Walters and Bill Lloyd all tried the car out and were 'amazed and delighted' with it.

On 1 February 1955, it was announced that the Cunningham team would enter D-Types for North American events and Le Mans. Before Le Mans, though, were two events – the Daytona Beach speed trials and the Sebring 12-Hour race. Phil Walters stormed home in the speed trials, a clear 12 seconds ahead of the field, and at Daytona, Mike Hawthorn and Walters won by 26 seconds from Phil Hill and Carroll Shelby.

Cunningham's Jaguar distributorship was based in the New York borough of Queen's, nearly next door to the Momo Corporation, which was run by expatriate Italian Alfred Momo, but partnered financially (indeed, guaranteed) by Cunningham. The Momo technicians prepared the cars as they arrived from Coventry, whether for racing or for sale to the public. For Jaguar, the exposure given to the marque by such a well-funded and enthusiastic entrant/distributor as Cunningham was vital in developing their North American market share. Cunningham did as much as anyone, and more than most, to build up the reputation of Jaguars in the United States.

Certainly the WSCC 3-litre capacity limit effectively vetoed any possibility of Cunningham using rebuilt D-Types with which to fly his racing flag. The weight of the car, even in 3.8-litre form had already given it problems against lighter Italian opposition in 1957 and it could be no better in 3-litre guise, where the most which could be reliably coaxed out of the engine would be in the region of 230 bhp. Cunningham needed a lighter car than the D-Type.

Brian Lister already had one. News of Archie's whitewash in the 1957 season had naturally reached America and Cunningham was minded to take a look at the Cambridge works. He was not the only one – Lance Reventlow, architect of the Scarab racing car, had already been there at the close of the 1957 season to kick the tyres and have a look. He thought that he could do better than the Lister chassis, but Cunningham realized that he probably could not.

Cunningham and Alfred Momo arrived at Abbey Road in September 1957. A deal for two 3-litre Lister Jaguars was struck, using the works' own engines. So, while Archie was getting in amongst the opposition in New Zealand, the cars were completed ready for a quick shakedown before being despatched to Sebring for the first event of the 1958 calendar. Archie would share one car with Walter Hansgen, while Ed Crawford and Pat O'Connor would drive the other. Already, Archie's 1958 calendar was filling up.

Carroll Shelby was also showing an interest. He knew that, as a sprint car, the Lister was more or less unbeatable, but was minded to discuss the installation of an American engine. Accordingly he followed in Cunningham's footsteps and reached Cambridge in November 1957. Brian decided upon three US distributors. For the east coast, Cunningham would import the cars through his Jaguar operation, and Shelby would cover the rest of the US except the west coast, which would be catered for from Seattle, first by the Carstens company, and later by Qjell Qvale. Shelby was hugely optimistic about potential sales; he seriously thought that he could shift at least a dozen cars a month. This was not hyperbole on Shelby's part, merely an error.

Shelby also cherished the idea of a Lister-Maserati. While such a concept immediately triggered flashbacks of the most traumatic kind for Lister, the Texan was all for it. The engine was, of course, one of the 4½-litre V8 firebreathers which had first been seen in 1956. Shelby's idea, one of many he had along the same lines, was to put this 400 bhp monster into a Lister chassis. Eventually he would make the AC Cobra.

Cunningham's technical guru, Alfred Momo, was to make a few changes to the team cars, albeit at the very margins. The battery was relocated away from the fuel lines; the hydraulic cylinders were placed further away from the exhaust; the chassis was strengthened with extra gussets, and assorted louvres were cut into the body at the sill to enable front brake heat and exhaust heat to dissipate more easily. A roll-over hoop was also added to the headrest in the interests of safety. The first two Listers were despatched in time for Momo to make his preparations for Sebring, the opener for the 1958 International season. They were to be fitted with Jaguar's 3-litre version of the D-Type engine, with an 85 mm bore and an 88 mm stroke, giving 2997 cc.

Chapter 12

Acceptances

THE invitation to attend the Tasman series of races, to be held in New Zealand in January and February of 1958 was greeted with predictable enthusiasm by Archie. MVE 303 was to be shipped out to Auckland, and Archie would be accompanied by Dick Barton and, at Bryan Turle's request to Sir William Lyons, head racing mechanic from Jaguar, Len Hayden. Archie and Hayden already knew each other, of course, through competition, but there was another connection which was a nice coincidence. Hayden's war service had been in the Royal Air Force, working on rather bigger engines than these little 300 bhp units. Hayden had in fact been a fitter working on Douglas Bader's plane at Duxford, when Bader commanded the 'Duxford Wing'. Archie had corresponded with Bader and appeared at several charity events with him in the cause of handicapped children.

The team decided that the car would remain in Appendix C trim, despite the Formule Libre classification of the tour, and keep its 3.8-litre engine. The works were too busy building production cars to interfere with it overmuch. Basic spares would be taken, but only one engine. There were six major races to be contested in the series, but flexibility was the key, as there was a slightly *ad hoc* flavour to the whole thing. The trip was to be the 1957 car's swansong. It was already a hard-worked machine, despite the attention which it had received, but Archie knew it well enough to be happy with it. It was to be the star turn, in fact.

Archie, Barton and Hayden spent 47 hours, via Viscount and DC6, to arrive at Auckland via Greenland, Vancouver, Honolulu, Canton Island and Fiji. The car, with its spares, was sent by sea via the good offices of LEP Transport, arriving, not unusually in those pre-container days, minus a few bits and pieces but in time for Hayden and Barton to race-prepare it for the first event ten days later.

The New Zealand Grand Prix, a Formule Libre event which

Top As Archie leaves Tatts Corner and approaches the back markers in the Aintree race, the spray becomes difficult to see through. Here he is seen pulling off his goggles in order to see properly. His eyes needed medical attention afterwards. (Autocar)

Above Salvadori's revenge. On 14 September 1957 Aston Martin achieved their first domestic victory over the Lister at Silverstone. Here, Archie is chasing Salvadori around Copse Corner. (T. C. March)

Below The second Formula 2 car under construction at Abbey Road. It is easy to see why Archie thought it resembled a coffin. The use of square section tube is a departure for Lister. Note the side-mounted fuel tanks and canted-over engine. (Brian Lister)

Left The completed Formula 2 chassis. Again, like the Lister-Jaguar, the engine is as far back as it will go. Archie hated it. (Brian Lister)

Below left The finished product outside the Abbey Road works. (Brian Lister)

Right Archie and Jay at home in Portugal Place in late 1957. The winged lion is the motif designed by the College of Arms for the Connaught company.

Below Cavendish Morton's three-quarter view sketch of Lister's proposed 1958 car. It was more or less correct. (Autocar)

Bottom A profile of the proposed car. (Autocar)

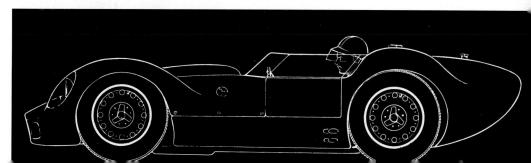

Above The Lister table at the BRDC end-of-season dinner dance at the Dorchester in London. Archie is making a quick check on his tie. Clockwise from him: unknown, Mottram Rankin, Babs Moore, Don Moore, Bryan Turle, Jo Turle, Jose Lister, Brian Lister and Archie's girlfriend – one of many.

Left Coming in to win the Lady Wigram Trophy. (Edwin Barton)

Below Archie and Ross Jensen in front of Jensen's Maserati 250F at Invercargill, NZ. (Edwin Barton)

Above Sebring 1958. The Cunningham team at their trailer. Alfred Momo is sitting on the steps. (Edwin Barton)

Right Briggs Cunningham.

Below The first 'Knobbly' Lister, destined for Briggs Cunningham, being gently eased aboard its cargo plane, on its way to the USA. History relates that they got it in somehow, although it is hard to see how. (Autocar)

Left Walt Hansgen and Alfred Momo in the winning Lister-Jaguar at Virginia International Raceway, Danville, Va, on 4 May 1958 after the final race. Note the roll-over hoop and louvres let into the sill. (Warren Ballard)

Below A view of the Chevrolet engine installed in the 1958 Lister, requiring an even bigger hump than the Jaguar car. (Brian Lister)

Bottom A close-up of a 1958 'Knobbly' Lister-Jaguar cockpit. The horn button is the only control on the right of the dash. (Brian Lister)

Right This six-frame sequence shows the Sebring episode when Gendebien's Testa Rossa attempts something quite unnatural with Archie's Lister, a procedure which pushes both cars outside the marker limits. In frame three, Gendebien is seen attempting to dislocate the Ferrari as Archie hops out. Courteously, Archie guides the Belgian driver off the Lister and watches ruefully as the Ferrari departs. Archie's 3-litre engine had expired, leaving him coasting along on the racing line.

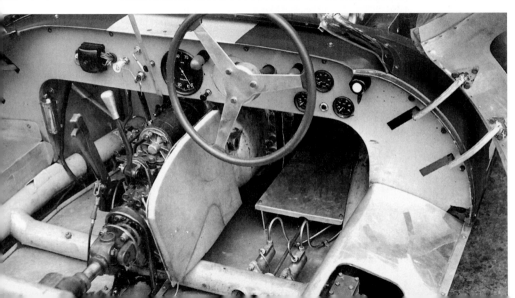

Above Don Moore explaining to Archie the finer points of exhaust pipe fabrication. (John Bull)

Below A publicity shot for John Bull magazine (not used in the end) of Archie relaxing outside the Anchor pub on the banks of the Cam. (John Bull)

Top right A moment of tension – Brian Lister and Don Moore, with Peter Whitehead, at Oulton Park, waiting for Archie's Lister-Jaguar to come past the pits again. He was late; a steering arm had broken. He was to finish this race in Bruce Halford's car. (John Horsman)

Right A shambolic start at the Easter Monday Goodwood meeting, 1958. Archie's Lister slews wildly as he struggles to reach the pedals. He has dragged the seat back down and is sitting on it, reducing his reach to the pedals even more. (Geoffrey Goddard)

Below right . . . After passing Moss on the Lavant straight, he leads him through the Members' Chicane – just. (LAT Photographic)

Above . . . After nine laps, Archie is forced to slow. A lap later, he retires with 'stiff steering'. In fact his steering rack had come adrift. His expression says it all. (Geoffrey Goddard)

Left A good shot of Masten Gregory and 'Wilkie' Wilkinson of Ecurie Ecosse at Silverstone in 1958. (Graham Gauld)

Above right Archie and Brian Lister relaxing during practice at Spa, 1958. (Edwin Barton)

Right Archie looking pensive before the race at Spa. (Van Bever)

Far right The Lister in the middle of the front row before the start at Spa. (Edwin Barton)

This picture captures Archie's mood in the cockpit before his last race. It had not yet begun to rain. (Van Bever)

Archie is hurried away from the crash towards the dressing station at Spa on 18 May 1958. Although he cannot be seen clearly, this is probably the last picture ever taken. Peter Garnier, then of The Autocar, remembers being scandalized when offered the most prurient pictures of the crash from Belgium, none of which is in this book. Racing drivers die a public enough death as it is. (Van Bever)

The wreck of VPP 9. (Edwin Barton)

ARCHIE

W A SCOTT BROWN
1927-1958

HE REPRESENTED
EVERYTHING THAT
WAS BEST IN
THE SPORT

71 FIRSTS
34 SECONDS
12 THIRDS

The bas-relief plaque unveiled by Bill Scott Brown at Snetterton circuit in Norfolk at the end of the day's racing at the opening of the 1959 UK season. Sadly, Brian Lister could not be there – he was at the Sebring race in Florida. The plaque was the work of Cavendish Morton. A report read: 'At the end of the day of furious activity and strident noise, an almost uncanny silence settled on the circuit when the beautiful memorial plaque to Archie Scott Brown was unveiled by his father. The vast crowd on both sides of the course was completely stilled as it paid its respects to that fine man who, as the inscription reminds us, if a reminder should ever be needed, represented all that is best in the Sport. If ever a man was genuinely admired, by those who knew him personally and by those who only applauded his great skill and indomitable courage from the spectators' enclosure, that man was Archie Scott Brown; it is fitting that his home circuit should have this perpetual tribute to his memory.'

Stirling Moss, hired by arrangement with BP's Bryan Turle, at the 19 July 1958 British Grand Prix meeting at Silverstone. Brian Lister was determined to trounce David Murray's Ecurie Ecosse that day, and he did. Note the scoop cut into the rear deck to direct cooling air down to the rear inboard brakes and final drive, and the slot let into the bonnet above the number plate to aid engine cooling. (Geoffrey Goddard)

The resurrected identity, VPP 9, with its periscope intake – a Frank Costin development of the effort made to cool Stirling's car at the British GP meeting. From this angle the modified front wings, now extended back to the screen, can be seen. The box in the nose intake is an oil cooler and the inverted cup on the windscreen is to deflect air from the driver's face. This car was driven by Walt Hansgen in the British Grand Prix meeting, but the clutch burned out. (Brian Lister)

The 1959 Costin-bodied car outside Abbey Road. It illustrates the skill of Williams and Pritchard very well. Note the separate aerodynamic shapes of the rear wing, bonnet and front wings, also the high radiused screen. (Brian Lister)

The passenger door of the Costin car. You can say what you like about its effectiveness, but it was certainly beautifully made. (Brian Lister)

Ivor Bueb in the finished vehicle outside the Abbey Road works. Frank Costin, in dark suit, and Brian Lister seem very happy with it. (Autocar)

One of the remaining original Lister-Jaguars, now restored and owned by Lister enthusiast David Ham and still raced today, with a gathering of members of the Lister team from the 1950s, most of whom are still with the company. Left to right: 'Dick' Barton, Ken Hazlewood, George Tyrell, Brian Lister, Brian Elliot, Colin 'Chippy' Crisp, David Ham, Bob Gawthrop and Don Moore. (Brian Hamilton)

allowed both single-seaters and sports cars to compete, was held at the Ardmore aerodrome circuit on 18 January. Most of the competition was of the open-wheel two-seat type. There were two Connaughts there, in fact – one of them an old mount of Archie's (to be driven by Roy Salvadori), the other, the low-drag 'toothpaste tube' car driven, as it had been the previous season, by Stuart Lewis-Evans. Both cars were there to be sold, as was the custom, rather in the manner of an equine 'selling race'. They were the property of Bernie Ecclestone, who had bought them at the Connaught liquidation sale. Lewis-Evans was appointed as the salesman. According to Salvadori, he nearly swapped them for a stamp collection, but came nowhere near realizing any cash for them, which was rather sad. The ubiquitous Maserati 250Fs were there, one being driven by Ross Jensen, as well as a clutch of Ferrari Formula 1 cars. Archie was driving the only sports car. It was not for sale.

Archie was placed well in the heat, second to Lewis-Evans, and he led for three laps until a procession of cars, led by Jack Brabham's Cooper, a Ferrari driven by Lex Davison and the two Connaughts swept by. It was something of a struggle for Archie, compounded by what he thought was a puncture three laps from the end. He slid crab-like into the pit area, howling for a new left front wheel. Barton and Hayden exchanged glances. It was clear that Archie could not see that the wheel was almost off; the kingpin had snapped clean through. The wheel had been flailing along the ground and the Dunlop tyre was scorched and melted by wheelarch contact. Barton was awed by the thought that Archie had come blasting along the straight, doing well over 120 mph, with only three wheels properly attached to the car. What was more perplexing was that he simply hadn't felt it. When they persuaded Archie that there was nothing for it but to retire, he calmed down a bit. He hopped out and helped the others push the car out of the way, at which the whole thing folded up at the front. To Archie, handling problems implied tyres, and that was more or less that.

A new kingpin was mounted and the tyre was replaced in time for the trip to the Lady Wigram Trophy race, to be held on 25 January at Christchurch. On the way they stopped off at Levin, where Archie entertained the locals and came second at the 'International' event. He drove fastest lap, which was a new absolute record.

At home in Cambridge, Brian Lister had an oddly disturbing dream, notable not for its sentiment – as he constantly fretted over Archie as he did over every driver who drove the cars – but in a particular detail of it. While asleep, he had imagined receiving a telephone call from the BP representative in New Zealand, saying that the Lister had crashed, Archie had died and that BP were taking down all their circuit flags. Brian, after naturally checking that all was well in New

Zealand, shrugged it off and carried on with the business of finishing the customer cars. He told Jose of the macabre dream in all its detail, and the small matter of the flags was to come back to him vividly three short months later.

Once at Christchurch, Archie set to in practice. He nursed the slightly creaky Lister along, turning in a new lap record in the process. He did better the next day, breaking the record again, and took pole position on the grid. After a struggle with Jensen's Maserati to hold on to first, he pulled away, setting another lap record and won the race in a record time at an average speed of nearly 91 mph.

He retired from the Dunedin race held the next weekend, when vibration from the paved circuit cracked the differential mountings. The car was by now feeling its age, or at least its mileage.

The final event of the tour was the International race at Teretonga Park, Invercargill. Barton and Hayden hastily welded up the rear end, and Archie had a go in two events. The first, a short sports car race – almost a sprint – he won going away; the second, a Formule Libre competition, was more problematical. The surface was terrible, a fact he communicated to Barton, who was unconvinced. A lap in the passenger seat changed his mind.

Archie was on the front row, and again struggled with Jensen for the lead, but the Maserati 250 had the edge this time. On the 15th lap he over-egged the pudding a bit and parked the Lister against a bank, sliding it over a ditch in the process. He rejoined the race and finished in sixth place. This race was notable, in that it was the last International event to be won by a Maserati 250F. The factory was in deep financial trouble, a situation brought about in part by the collapse of the Peron regime in Argentina, where, thanks to Fangio, rather a lot of business had been done. Debtors there were rather harder to catch than Juan Manuel, however, particularly when repudiation of obligations was so straightforward. From then on the firm operated in administerial receivership, which prevented competition. It was a tragedy of operatic proportions, but possibly a timely one. Maserati had little new to offer for 1958, and better a sudden finish than a slow decline into has-been status.

After his return from New Zealand, in the few days left before going to Sebring, Archie leaped straight into the final testing of the new 1958 Lister-Jaguar. He found it transformed – luxurious, even. Unlike the Bristol-engined car, little had been done to the 1957 car throughout that season, aside from the Appendix C modifications, larger brakes after the Empire Trophy and the switch to the 3.8-litre engine. Most of what had been learned on the 1957 car was put into effect for the new model. Archie particularly appreciated the slightly more comfortable seats and the roomier cockpit. The car had been less thoroughly tested than before, partly because the star driver was globetrotting, and partly because little that was radically new was involved. The new bodywork was the main feature. There was, though, one major improvement – the tyres. Lister had always remained resolutely faithful to Dunlop, but Avon, who equipped the Aston Martin team as well as supplying the Feltham road cars' footwear, seemed to have the edge at the start of the '58 season. However, they would not countenance supplying Lister, almost certainly for fear of upsetting David Brown. Nevertheless, Dunlop were on the verge of producing a new generation of tyre, the nylon-braced R5. This gave such grip that it was possible to raise lap times by a matter of whole seconds over the previous season, although not without a price. The loadings imposed upon the front end geometry were altogether of a higher order than before, which was to cause operating difficulties.

In America, Cunningham, their affluent and considerate host had arranged everything, down to a Cadillac Eldorado for Archie, Barton and Len Hayden to drive about in, and accommodation at a decent hotel while the group were in transit down to Sebring.

At the race itself, the team decided that Archie and Ed Crawford would be first away at the Le Mans start. The opposition was of the usual quality, with a works Aston Martin team of two 3-litre DBR1s, works Ferrari Testa Rossas driven by Hawthorn, Phil Hill and Olivier Gendebien and a good selection of local offerings. The Astons were far and away the quickest, though.

It was hard work. Archie circulated in the top half dozen in the very early stages before his engine gave up the ghost. The car slowed rapidly through engine braking just before a sharp bend near the pits. Olivier Gendebien was chasing Archie very closely, attempting to link up with the other Ferraris. As the Lister slowed, Gendebien ran up the right-hand rear wing with the front left of his Testa Rossa, severely damaging the Lister and nearly decapitating Archie in the process. The two sat there for a moment, like a pair of mating tortoises, before Archie twisted in his seat to avoid the tyre which had thumped him hard on the head, and waved Gendebien out of his car. The Belgian climbed out and gingerly hopped on to the road to inspect the damage. Archie managed to extricate himself and sportingly offered to guide the Ferrari back off the wreckage. Gendebien reversed off the Lister and rejoined the race. Archie took off his helmet and limped over to Don Munson. 'Odd sight, that ... to have a bloody Ferrari sitting on your head. I bet you laughed.' Munson didn't laugh at all. The Pirelli tyre tracks on Archie's helmet and shirt told a succinct story. Had it not been for the roll-over bar fitted by Momo to the Cunningham cars, this might have been a terminal accident.

Crawford's engine failed a little later, as did all the Jaguar 3-litre units. Cunningham resolved to re-engine the Listers with 3.8 engines for the balance of the season and enter domestic races, a decision which was to prove wise. Hansgen was to become an even more outstanding driver in the re-engined Lister than he had been in 1957, when he was clearly the SCCA driver of the year. The 3.8 Listers would be entered in Category C Modified for 1958, as had the D-Types before them. It was to be almost a perfect season for Cunningham in terms of results, and it confirmed his decision to stay with British machinery and American drivers. Certainly, his Listers were to prove as dominant over the D-Types as Archie's 1957 car had.

Chapter 13

Nightmares

RACING IS A VICE, AND AS SUCH EXTREMELY HARD TO GIVE UP.
– Alfonso de Portago

CUNNINGHAM was not the only racing team casting about for a new car. David Murray had already been informed that Jaguar were not about to take up racing again in 1958. He, like Cunningham, realized that the D-Type was close to obsolete and ordered a Lister for 1958, still trying to manoeuvre Archie into driving it. He also, by way of hedging his bets, arranged to have call on the loan of a Tojeiro-Jaguar from John Ogier.

When it became clear that he was unable to obtain Archie's services for the season, Murray contracted with a man who knew a bit about Jaguars, having owned his own C-Type in 1954, but whose main experience was in Italian machinery.

Masten Gregory, from Kansas City, Missouri, entered his first race at Caddo Mills, Texas, in 1952. He was a man of some leisure, having inherited a tidy sum in 1951. Deciding that the racing life was for him, he bought a C-Type Jaguar in late 1953 and campaigned it in both North and South America. After it broke down at Buenos Aires in 1954, he sold it. He then set out on the established method of progression for many affluent drivers in a hurry – he started buying the winning cars in events and campaigning them as owner-driver. By the time Murray hired him in the spring of 1958, Gregory had already notched up an impressive resumé. For example, at Reims in 1954 he had pipped two Cunninghams for fourth place behind three works Jaguars, as well as partnering Duncan Hamilton to sixth place in the 1957 Le Mans event. His predilection for Italian cars had led him to sign for the Formula 1 team, Scuderia Centro-Sud for the 1957 season. Despite his international activity, Gregory was an unknown in Britain. He was a fine driver, but thought to be totally wild by some who drove against him. He was himself to say much later that he fully expected to die in an accident, a price he was apparently quite happy to pay in order to live the life of a racing driver.

The car which Murray ordered, BHL 104, was among a clutch manufactured in January 1958. It was bodied in aluminium, and registered 341 SG. At that stage, Murray had been attempting to lure Archie away from the works team and was thus uncertain who would drive the car. Archie finally put his foot down after his return from New Zealand, partly because he was well and truly tired of the game, but more to reassure Brian Lister. In March 1958, Gregory was confirmed as the Ecosse driver.

The first event of the British season was an SMRC spring meeting at Snetterton on 30 March, which included both unlimited sports car and Formule Libre races. Archie won the sports car race going away from John Bekaert, as well as setting fastest lap, and won the Formule Libre race with little difficulty. There is not much doubt that the R5 tyres, beneficial though they were, probably made the Lister harder to drive in the Scott Brown style. It was also to be noted that the extra grip made the steering gear work much harder than before. This was to be rudely pointed out within a week.

Next weekend was the Goodwood orgy of speed, the opener for the UK leg of the International season. The competition was well up to the previous year, the main threat being Moss in the Aston Martin DBR2 car, powered by a 3.9-litre engine, a single-plug version of which would eventually go into the DB4 road car as a 3.7. Archie's wasn't the only Lister, either. Peter Whitehead was there, as well as Bruce Halford in HCH 736, the superbly pretty Maurice Gomm bodied car owned by Dick Walsh. Peter Collins drove a Ferrari 206.

The race began with a Le Mans type start, an activity at which Archie usually excelled. In this case, though, as he leaped into the car his foot dragged the backrest on to the seat and he dropped in on top of it. Not only did it make the pedals hard to reach, but it shoved his head out into the airstream which must have been less than comfortable. He made a poor start, sliding around untidily in third place behind Moss and Collins, but soon passed them both to hold the lead for nine laps, whereupon he slowed dramatically, the steering rack mounting brackets unable to take the strain of the loadings imposed by the new tyres. That was it. Unable to steer with any semblance of accuracy, he retired. He had learned much in New Zealand.

The Glover Trophy for Formula 1 was also on the card. Archie came in a poor sixth, his privately-entered Connaught completely out of contention now.

The most promising event of the whole 1958 calendar was the British Empire Trophy, held as usual at Oulton Park. The performance of the Lister in practice for the first heat was, to say the least, startling. Archie comprehensively destroyed his old lap record and grabbed pole position at over 90 mph. Moss was there in the Aston DBR2, supported by Brooks in a similar car. Whitehead and Halford were again in attendance. Archie scorched off the line to take the lead, which he held for nine laps. He slowed up as he scanned the instruments, which revealed that the oil pressure and temperature were not all they should be – the first low, the second high. He had already set fastest lap and, rather reminded of the 1955 race, there was no need to win the heat by a country mile. His place in the final was more or less assured, so he backed off a little.

Lucky he did. After Goodwood, the steering rack mounts had been replaced with stronger units. This time, they held, but the steering loads were merely fed into the steering-arm, which failed. This was worse than Goodwood, as this time he had no steering at all. He pulled up.

Walsh and Halford stuck their heads together and agreed that Archie would have a good chance in HCH 736. Although the privateers had lapped four seconds slower than the works Lister, that was still faster than Archie had done last year, when he had won by ten seconds. The Astons were, oddly, no quicker than their 3-litre precursors last season, so it seemed reasonable that the Scot would have a fighting chance. The Stewards were inclined to agree. It was a generous offer, honestly made; besides which, none of them relished the prospect of the motor racing media bearing down upon them for excluding a man who was now at the top of the tree.

There was a problem, though. HCH 736 was a standard chassis, fitted out to accommodate someone of about average height. Halford is about 5 ft. 9 in., about eight inches taller than Archie was. There was no time to block the pedals or alter the steering column. The only thing to do was to pack Archie from behind with coats and cushions. He started on the second row of the grid. In the event, the Aston Martins scored a slightly hollow 1–2 and Archie was a sad but philosophical third.

The steering problem concerned Lister greatly; probably even more than it concerned Archie, whose slightly childlike faith in Lister and Moore was fully restored after the problems over the Formula 2 car. The professional engineer in Brian insisted that first a modification be designed, and second, all his new clients be told about it. He viewed racing as an extension of his business; not to keep customers up to date on developments was anathema to his philosophy.

A week after Oulton Park, just up the road at Aintree, the BARC meeting was held on 19 April. For the Formula 1 event, Archie came fourth in his trusty Connaught.

In the sports car event, for cars over 1100 cc, the competition was as stiff as usual. There were two Astons – Tony Brooks in one, and Archie's old rival, Roy Salvadori (who had replaced Stirling Moss) in the other. Ecurie Ecosse had finished their Lister, which was to be driven by Masten Gregory.

It was a memorable race. Lister's modification clearly worked, as

Archie's steering held together. Archie set a new lap record at 2:04.4, but Salvadori broke it later in the race. The two pairs, Listers and Astons, howled around the 200-mile course, Archie holding the lead, but with Salvadori feet from his tail, and Gregory feet from his. The third Lister, HCH 736, Bruce Halford back in the cockpit, spun out at Tattenham corner. Archie won, Salvadori second, Gregory third. Salvadori had effectively separated the two Listers for most of the race.

The day after Aintree, the news reached Cambridge that Walt Hansgen had won the 40-lap President's Cup at Marlboro, Maryland, in the Cunningham team's new Lister-Jaguar. It was a walkover for the New Jersey driver, helped by a torrential downpour while he was in the lead, but he won by nearly a minute. It was a significant American debut for the re-engined car. Hansgen would win the next five races as well, supported by Ed Crawford in the sister car.

At Silverstone, Lister had been hoping to attract Jean Behra to drive the second car, but the arrangement fell through at the last minute. Lister's fuel sponsors, BP, who had done so much to create this car, managed to hire Wolfgang Seidel, who was delighted to compete in a works team with the great Archie. This time, Aston Martin fielded Brooks, Salvadori and Moss. The Ecosse Lister was back, but looking a little different from a certain angle. The front body had been modified, smoothing out the well-defined front wing and fairing it back into the body just forward of the door. It was a hastily-contrived effort, as revealed by the pop-rivets which held the new panels in place. Indeed, underneath the body was standard Williams and Pritchard 'Knobbly', as the cars had come to be known. It seemed to work, or rather not to hinder, as Gregory made second fastest in practice, 1.6 seconds slower than Archie, and the two shared the front row of the grid. For a while, it was a re-run of Aintree, with Archie, Gregory, Salvadori and Brooks fighting it out, but gradually the order was teased out. Archie lost his lead on lap seven, and never regained it. Gregory trounced him by 26 seconds. Archie was simply astonished. Babs Moore, Don's wife, found him totally disheartened in the paddock; initially monosyllabic as he peeled off his soaking wet polo shirt, slow in coming to terms with what had happened. Despite the cool and realistic approach taken by Jay towards the more Darwinian elements of Archie's prospects when he was young, he had become rather used to winning.

The immediate assumption was made that there was something wrong with the car; Archie was the first to refute this, with the statement: 'There was nothing wrong, nothing at all – I drove as hard as I could, but I just couldn't win!' Certainly, nobody had seen him as lowered as this since his licence was taken away. Bill Scott Brown was of the opinion that the fairings riveted on to the Ecosse car had made a big difference to its roadholding. Whatever, Archie had never been beaten by this margin in his first-class career, except by cars of a much higher specification, and the episode shook him rigid. Clearly, the Ecosse car was the one to beat, and Gregory the man to beat. Later, he made light of the episode in The Saracen's Head at Towcester, gently chiding Jose Lister that she had forgotten to wish him luck.

On 4 May Hansgen won the feature race at the Virginia International Raceway, Danville, driving Cunningham Lister No. 60. As the Cunningham team limbered up for 1958, it became clear that the machines completely outclassed their opposition – a certain predictability was emerging in the eyes of the SCCA competitors, which was to persist for two years. Hansgen was even more formidable in the Lister than he had been in the similarly-engined D-Type the previous year.

Both VPP 9 and 341 SG were absent from the BRSCC race at Mallory Park on 11 May, as the Ecosse team were taking no chances with their Lister ahead of the Spa race the next weekend. Archie drove the ex-Seidel car to victory, setting fastest lap ahead of Bruce Halford who was still using a 3.4 engine; but Spa was the race which was uppermost in most minds, and VPP 9 was being prepared for it.

The unconditional acceptance of the entry to the Spa Grand Prix for sports cars was seen as a major breakthrough at Abbey Road. The organizers had had, they claimed, to pay an extra insurance premium of 50,000 Francs, which was not very much, to allow Archie to compete – which news Archie greeted with a small sniff. There had even been a possibility of an entry for the Monaco Grand Prix on the same day, as the two events clashed, because Archie had discussed the possibility with Archie Butterworth, architect of the AJB engine which powered the Elva. The plan had been to install this unit in a Cooper chassis, but it came to nothing. The chassis is rumoured to be hanging on the wall of the basement of a seminary near Guildford. It is further thought that it is possessed of the torsional strength of damp spaghetti. Anyway, the problems were legion with the Butterworth engine, an air-cooled flat four, the most irritating of which was its propensity to chew valves. Archie actually loved the engine, as it reminded him of the Porsche 356 which he hankered after but could never afford. As Archie Butterworth put it: 'As with so much in motor racing, it just never happened.' So, Spa it was, at last.

The Spa circuit was, and still is today, an awesome ordeal for car and driver. Situated in the foothills of the Ardennes, Spa Francorchamps is on the other side of Belgium from where Bill had been downed during the Great War. Some drivers adored the track, others hated it. Few had no opinion at all. As a road circuit it had few equals for speed – Monza could be lapped almost as quickly, but that was a purpose-built track. All were agreed, though, that it was one of the most potentially dangerous tracks in the world. Facilities were limited, but that issue was seldom raised in the 1950s as the gladiatorial element of racing, with its brutal element of natural selection, was one of the supremely popular things about it.

Archie went out with the Lister and Walsh teams. They spent the night in Ostend before driving down to Spa in time to celebrate Archie's 31st birthday on Tuesday. They stabled the car at Stavelot, at the garage Lecoq, where many teams used the facilities. Bill followed by train and taxi. Upon arrival, Archie realized that the team mascot, the black cat, had been left behind. This vexed him, although he did not mention it to Jose Lister, who had telephoned on the pretext of reminding Brian that he had forgotten his toothbrush. Jose took care to wish him luck but also pleaded with him to 'take care and don't overdo it – it's not worth it.'

BP had booked their hotel rooms. As Brian and Archie walked into the lobby, the first thing Brian saw was a pair of crossed BP flags fixed to the wall, which made him rather uneasy, reminding him of his dream about New Zealand.

Many present agreed that Archie was somewhat tired and reduced. As to why is a different matter. Certainly his love-life, for example, seemed to be sorted out – he had become engaged. It was not to Marion, though, but to Jill Fenner, from Hull. He had given up on other fronts, it seemed. There was, however, tension there. There is some thought that Jay had engineered the match, as Miss Fenner was actually one of her finds, rather than Archie's. It put him in a tricky position with Marion, although he seemed now to have accepted 'good friend' status as opposed to that of ardent suitor. Despite this, he had arranged to travel to Nürburgring with Marion for the 1000 km race on 1 June, which was perhaps naughty of him, despite the platonic nature of their relationship.

A further concern was his mother. She had been pressing him more than usual to settle down. Archie knew Jay well enough to realize that marriage would probably be used as a fairly unsubtle ambush to force him to give up racing, which he loved dearly, and start breeding – a prospect which not unnaturally filled him with horror. His mother was ill, anyway, having been admitted to a clinic on the day of the departure for Belgium for a minor but painful operation. Despite their occasional noisy antipathy over his career choice, he worried deeply about her.

Archie's childhood and adolescence, brief though both had been, had left him with a reverence for plain dealing. He disliked bad behaviour, in both himself and others, and was certainly not at all hypocritical in identifying it. The knowledge that someone, probably him, was going to behave badly over the issue of his private life may well have lowered him a little.

If all this was not enough, he was totally exhausted after the Sebring and New Zealand trips, both of which had provided ample dark hints about mortality, and neither the garage business nor the racing had been going brilliantly. So far in the season he had not really progressed over the previous year. His Formula 1 ambitions seemed well and truly capped, which was particularly irritating now that BRM seemed to have sorted out their problems. It had not escaped his notice that, bad though the cars had seemed to be, no-one had actually died in them. The situation with Murray had irritated him as the Ecurie Ecosse chief had constantly moved the goalposts, and in attempting to come to terms with him for entries in International races, he had had to run the risk of compromising his relationship with the Lister team where, when all was said and done, he was extremely happy. So, in a period of a very few months, he had risked alienating both colleagues and friends and advanced his career not one inch. For someone who prized proper behaviour almost above all else, it was a fairly poor position in which to find himself. Professionally, he was also aware that the cars were changing. He was, one way or another, probably at least contemplating the end to his career, even though 1958 was his most promising year yet. As a totally committed racing driver, he also realized that to target beating just one driver is silly; the object is to beat them all. The episode at Silverstone, though, had given him pause for thought.

The circuit length was just under nine miles. Speed and precision were the twin objectives of any competitor on as fast a circuit as this, and practice was brisk. The race was set for Sunday 18 May and practice started on the Friday. Salvadori and Brooks were not there, as both were engaged for the Monaco Grand Prix. Aston Martin fielded two 3.9-litre DBR2's for Carroll Shelby and Paul Frère. Frère, being local, knew the circuit well, and liked it not a lot. The issue which emerged quickly was not whether Aston Martin or Lister-Jaguar would win, but which Lister-Jaguar.

The Ecosse car was in the same trim as it had been at Silverstone. VPP 9 had had the usual attention to the cooling, this time via louvres cut into the scuttle. The weather was cool, but wet on the Friday, dry on the Saturday. Dick Barton noticed what appeared to be a crack on the supplementary steering arm of VPP 9 and the team was faced with a crucial decision. They debated whether to scratch the entry or repair the arm. Archie was consulted, of course, but he wouldn't hear of cancelling the race. Barton repaired the arm to everyone's satisfaction and the practice session proceeded.

Frère set fastest time of the day on the damp Friday at 4 min. 21 sec., with Archie 2/10ths of a second behind him. The next day, when the rain had stopped, Archie managed 4 min. 13.7 sec., an average of just over 125 mph. Gregory improved that by three seconds, so the line up was Gregory, Archie and Frère on the front row, with Shelby and Bueb, driving a D-Type, on the second. The front row was fine, though. Archie's pleasure was somewhat marred by discovering that £30 had been stolen from his coat pocket while it was hanging in the transporter during Saturday's practice.

Back at the works, Ken Hazelwood, one of the mechanics working on the production cars, had slept badly the previous night. He confided to his wife that he had dreamed that something would go wrong with the car – he imagined it was a hub, and repair would be needed. The nightmarish part was that Archie would be killed in the race.

Frère had, on the Friday afternoon, pointed out to Leon Sven, the Clerk of the Course, that a road sign at the end of the Seaman bend, which was really a kink in the very fast stretch between Blanchimont and La Source hairpin, was a possible hazard. There was hardly any run-off on the Spa circuit, unlike the aerodrome circuits in Britain, so whatever space that there was was precious from the safety point of view. It was a supremely dangerous corner, with no margin for error whatsoever, given the speeds at which it was taken. Sven promised Frère that the sign would be taken down, but it was overlooked.

Archie complained of some lifting of the Lister's nose in practice. He had not expressed any opinion of the Ecosse modifications when beaten at Silverstone, but it seemed that the Gregory car was a little more stable at speeds in excess of 120 mph than was his own. Bill, slightly unhelpfully, was still convinced that the modifications to the Ecosse car were significant. There was also some speculation that Gregory's car was fitted with a special differential. Whether it was or not is hard to determine, as the car was later written off. It might well have been a Halibrand unit from America, as discussion revealed that the ratio was not available in the UK. Either way, there was concern that Ecosse had the edge in adhesion and acceleration. The idea that the Ecosse car had any advantage mechanically in the engine room over the Moore-prepared unit of VPP 9 is laughable, and even from this distance can be dismissed out of hand. The Ecosse team had had their knuckles rapped by Jaguar on more than one occasion by inventing skills and insights for themselves, or more particularly Wilkie Wilkinson, their chief engineer, which rightly resided at Brown's Lane, Coventry. The truth was simple; both cars used works engines, and the Lister unit probably had a slight edge, given the Don Moore exhaust.

Archie sat in the middle of the front row, chewing his habitual wad of gum to ease the mounting tension, under a bright golf umbrella to ward off the sudden gusts of drizzle which often characterize the Spa circuit. It was drying, but there was still some ground water left from a shower after lunch. The race theoretically started at 4 p.m., but it was late, because of a wrecked Alfa Romeo which had to be cleared off the track near Seaman bend from the preceding sports car race. The road there, which passed under overhanging trees, was wet.

Fastest away were the Astons, able to outdrag the Listers thanks to their lower indirect gearing. Shelby and Frère took the lead immediately, to be displaced by Archie and Gregory before the end of lap one as their private duel started to dominate the race. The two Listers went into the lead by several hundred yards by the time the lap was over. They then swapped the lead between them, literally inches apart. The competition was so fierce that VPP 9 dented its nose on the rear of the Ecosse car on lap three. The crowd had never seen anything like it as the two Listers had the race to themselves. The rain was intermittent, wetting some parts of the course, leaving others dry. On lap five, a brief but heavy shower landed suddenly on Seaman bend after the Listers had gone through and they hit the water as they came round for lap six. Archie, in the lead, lost adhesion. He was travelling flat out. Reports indicated that he was not quite out of control, one account suggesting that he was trying to avoid Gregory who was right behind him and therefore veered toward the infield. There was never any suggestion at the time that Gregory had nudged him. The green Lister ran along the right-hand side of the road towards the Club House wall, its wheel spinner actually gouging a scar in the Seaman memorial as the car ran toward the grass verge. Observers at the time noted that there was a chance that Archie was getting the Lister under some semblance of control after his huge slide, citing as evidence of this that he had managed to avoid Leon Dernier's dawdling Ferrari by visibly changing course, but what happened next ensured complete disaster. After sliding up on the verge, the right-hand front hit the road sign which had so concerned Frère, and the track rod snapped, tearing off the wheel and collapsing the steering. Archie was merely a passenger now. The Lister bellied hard over the edge of the verge, smashed down a wire fence and dug its nose into the soft, wet ground, careering towards the infield paddock bounded by the La Source hairpin. The area had been wooded until a few months before, and although it had been cleared, it was littered with tree stumps and straw bales, which spectators were using as vantage points. They scattered, screaming, as the green car somersaulted towards them. The Lister came to rest semi-inverted on a bale with poor Archie half in and half out of the car.

Thirty gallons of fuel were still aboard and started to pour out from the ruptured tank. It ignited powerfully. Two gendarmes, M. Dasthy and M. Bleret, started forward to ensure that no spectators were injured, which happily they were not. Most of them were fleeing in terror from the spot. The pair bravely sprinted towards the blaze, but were beaten back as a series of explosions rocked the stricken Lister. As soon as they could, accompanied by marshals, who had eventually started running the right way, they waded into the fire and pulled Archie out as the Elektron body was flaring cruelly alight. With careful haste, Archie was taken to the dressing station, supervised by the track doctor, Dr Collette.

Bill Scott Brown was in the pit area after the La Source hairpin when the crash happened:

> My first intimation of anything wrong was the crowd in front of me, in the stand, a giant collective gasp. I knew one had crashed. I didn't know which. I had to wait until the drivers came round [La Source]. Then Masten Gregory came round alone. I should have been able to run across a narrow neck of ground, but I came up against a high wire fence. I tried to claw my way up it, but I couldn't do it. I could see a column of black smoke. There was nothing to do but wait, after I got round it. They were pretty slow in getting him out. They must have given him a good jab, because he was a little high, morphine, something like that. His first words to me when he was carried into the dressing station were: 'Hello Dad, I must have been going too bloody fast. Am I badly burned?'
>
> I said, 'You're no beauty, but I don't think there's too much to worry about.'

It was all he could say. Archie was in dreadful shape. Dr Collette glanced at his watch and estimated that he would be dead by six o'clock. One who overheard this was Mme. Collette Stasse, wife of the director of the Ecurie Nationale Belge (ENB), Pierre Stasse. She was tempted to erupt at Dr Collette, but instead threw her considerable energy into making things as easy as possible for Archie and Bill, who was beside himself. Dr Collette decided to send Archie to the St Elisabeth clinic, Heusy, where he had sent Seaman. He did not accompany him. Archie received blood transfusions and morphine in the dressing station, but was not moved to Heusy until the end of the race, as the organizers preferred not to halt the race. Bruce Halford, who had pulled up with gearbox trouble, moped about outside the dressing station, powerless to help. It was his birthday.

Brian was appalled. The first conclusion to which he jumped was that the repair to the steering arm was responsible. Reg Parnell, who could well imagine what Lister was going through, inspected the cooling wreck and reassured him that nothing had broken off except as a result of the impact. Brian was somewhat relieved by this. Despite the intense competition that existed between the Lister and Parnell's Astons, Parnell, who had a huge respect for the Lister effort, had stood solidly at his side at the worst moment of his life.

Mme Stasse called Bill at the hospital upon Archie's arrival, offering assistance, any time, day or night. He took her at her word and phoned at 5 a.m. on the Monday morning, aghast that a burns doctor had not been to see Archie; only nuns and the resident doctor, Louis Grenade, who were unable to do anything much except sedate him heavily. Mme Stasse telephoned a burns specialist of her acquaintance, getting him out of his bed, only to discover that he was engaged first thing in the morning on an operation in the north. He agreed to come down as quickly as possible, arriving after lunch. There was little he could do. Archie's kidneys had failed and he was dehydrated and in massive shock – although heavily sedated and feeling little pain. The burns had been largely ignored, except from the most basic treatment. It was, in short, too late. No-one knows whether any of the lessons learned in the war could have been applied in Archie's case. Had they been available, there was perhaps a faint chance. Dr Collette was, though, a pre-war doctor. He had actually treated Dick Seaman nearly 20 years before, or not, as the case may be. His assumption was that Archie could not be saved, and that was that, however solicitous his demeanour to Brian Lister and the works crew.

The Belgian press released bulletins on Archie's condition almost hourly, not only for the benefit of the numerous British correspondents who were waiting patiently for news, but for the Belgians themselves. Since the little Scot's arrival in the country, a small mythology had already grown up around him, one of the oddest being that he was an ex-RAF Spitfire pilot who had been wounded during the war. Those who circulated this theory had failed to do their sums in the same way that Peter Riley had, seven years before. Brian Lister tactfully left Bill to his son, but besieged the hospital for news, both personally and by phone from the hotel. The Italian manager, saddened by the news, was consideration itself.

Back in Cambridge, Jose Lister was attempting to tell Jay of the accident, but the Evelyn Nursing Home, where she was recovering after the small operation, would not put her through. Jay had remarked that she would prefer not to be disturbed, and the staff, despite being told by Jose what had happened, took her at her word, with the result that she was not told at all – none of the staff being prepared to break the news. Iain McWilliam had seen the news of the crash on the six o'clock news on Sunday. He was on a TA camp in Stirlingshire. He, too, tried to ring Jay, not knowing she was in a nursing home. He found out where and pestered the place until they put her on the line. He arranged to meet her at London airport on Monday and took an overnight train down.

When the pair arrived in Brussels they were somewhat startled to find Collette Stasse and her chauffeur waiting for them. She whisked them down to Heusy at breakneck speed, arriving at the St Elisabeth clinic at eight in the evening, to no avail. Archie had died 20 minutes earlier.

The wreckage of VPP 9 was left at the track, locked in a garage until the morning when the depressing task of loading it on to the transporter began. Jack Fairman and one or two other drivers, including Bruce Halford, lent a hand, as clearly the Lister personnel were very distressed and barely up to the task. The sorry procession made its way towards Ostend, accompanied by the HCH 736 team. Brian Lister stayed behind to await news of Archie. When they reached the border, they realized that they had no documents, so Naylor went back to retrieve them from Lister. Barton stayed at the border, trying to convince the officials that the wreck they had in the back was indeed the same car that they had brought through the previous week. When Naylor arrived with the tryptique, the news of Archie's death had been announced on the radio and they were allowed to leave. 'I'll never forget the stink of that thing sitting in the back,' Barton later said.

Tellingly, Bill Scott Brown, who had found the time to talk with Brian Lister at the St Elisabeth clinic after Archie died was, while as distressed as anybody could be, also philosophical. He knew, like Jay, that the lease of life granted to his son by the efforts of Naughton Dunn was not infinite. Archie had suffered from persistent tiredness all his life, there always being the possibility that his handicaps were not all visual, and he had always had a problem with his tiny legs, which were less and less able to support his weight as he grew older and even stouter. It was a typical Bill Scott Brown observation. He owed much to his son, as Archie had really given him the impetus to dry out properly. Even outside the hospital where his son had just died he was able to find it in him to offer some crumbs of comfort to Archie's stricken friend, which included a message from Archie: the crash had been his fault for going too fast and nothing to do with the car, and 'not to feel too bad about it.'

Jay was, of course, beside herself. Despite the support which she had offered to her son, this was her nightmare come true. She too was able to create at least a thin layer of objectivity, and mindful of the strain which Bill had been through in his constant vigil at Archie's bedside, suggested artlessly that he might like a small whisky. His response was straightforward; he would never touch another drop. He hadn't done for ten years and was not about to start now. His role as witness to his son's success, followed by his presence at his death had confirmed that Bill really was cured.

Brian Lister trailed back to the hotel and conveyed the news to the other concerned guests, many of whom were directly connected with the race, and some of whom knew Archie well. The manager was predictably upset by Brian's tidings. He walked over to the BP pennants on the wall. 'We might as well take the flags down,' he said. Lister went cold.

Bill and Jay, accompanied by McWilliam, flew back to England together. They were to speak of remarriage, but Bill's life, so changed by his son, had taken a different route, and the umbilical which had connected them was now cut forever.

The shock felt at Archie's death was profound. In the time that he had taken to grasp the Lister-Jaguar by the scruff of the neck he had started to become thought of as indestructible. The 40 staff at Listers were stunned; so was the rest of the racing world. Bill, Jay and Brian Lister were the recipients of mail literally by the sackful, much of it sent within hours of the accident, to be augmented by more when the news of his death the next day was announced on the radio. It had not been a matter of public knowledge that he had been so critically injured, so many were breezy notes sending best wishes to Archie, even congratulating Lister on Gregory's fine win.

The papers were gloomier on the morning of the 19th than had the radio broadcasters been the night before. Dr Grenade had stated Archie's condition to be 'extremely critical', so when the terrible news finally broke on the evening of 19 May, the tone of the letters changed. Schoolboys, pensioners, and particularly the handicapped, as well as personal friends and the racing fraternity, were all moved to write. One letter, which we should leave anonymous, but from someone who should know, said: 'We have always looked upon him as one of the finest sportsmen ever in motor racing and there has certainly been no-one like him since the war.' Two schoolboys wrote from Warrington, not only to send their clearly sincere condolences, but to thank Brian for letting Archie drive his 'wonderful products'. There were many more in similar vein.

The funeral was a truly miserable affair. Many from Scotland could not manage to make it at such short notice, as plans were not finalized immediately and Shell-Mex encountered some small bureaucratic delay in repatriating Archie's body. It was a dismal wet, windy day, the weather matching aptly the mood of the gathering. After a service at the Round Church in the centre of Cambridge, Bill took Archie's ashes away from the Cambridge crematorium and brought them back up to Scotland. He scattered them on the Clyde side of the Isle of Arran, overlooking the waters they had sailed together, on a hill known as the 'Sleeping Warrior'.

Upon his return, Bill telephoned Brian Lister. Had Brian insured Archie's life? Brian, shocked, told him that he had not. Bill told him that he had had a call from an insurance company who had written a policy on him and that Bill was listed as the next of kin; if Brian hadn't insured him, who had? Brian phoned John Eason-Gibson who contacted a Lloyd's underwriter who was a BRDC member to ask him to find out. A few weeks later, back came the answer – David Murray.

There had, of course, been inevitable speculation that the accident was in some way connected with the steering problems which had plagued the cars earlier in the season. Reg Parnell, who couldn't do enough for Archie's stricken colleagues, had reaffirmed his opinion that there was no question of a mechanical failure. Two independent RAC scrutineers, brought in by Brian Lister as soon as the car was back in the UK, were to agree unanimously on the issue. The consensus view which emerged, from witnesses and competitors alike, was that Archie's eagerness to win, particularly after having been trounced at Silverstone by Gregory, coupled with his inexperience of treacherous weather in combination with a very precise circuit, contributed to his leaving absolutely no margin for error. The error, when it came, left little room for recovery.

Paul Frère, who came second to Gregory in the race, made extensive reference to the crash in his autobiography *From Starting Grid to Chequered Flag* (Batsford, 1962):

> If I may state an opinion, I shall say quite definitely that the accident could in no way be attributed to the fact that the brilliant British driver had the use of his left hand only. For three years he had competed regularly in England and the previous winter he had done a brilliant tour of Australia [sic] and New Zealand. In three years he had accumulated an impressive list of victories, and they were not Pyrrhic victories because he often beat aces like Moss, Collins, Brooks, Salvadori and so on. Not only was he an extremely brilliant driver he was also very steady and up until then had never had a serious accident.
>
> However, his favourite terrain was the British type of circuits which are mostly sinuous and often laid out on disused aerodromes where a driver who makes a mistake can leave the road without much damage since it is bordered by fields. On these relatively safe circuits the British drivers have alarming dices with each other, with their cars a few inches apart and driving on the very limit. But they do sometimes forget that on real road circuits one is not as likely to get away unscathed after a mistake, particularly when, as at Francorchamps, the race average is of the order of 125 mph. If one takes certain risks on an aerodrome, they must definitely not be taken on a circuit like Francorchamps and it seems that this is what Scott Brown and Gregory had forgotten. . . The trace left by Scott Brown's wheels showed that when he had left the road it [the car] continued for a few dozen yards along the grass verge which separates the road from the ditch. It is very likely that the driver could have saved himself if the car had not hit this post, which tore off its right front wheel. From that moment the car was completely out of control and the accident became inevitable.

The crash was never put down to anything other than Archie's error; there was no suggestion that Gregory had a particular role to play in it, despite the intensity of the dice that the two Listers were having. Later, there was to be speculation, mainly from the uninformed, that Archie had been run off the road. Given that he was in the lead at the time, and had held his own against very tough competition indeed, this can be discounted as mischievous gossip, intended to rationalize an apparently inexplicable accident that had happened to an exceptionally well-liked man.

Gregory was not a particularly popular man. He was considered dangerous by some of his peers, and was even actively disliked by a few. He may have been a little weird, but that is not of itself inconsistent with his chosen career. That he was aggressive and erratically inconsistent is undisputed. That he was an habitual drug user (a rumour I encountered more than once in researching this book) is, if I may use this as a forum to say so, totally unproven and, were he still alive, libellous; but it is a view probably fertilized by Gregory's early death in 1985 at the age of 53.

Put simply, Gregory was doing his job, and so was Archie. Many of the letters which Brian received from people who knew Archie well were at pains to point out that he had died doing something which he loved and that Brian should be content as being the man who'd had the honour of providing the means – these are sentiments which do great credit to their sources as well as their recipient, but which were not to offer Brian much immediate comfort.

Chapter 14

After Archie

OF course, it had been Brian Lister's first instinct to withdraw from racing altogether after the catastrophe at Spa. Archie had been with him from the start of this great adventure, after all, and the works had never operated with any other driver, apart from the occasion when Archie's licence had been temporarily revoked when there had to be one or two guest appearances by others. The Abbey Road team was a very close one, and every member of it had thought the world of him. His temperament, enthusiasm and raw ability would be hard to match, let alone replace, however hard Lister looked around. There was now a huge vacuum – on many levels.

On the other hand, the work that the trio of Brian, Don Moore and Archie had put in had finally started to gain an enthusiastic customer base as well as a commercial following. Brian had a fuel and oil sponsorship contract with BP, as well as Archie's tyre-testing contract with Dunlop. Neither of these two concerns was remotely interested in pressing any points, however, as they realized full well that the whole Lister operation was devastated, and therefore threatened by the disaster – an impression which the Cambridge concern emitted in waves.

Had Lister's been a racing car manufacturer first and foremost, the idea of retiring from racing would have been absurd. Most manufacturers had seen their cars crash and their drivers die, but pressed on. The disaster of Archie's death, though, had thrown the purpose and the priorities of both George Lister and Sons and Brian Lister (Light Engineering) Ltd into very sharp relief indeed, and there was an obvious conflict between the two, at least in Brian Lister's mind. The overwhelming mood, however, was grief.

Lister's was not the only business which suffered. The Autodel Garage was in financial difficulties (as it always had been) and Jill Fenner, Archie's fiancée, who was wealthy in her own right, injected some funds to keep it limping along until the business was wound up. There was desultory talk of carrying it on, but no-one was really interested now that its mainspring was broken. But back at Abbey Road,

Brian Lister was considering his own options. To most observers, he seemed pole-axed.

Salvadori commented:

> Brian Lister was brilliant – he had this fabulous contact with Archie and they worked supremely well together, like Chapman and Clark later. A good partnership. I knew Brian well and it seemed to me that he lost interest when Archie was killed …

Salvadori makes a typically perceptive observation here. The relationship between the builder and the driver is seldom as close as it was between Scott Brown and Lister and so the Clark-Chapman parallel is apposite, so far as it goes, but Brian's view of the issues as an employer, businessman and race entrant were naturally at odds with his reaction to events as a man. His doubts about continuing were the natural responses of a sensitive man who had just lost a close friend. On the other hand, he had customers, one of whom (Dick Walsh) had entered, along with another (Ecurie Nationale Belge), their Listers for the Le Mans 24-hour race in June, barely a month after Spa. Brian had, of course, abandoned any idea of his own entry, and Ecosse were not entering a Lister but a pair of D-Type Jaguars.

After the huge help which the Stasse family had provided – not to mention Walsh, Naylor and Halford – Lister was reluctant to let them go through the ordeal of the Sarthe circuit without a measure of interest and moral support. He accompanied his customers to Le Mans, with Dick Barton, in a private capacity – a much-needed displacement activity and one which had real purpose – to give moral support should the need arise, as well as to receive some.

Well, the need certainly arose. The 1958 Le Mans race was one of the most gruelling on record. The weather was unusually filthy and, for those cars using the short-stroke 3-litre Jaguar engine, the largest capacity allowed in the event, there were more problems in store. The ENB car, wearing its yellow and green livery, a mirror image of the Lister works, was driven by Claude Dubois and Freddy Rousselle. Brian Naylor and Bruce Halford were in HCH 736.

In practice, the Belgian Lister was a little smoky, but they decided to press on anyway. In the event, they lasted four hours into the race before one of the fragile Titanium conrods gave out and ventilated the block, dumping their oil out on to the track. There is a theory that the conrods, in effect the same as those used on 3.4-litre engines, were over-machined down in order to clear the narrower bores. Given that the crank was of a similar throw to the 3.4 engine, it would have over-stressed the neck of the rod, with predictable results. This may have been true – certainly, conrod failure was a consistent feature of the 3-litre Jaguar engine in all its surprisingly assorted bore and stroke ratios.

Despite retiring, the Belgian team did rather better than the Ecosse D-Type, driven by Ninian Sanderson and John Lawrence, which started to lay an expensive-looking smokescreen down after less than two laps, closely followed by the Fairman/Gregory Ecosse car minutes later. It started to rain after two hours, and never really stopped. By the eighth hour, there were only two Jaguar-powered cars left in – Duncan Hamilton and Ivor Bueb's privately-entered D-Type, 2CPG, and the Walsh Lister. Naylor and Halford were doing quite well, lying sixth when, by way of a change, the exhaust camshaft snapped. They had no spare.

As it happened, the place was littered with both spare parts and spare mechanics for Jaguars, most of the cars having expired, and the Coventry mechanics who were attending the Ecosse cars soon produced one. They stripped and rebuilt the top end of the engine, replacing the bent valves and the broken cam and fitting new gaskets. When they proudly restarted the car, they discovered that the engine would not run smoothly below 3500 rpm; the cam timing on the Ecosse cars was radically different from that of the engine in HCH.

They kangarooed off again, relieved at having only lost a few places. A quick check around the circuit revealed why – nine other cars had retired during the time, about an hour, mainly down to accidents. By the time Naylor and Halford rejoined the race, there were only two dozen cars left in, out of 55 entered. They ploughed on through the night until the 20th hour when, while in ninth place, the gearbox jammed as Naylor was attempting to change down. Naylor pulled the car up at the end of the Mulsanne straight and the faithful Jaguar mechanics wandered over. Carelessly, one or two of them dropped some tools. By a coincidence, Naylor found a King Dick spanner and a screwdriver by the side of the road. He levered off the top cover and hammered the change lever into top. The high minimum idling speed occasioned by the new cam assisted his take-off, but it is a tribute to the torque of the Jaguar engine that he managed to get away at all. There was no time to replace the cover, so the inside of the cockpit became coated and filled with a dismal coulis of rain, metal filings and gear oil. After a brief sojourn in the pits, where a slightly more professional running repair was made, the car restarted again, only to begin losing its brakes. Back to the pits again, they nearly withdrew, but decided to improvise one more time by the simple expedient of sawing through the rear brake pipes, isolating the leak and crimping off the ends to avoid total fluid loss. They sauntered round gingerly, with no rear brakes, to be classified 15th at the end of the race. Theirs was the only 3-litre Jaguar engine to ever finish at Le Mans, as well as the only Lister.

Lister was awed by this effort, and it gave him pause for thought. What may have finally helped him make up his mind to return to racing was a dinner which all the Jaguar entrants attended the evening after the race at the Ricardeau Hotel. Given that the only Jaguar-powered car to finish was a Lister, it all got a bit out of hand, and some disparaging remarks were made concerning, not only the merits of the Lister, which was merely ribbing and therefore entirely expected and acceptable, but about Archie, which was not.

Archie's death was still a raw wound, and Murray and Wilkinson probed it cruelly. The knowledge that Murray had held an insurance policy on Archie's life, a legacy of both the Swedish Sports Car Grand Prix and his attempts to lure Archie to a 'Scottish team', brought relations between Lister and Murray to a new low. That Lister was not merely being touchy is confirmed by the fact that Bob Gibson-Jarvie, an Ecosse supporter, was at pains to apologize for Murray's tasteless behaviour.

Lister, for better or worse, resolved to re-enter racing. He lacked a works driver, of course. When he informed Bryan Turle that it was his intention to carry on as an entrant as well as a manufacturer, the BP executive, predictably delighted, proceeded to shortlist some options. After Hawthorn, who was the 'property' of the wrong oil company, one of the most obvious choices was Ivor 'the driver' Bueb, the enthusiastic garagiste racer from Cheltenham. He was a Le Mans veteran, mature and well-versed in matters Jaguar. There was also Bruce Halford, but he was, for the moment busy campaigning HCH 736, and was to do so until the car was sold to the Border Reivers, the 'other' Scottish racing team, for Clark to drive.

Ivor Leon Bueb, originally from Dulwich, was based in Cheltenham where he ran, or at least owned in partnership with Geoffrey Turk, a garage business. He had first raced in 1952 and his first drive for the Jaguar works team had been to partner Hawthorn in the tragic 1955 Le Mans race, which they had won. Hawthorn and Bueb reappeared in the 1956 event, coming sixth. Paired with Flockhart, Bueb had again won in 1957, driving for Murray. He, too, had had his Formula 1 debut with Connaught, coming fifth at the Syracuse Grand Prix in February 1957 and third at Pau in April of the same year. He had retired from the Monaco Grand Prix, Connaught's last entry before the firm finally succumbed to bankruptcy. Arguably, Bueb had bumped Archie out of his Formula 1 drive. Thus, if Lister had serious ambitions in the area of endurance racing, Bueb would be a logical choice. Few other drivers were available with the relevant experience or attitude. Bueb, though, had commitments that season, already sorted out before Archie's death, so Brian was obliged to pick his drivers on a rather piecemeal basis. As things transpired, the balance of the season was to work out quite well.

A few changes were made to the cars. The most obvious was the colour scheme. The characteristic yellow stripe, always to be associated with Archie, was modified to sweep back around to the leading edge of the front wheel arch and the trailing edge of the rear one. The whole of the nose cone was thus painted yellow. In a typically nice gesture, the Ecurie Nationale Belge, whose yellow and green colours mirrored Lister's, modified their own car accordingly.

The possibility that the faired-in wings of the Ecosse car gave a real advantage was acknowledged also. Lister had the bonnets of the works cars modified to imitate the shape of the Ecosse cars, with panels riveted on from the top centre of the front wing curve, merging just in front of the screen. The nose of the car was also lengthened by several inches. Naturally, for the UK season, the works cars were all running 3.8-litre engines.

So, for the balance of the 1958 season, a number of drivers were entered in Lister cars, the most regular being Bueb, whose first victory came quite soon – a fortnight after Le Mans, at a BRSCC meeting at Crystal Palace on 5 July, when he won from Halford and set a new sports car lap record in the process. Bruce was, of course using the 3.4-litre engine which the car had always had, giving away nearly half a litre of engine capacity as well as driving a car which had just competed at Le Mans – it was a considerable achievement for both car and driver, but Halford is well-known as a 'tryer' and the car had plenty left in it as its later history would show.

After the distasteful episode following Le Mans, Lister uncharacteristically resolved to stomp all over Ecurie Ecosse, and telephoned BP. Turle was most understanding, both from the personal and professional point of view – after all, Ecosse were an Esso-sponsored team. Turle arranged a one-race deal with Stirling Moss for the BRDC/RAC International at Silverstone on 19 July, who would drive MVE 303 (still with a magnesium body), while Lister arranged with Cunningham that Walt Hansgen should come over on a visit and drive a second works car – another VPP 9, rebuilt in aluminium using the Spa wreck's identity. It was over-egging the pudding a little, perhaps – probably the two best sports car drivers on their respective sides of the Atlantic – but Lister was determined. Moss had had little to do with the Lister marque. He had, of course, driven the Lister-Bristol at Goodwood years before and tested the 1957 car at Crystal Palace, but more out of interest than anything else. He and Archie had been friends, too. Ironically, Ivor Bueb was driving in the same race in a brand new Tojeiro-Jaguar, borrowed by Ecurie Ecosse from John Ogier, a long-standing arrangement.

Stirling had of course, like everyone else, been aware of the steering failures which Lister had suffered prior to redesigning the components and, seldom one to mince words about such things, justifiably asked Brian if they had been responsible for the crash at Spa. Given the report which had come back from the RAC, coupled with the on-site inspection which Parnell and others had made, Brian was well-supported in giving Moss and Hansgen the reassuring news that the cars were as safe as they could possibly be. Hansgen already knew this; he had suffered no such failures during the early part of the USA season, a fact possibly attributable to the Cunningham team favouring Firestone tyres over Dunlop. The Cunningham team had of course fitted Brian's new steering arm as a matter of course in May, when advised of the precautionary nature of the modification, but they had never had even a hint of trouble with the old one.

The event was satisfactory from the Cambridge team's point of view. Lister's strategy worked rather earlier than anticipated, as Gregory wrote off the Ecosse Spa-winning car, 341 SG, in practice, sustaining fortunately only light injuries. He saved himself from worse damage by jumping out of the car just before it ran into the banking. Gregory ended up in the crowd, but would probably have been killed had he stayed in the car. He was to repeat a similar trick in a Tojeiro at Goodwood the following year. It was something of a party piece with Gregory, a later variation of which was to roll out through the windscreen aperture of a wayward Ferrari 330LM.

Stirling won the race, but didn't threaten to break Gregory's lap record in the process. Two 1500 cc Lotuses came in behind him, followed by Bueb in the Tojeiro. Bruce Halford was sixth in his Le Mans car. Hansgen had rather uncharacteristically wrecked his clutch at the start and retired after a few laps.

The Vanwall Trophy meeting at Snetterton came next on 27 July. The year before, this had been the occasion of one of Scott Brown's clean sweeps, and the Lister drivers affirmed their intention to produce a creditable result. The one-race deal with Moss was over, but Ross Jensen, Archie's opponent from the New Zealand tour, was over for most of the season and accepted with alacrity an invitation to drive. The unlimited sports car race was no problem; Hansgen first, Jensen second, Halford third. The Formule Libre event for the Trophy itself was less sequentially perfect – even though Hansgen won it convincingly – as Henry Taylor, Archie's companion from the Nürburgring, got in the way and came second, driving a British Racing Partnership Formula 2 Cooper, just ahead of Jensen, with Halford in fourth place.

A tidier win for Lister came on 4 August at Brands Hatch. Bueb drove VPP 9, Hansgen's mount at Silverstone, and Ross Jensen took MVE 303. They took first and second respectively in the Kingsdown Trophy followed by Halford in the venerable HCH 736 in third place.

There was a slight sense of *déjà vu* about some of this. If Bueb or Jensen had any doubts about their suitability to take up the Scott Brown mantle, they were groundless. Archie would always enjoy a special place in the affections of the Lister team, but the winning pleased everybody, particularly with the two works cars being so well backed up by the privateer Walsh and the ever-professional Halford.

Snetterton on 7 September saw Bueb and Jensen pass into Archie's giant shadow. The Snetterton Club had started a Scott Brown Memorial Trophy Meeting, the prize for which would be presented by Archie's mother Jay. All a little mawkish, really, but she had allowed herself to be persuaded. The Trophy itself was a Formule Libre race, which Bueb just managed to win from a Formula 2 Cooper driven by Jim Russell. Jensen won the unlimited sports car event which followed.

This was all going rather well. It was lost on nobody that the 'Knobbly' Listers, with their 3.8-litre works Jaguar engines, were winning races and delivering a remarkable consistency, but that they were not producing the kind of wins that such cars had enjoyed the previous season. This was nothing to do with Archie not being there – Hansgen, after all, had broken Scott Brown's old record comprehensively during the Vanwall Trophy meeting – but it had a lot to do with the types of cars that were chasing the Listers home, Formula 2 Coopers and 1500 cc Lotuses in particular. If the thought worried anyone at Cambridge, or Feltham for that matter, it didn't show much for the time being.

The weekend after the Scott Brown Memorial, VPP 9 and MVE 303 were entered for the RAC TT at Goodwood. It was to be a rough experience. John Bekaert and Bruce Halford were drafted in to support Jensen and Bueb respectively. The traditional problem of brake cooling on the Listers had been addressed again. Enough slots and louvres had been cut into the body by now, and this time round Brian had hired aerodynamics expert Frank Costin to consider the problem. What he came up with looked rather like a periscope and, indeed, that was somewhere near its function, but using air, not light. The appendage, mounted on the rear deck, was designed to drive a gust of cooling air down to the rear brakes, enclosed as they were in a low-pressure area next to the final drive. It worked sufficiently well, for Costin was to be retained after the season to modify the body designs into 1959.

A full team of three Aston Martins were present, all 3-litre DBR1 models. Stirling Moss and Tony Brooks drove one, Roy Salvadori and Jack Brabham another and Carroll Shelby and Stuart Lewis-Evans the third. The race was a half-distance, half points event and Ferrari, having secured the championship already, didn't bother to attend. Duncan Hamilton was there in a D-Type and Jean Behra in a Porsche, with assorted Lotuses and smaller capacity cars.

In practice, the kingpins were discovered to be defective on VPP 9 and as a result were replaced on both cars. The race was 148 laps, but after only ten Bueb crashed while avoiding a mêlée on the track at Madgwick corner. Lister called Ross Jensen in to give MVE 303 to

Bueb and Halford but, again, a kingpin failed before long while Halford was driving. Once the Listers were out, Aston Martin managed to engineer a Mercedes-style 1-2-3 parade, the three Feltham cars finishing within 8/10ths of a second of each other. Moss and Brooks were first, Salvadori and Brabham second and Shelby and Lewis-Evans third. Poor Lewis-Evans was to die a month later under circumstances even more horrific than those which had killed Archie at Spa, when his Vanwall crashed and burst into flames during the Moroccan Grand Prix at Casablanca.

The season was winding down now. On 20 September, the MCMC ran an International meeting at Oulton Park, the scene of so much Lister drama. Only one Lister was entered by the works, that being MVE 303 driven by Bueb. Halford drove HCH 736. It was a wet race, won by Roy Salvadori in a Lotus Climax, with Bueb second and Halford third. After the promise of the middle of the season, which had done much to boost morale at Abbey Road, it was a slightly limp result, but much had been proved by the brave return to racing. First, that Archie, although he would always be desperately missed, was not as irreplaceable in competition as everyone had feared. Second, that the cars, at least within their ageing universe, were still competitive. And, third, the morale of the factory and the customers was, after an almost terminal dip at the time of Archie's death, still intact.

One of those customers, Briggs Cunningham, had been having an extraordinary season in the SCCA events in America. After Sebring, the white cars, back to full 3.8-litre specification, were almost unbeatable. After Hansgen's victory at Marlboro, he went on to win at Danville, Virginia, followed by Cumberland, Maryland. A week after Archie's death, Hansgen and Crawford delivered a 1–2 at the Bridgehampton, New York, meeting. The pair so outclassed the opposition and developed such a lead that, in order to make the race interesting for the spectators, they swapped the lead once or twice over the 25-lap course.

By the time of the mid-year Lime Rock meeting, a third Lister was entering the fray. This was BHL 114, owned by Mrs Henry Clark Bowden, a member of the Du Pont chemical dynasty. It was fitted with a Chevrolet Corvette engine and driven by Fred Windridge, who was pleased to be able to get a little closer to the leaders than he had earlier in the season. Windridge came third in the C modified class at Lime Rock, which Hansgen won, although their places had been reversed earlier in the meeting with Windridge's Corvette beating Walt's XK150. From then on in the 1958 season, Windridge was always a potential threat, but never managed to trounce the Cunningham Cars.

A fortnight later, another New York region event at Lime Rock offered Hansgen and Crawford the opportunity of another 1–2.

Windridge was bumped off when lying third, but to prove that there was actually some competition going on, this time round Crawford came first. And so, more or less, the season went for the Cunningham team.

As a rule, Cunningham tended to enter races in central and eastern USA, where the results started to become rather predictable. Lance Reventlow and Chuck Daigh, driving a pair of Reventlow's Scarabs, had tended to stay closer to their Californian home. The two teams finally met, albeit in different classes, at the Thompson National Races, organized by the New England region of the SCCA in the late summer. Hansgen had a puncture while in the lead, allowing Daigh to win the race, but at the Labor Day meeting at Thompson, Reventlow beat Hansgen handsomely, and the New Jersey driver's total dominance was suddenly in question. The weekend after, at Elkhart Lake, Wisconsin, both Lister-Jaguars retired from the Road America 500. Crawford's usual car, driven by Phil Forno, lasted 37 laps and Hansgen lasted 41 before they both retired with oil seal problems at the differential. It was a recurrence of the dreaded Lister brake syndrome, the inboard rear brakes generating too much heat with nowhere to go.

However, despite the slightly mixed results towards the end of the year, the Cunningham team looked forward to getting their hands on the 1959 Lister-Jaguars. Fred Windridge, having seen the effectiveness of Reventlow's Scarabs, advised Mrs Clark Bowden to invest in a Scarab engine, which she promptly did. The Scarab used a Chevrolet block, like Windridge's Corvette, but was tuned in the way that they only seem to manage in California.

Back in Britain, with Archie gone, the competition pace had not been as furious as before, and much consideration was now given in Cambridge to what future cars should look like. There was never any serious route to go other than to capitalize upon gains already made. The Lister name was synonymous with muscular vehicles with the engine in the front, but it was feared that the design of the 'Knobbly' body was already a little dated. To our eyes, of course, it is a deliciously styled masterpiece, all swooping curves and bellowing engine; to the cognoscenti of the late 1950s a purer form was deemed more attractive, which owed more to the aircraft designer than the motor engineer. Malcolm Sayer had started it – Frank Costin continued.

Chapter 15

Swansong

FRANK Costin had done seminal work for Chapman at Lotus and, via that connection, Vandervell at Vanwall. Having trained at de Havilland, he could call upon a vast experience of aerodynamics with total authority. Brian Lister retained his services in the autumn of 1958 to rebody the 'Knobbly', keeping the same mechanical layout.

Lister could read the writing on the wall on the subject of large-engined sports cars, at least within the context of the moment, with only the cast-iron Jaguar engines available to the team. There was clear evidence that history was repeating itself. The Bentley experience of the 1930s when they came to be beaten by much smaller cars, such as MGs and Bugattis, was a clear parallel. Lister hoped that Costin, with his obvious credentials, could embark on a new chassis frame that would save weight; and by that time, rumours concerning a light alloy Jaguar engine might well prove to have been well-founded.

The first priority was an efficient aerodynamic body which would be useful at both short circuit races and Le Mans. The existing chassis was well-proven on shorter circuits and clearly had no problems at Le Mans, a race in which roadholding came second to reliability as a pre-requisite. Lister was the first to admit that the 'Knobbly' body, although low in frontal area, was high in wind resistance.

Lister had a fine car already. It was the finest of its sort, better in some ways than that great British bellwether the D-Type, and not merely because it used the same engine suspended in a better chassis. The Lister-Chevrolet gave eloquent testimony to that, as had the Lister-Bristol before it.

Costin adhered to the fundamental principles which had made the Lotus such a success. The four wings and the body were each designed as separate aerodynamic shapes; where they met and were connected, the points of contact were smoothed by separate panels. He committed the ideas to paper for Williams and Pritchard to execute.

The Lister chassis was left largely untouched, apart from the addition of a square section lateral tube amidships, which purported to make the structure more rigid. This modification was only carried out to the Costin-bodied cars, so any other body found on such a chassis is a replacement. Several cars of this type can be seen, though as the new Listers were to gain a less than enviable reputation in comparison to their predecessors.

As for the running gear, the steering arm and kingpin failures which had plagued the works in the 1958 season were now well and truly sorted, as Archie had always known they would be. Costin reapplied himself, with imagination, to the issue of brake cooling which was always a Lister difficulty. He went about it in two ways; first, by installing ducted scrapers to remove physically the membrane of hot air which builds up near the surface of discs, and second, by building ducting in the undertray to cool both the rear brakes and therefore the differential, as well as another conduit which picked up cool air from under the car and blew it over the diff. directly. Both ducts exited directly at the rear of the car.

There was certainly plenty of air available under the car; the ground clearance was huge, a massive six inches under the chassis, which made the car look even larger than it really was.

It transpired that Costin might well have spent more time on cooling the driver than the running gear. One of the patent devices applied to the Lister, previously seen on the Le Mans Lotus 11 in 1957, was an inflatable tonneau which was blown up and held in place by air flow, improving the topside drag. In this application though, contrary to the experience with the Lotus, the smoothness of the line created had an effect rather similar to that experienced by the works when the 1957 car was forcibly modified with a taller screen. It reduced airflow in the cockpit, leaving the driver broiled and breathless. The Lotus had ducts to introduce cool air into the cockpit; not so the Lister. The new screen was possessed of another Costin trademark, a sharp inward curve at the front and sides, leaving a relatively small opening at the top. Stick on a tiny flat roof and it would have been a coupé.

The purpose of all this, of course, was endurance racing, specifically Le Mans and Sebring. The combination of a Lister chassis clothed in a fully aerodynamic body which offered the minimum of wind resistance should have been a sound one. The observed decrease in manoeuvrability on tight circuits was deemed to be a small price to pay in exchange for a crack at the big one. Lister, however, had already been here before with MER 303 – the Maserati specification was promising, but really failed to deliver. His hopes were high, but leavened by a certain scepticism. It was becoming clear to Brian Lister that racing car design, influenced by aeronautical and strictly scientific principles could become an extremely time-consuming activity. It was the perfectionist's way. Setting up experiments and borrowing a circuit specifically for one test, poring over the results afterwards and starting again until it was 'right' may well have been the way to proceed, but as far as Lister was concerned he had neither the time nor the money to support it. It was almost certainly the way to build aircraft but his own experience told him that as a strategy to develop race-winning cars in anything like a reasonable time, it was flawed.

The project interested Jaguar, who sent Malcolm Sayer to Silverstone on 27 February to have a look at Moss and Bueb driving, respectively, 3-litre and 3.8-litre cars. He reported back to William Heynes:

TESTS ON LISTER-JAGUAR – SILVERSTONE
The following points may be of interest:

1. Best lap times: Moss (3-litre) 1.45
                            Bueb (3.8-litre) 1.52

2. These were interim cars, to get the body right for use on the new space-frame car to be introduced this summer. The space-frame will weigh 62 lb., a saving of 70 lb.

3. The basic shape of the car is good, although designed purely by eye and without any wind-tunnel work, but so many exits and entries for cooling-air have been added that I think the drag will have increased considerably. Similarly, it has been found that the curved screen offers virtually no protection to the driver, so a perforated Perspex plate has been added as shown, which by spoiling the flow reduces the steady blast to a buffeting. This again must greatly increase drag.

4. Both bonnet and tail are simple skins, having no rigidity once detached. They hook on and are each held by 3 Dzus fasteners. This seems precarious to me, as cracks are already visible round some of the fasteners.

5. As in earlier cars, rear brakes are cooled by a scoop under the car, this scoop fouled the track and came off, and I was told 'They usually did, last year.'

6. At Mr Badger's request further holes were cut to cool the rear tyres, but proved too localized so that only the outer half of the tread was cool enough. We left before further tests were made ...

Mr Badger was the Dunlop representative present.

Walsh and Halford, meanwhile, had decided to sell HCH 736. It was a cruel decision to have to make, but it was plain that the 3.4-litre car, which had a host of places, but few wins to its credit, was destined to be the bridesmaid, rather than the bride, when up against the works' 3.8 machines. After the SMRC race meeting at Snetterton, where Bruce scored two second places, the car was advertised for sale.

The Border Reivers team had disposed of their ex-Murkett, ex-Gillie Tyrer, ex-Scott Brown/Taylor D-Type to Alan Ensoll, who had it rebuilt as a road-going XK SS, and were in the market for a slightly newer machine. Walsh advertised HCH in *Autosport* magazine. Jock McBain, the Reivers' founder, bought the car, to be entered by the team. Jim Clark, who had cut his teeth on the D-Type, was nominated to drive the Lister. He found it, initially at least, very cramped (a legacy of its chief tester) and the équipe took the tinsnips to it with a vengeance. Clark was fascinated by the Lister; he had seen Archie crash at Spa and, although he never remarked upon their having attended the same prep. school, even if he realized it, he clearly felt that the Lister offered a link with him.

For the works, bolstered by the 1958 season, which had pulled them gently but firmly back from the edge, events kicked off with the Sebring 12-Hour race on 21 March 1959. Cunningham entered the cars, with Lister there as an observer. Stirling Moss and Ivor Bueb shared the newest one, a Costin-bodied works chassis from 1958, number BHL 123, with Hansgen and Thompson coupled with Cunningham and Underwood driving the team's 1958 'Knobbly' cars. The Costin-bodied car was in effect outclassed by the 'Knobblies', but that is to rather discount who was driving it. Moss had already demonstrated his single-mindedness at the Nürburgring 1000 km the previous year, where he had driven 36 out of 44 laps of the race, to win against the full Ferrari team. This was a similar challenge. His impatience took over as the Hill/Gendebien Ferrari expired, giving Stirling third place, which he contested with great gusto until the sixth hour, when he made a fuel stop. The Cunningham pit crew started to dump fuel into the tank but Moss, up with the leaders, pressed on before the refuelling was complete. He ran out of petrol a mile from the pit lane. Hansgen attempted to push the Costin-bodied car with the nose of his 'Knobbly', but only succeeded in denting both. Moss was disqualified for getting to the pits on the pillion of a marshal's motorbike. It was an uncharacteristic error from the maestro, and one which Lister was convinced was unnecessary, putting the fiasco down to the fact that he did not take over the running of the car himself. Perhaps if Cunningham had not been driving, the management of the pits would have been a little tighter. Cunningham had said to Lister, Moss and Bueb that he would leave them to get on with it, and Lister feels now that he should have taken control and made it plain to Stirling that he was in charge. In some situations, particularly when he is not paying the bills, Lister tends towards diffidence. Moss's enthusiasm expanded into the vacuum left by the lack of strategy. The Cunningham organisation, with their habitual courtesy, did not interfere. It was a disappointment compounded by its silliness. Moss, no doubt annoyed with himself, did say to Lister, on his retirement from the race, that the best thing he could do was to revert to last year's body; he had found the car difficult to place; an attitude which eased Lister's discomfiture not at all.

Bueb and Halford, the works drivers for 1959, also had F2 schedules to keep that season. Bueb had been instrumental in setting up the British Racing Partnership in conjunction with George Wicken to drive the improbable-sounding Cooper-Borgward. Actually it was a tremendous car, as Stirling Moss was to prove.

Sadly, because of the overlap of the Sebring race with the first proper event on the British calendar, Brian Lister was not present at Snetterton to see Bill Scott Brown unveil a bas-relief plaque in memory of his son. There was total silence as the crowd paid its respects. The plaque, designed by Cavendish Morton, read, simply: 'Archie. W. A. Scott Brown 1927–1958. He represented everything that was best in the sport. 71 Firsts, 34 seconds 12 thirds.'

The works effort proper began a week after Sebring at Goodwood. Interestingly, the works colour scheme reverted back to something very close to that used during Archie's time, albeit with a background colour of a darker green and a lighter yellow stripe. After a tight race, which was a squabble between Salvadori's Cooper-Maserati, Graham Whitehead's Aston Martin and Peter Blond's Lister-Jaguar with a Costin body, Bueb stole the lead on lap 16 and increased his lead over the last five laps to win by a seven second margin. Peter Blond was second, the rest nowhere. Masten Gregory was racing, too, driving an Ecurie Ecosse confection, most of which had been made at Cambridge, but finished fifth. Bueb's chassis was possibly the same one, registration VPP 9, carrying the identity of the Spa car, which had been entered for Hansgen at the British Grand Prix meeting in 1958, but by then rebodied with Costin-designed coachwork.

The customer list was rather more diversified than before, with several private owners, as well as the proper racing teams, throwing their hats into the ring. Derek Wilkinson ran a car for John Bekaert; Jonathan Sieff for Peter Blond; Mike Anthony ran a Lister Corvette, a truly fearsome piece of kit, but with a little more success than Ray Brightman and John Ewer in similar behemoths. Bill Moss and Peter Mould both campaigned their own cars, the former a 3.8, the latter a 3 litre. The Border Reivers were to have a good season with Clark, Whitmore and Blumer at the wheel, as would Ecurie Ecosse, with whom Lister dealt on a coolly distanced but punctiliously professional basis.

The Reivers entered the Lister for 28 events in 1959. Clark drove it for most of the time, but both Sir John Whitmore and Jimmy Blumer also achieved wins with it, the former in July at Charterhall, the latter at Ouston in August. For the balance of that season, Clark won 12 races, came second four times and third twice. He retired twice, once running out of petrol, the second time when the hard-worked engine dropped a valve, suggesting that Walsh's timing was sound, even if the engine's wasn't. The car left a lasting impression upon him:

The Lister taught me a good deal about racing and I had fun with that car. It was a beast of a thing, mind you, really vicious, but it was more fun than any except maybe the Aston Martins I drove later.

Jim Clark's 1959 season was to change his career. The next year gave him his first Formula 1 drive, and his subsequent resumé is both a matter of public record and a source of national pride. Certainly, for this writer (in prep. school at the time), his death, on 7 April 1968 was a matter of much greater moment than anything else which happened that year. I think that it still is, really.

If there was a 'Lister Race', it was the British Empire Trophy, but for 1959 it was to be a Formula 2 event, which rather emphasizes the fascination which the category was generating. The unlimited-capacity sports cars were relegated to a slightly humiliating supporting role. Bueb had a hard time keeping up with the Cooper Monaco cars and finished fifth, while Halford parked in the lake. He waded out, not realizing that he had nearly been impaled on a submerged stanchion and that the car was perilously close to a landmine which had lain in the lake since the war. All in all, considering the possibilities, Bruce had quite a lucky day. Jim Clark, driving Bruce's old car, came eighth. The race confirmed what had been suspected at Sebring – that the Costin car was no better, and in many ways worse, than the old 'Knobbly' design. To revert back would, though, be a huge loss of face as well as the cause of an expensive financial write-off. In fact, it wasn't so much that the Costin-bodied car was uncompetitive; the whole genre itself was hard put to hold its own against the new elfin Lotus, Cooper and Porsche opposition.

There was more development back at Abbey Road. Costin, undeterred by the rather off-hand reception which his cars were receiving, had embarked upon designing the new chassis. It was a radical new departure for Lister and a long-held ambition for him; a completely new space-frame structure which was targeted to weigh only 62 lb. – less than half the weight of the original Lister-designed chassis. It was ferociously expensive to build and develop, of course, and was never to be fully completed by the works, but those who drove it when it *was* finished reported great things of it. In fact, when the car was eventually completed, which was not until after the factory racing programme had closed, it was found to weigh marginally more than the conventionally constructed cars. To be fair, though, the bodywork was completed in a much heavier grade than he had envisaged – 16 gauge as opposed to 18 or even 20 gauge, which added a lot of weight. It was really only a conceptual exercise, which would have required much more testing and development. Its subsequent completion possibly does not do justice to the real potential of the machine, for as a production reality it was still-born and revived by privateers rather than

Lister or Costin. It later entered two endurance races; Le Mans in 1963 and the Nürburgring 1000 km in 1964, completing neither event.

Brian Lister only had his eye on one event in 1959 – Le Mans. After the cock-up at Sebring he was anxious to prove that his cars were suitable for endurance racing, as if Halford and Naylor hadn't proved that the previous year. Nothing of Lister manufacture had gone wrong on that car, after all.

In the event, it was to prove both a tantalizing and lowering experience. Since the failure of all but one 3-litre engine the previous year, Don Moore had been experimenting with a number of ways of producing a reliable 3-litre D-Type engine. Despite the fact that Jaguar had issued a proprietary kit to build one from a 3.4 block – one or two of which Moore had built, with hopeful results – the relationship between Listers and Jaguar mandated that the internals of the engine had to be ex-works. The fragile conrods, so often the cause of failure, were still a feature of the engine, so the prospect of detached pistons still loomed large.

Listers themselves were messing about with a new Costin idea – aerofoil brakes (to assist the rather skinny Dunlop discs which they were using), but Lister dropped the idea before the event; feeling that the rather underdeveloped device was not yet ready. Nevertheless, the concept of a downforce wing on pylons, operated from the cockpit, was a prescient one.

They had good drivers. Ivor Bueb and Bruce Halford, the latter undeterred by the horrors of the previous year, were to drive the recycled BHL 2, suffixed :59 with a works-prepared 3-litre engine, EE 1305. Walt Hansgen and Peter Blond were listed to drive BHL 3:59 fitted with an engine which Hansgen knew well – it had powered his car at Sebring, No. 1302. Both units had been tested at a slightly hysterical 260 bhp at Coventry.

Le Mans was to be the race where David Brown finally got within reach of the World Sports Car Championship, after years of perseverance and the expenditure of an almost unimaginable amount of money.

Engine No.1302 blew up first, after 52 laps. Hansgen and Blond had lasted four-and-a-half hours. Don Moore, probing about under the car, picked out a piece of conrod which had holed the sump and stuck in the undertray of the car. Don removed the sump and extracted the offending rod from the crank. He gave it to Costin, who was examining it when someone from Jaguar (it may even have been 'Lofty' England), without a word, removed it from him and walked off. The weakness of the top end of the 3-litre engine, having effectively curtailed any thought at Brown's Lane of re-entering competition, was becoming an embarrassment.

After nine hours Bueb and Halford, driving as steadily as only they could, managed to ease into fourth place, within optimistic sight of the lead, before one of their conrods went and they too were retired. HCH 736's claim to fame from 1958 remained unchallenged.

This was all rather depressing stuff. The only arena open to the Listers was that in which domestic UK events were run – back to where they started. It was becoming clear that the days of the unlimited sports car class were coming to a close. Technology, as always, is best exploited by those who are first with it, and the development of that technology is expensive. Lister was not in that category, being essentially involved in the business of racing to promote the parent company. He could see that the exponentially rising cost could easily threaten the well-being of the very object of the exercise. The rude awakening came at the British Grand Prix meeting at Aintree on 18 July when the works Costin cars, driven by Bueb and Halford, finished behind Jim Clark in Bruce's old steed. That Clark was himself fourth behind three small-engined tiddlers sent a message loud and clear to Abbey Road.

On 23 July 1959 Brian made his intentions clear in this press release:

LISTERS WITHDRAWING FROM MOTOR RACING

After six years in the field this company is retiring from active participation in motor racing for at least a year.

During this six year period Lister cars, powered mainly by Bristol and Jaguar engines, have won practically every event of importance in their class at one time or another in this country and the USA.

It should not be forgotten that the late Archie Scott Brown, whose wonderful and courageous driving was an inspiration to all, was at the wheel of our cars for many of these victories.

The main reasons for our decision are:

1. The incessant changes made to sports car regulations by the CSI leading to unnecessary expense practically every year.

2. Competing for drivers with more powerfully backed works teams is making racing uneconomical.

3. Motor racing in 1960 is going through a most uncertain stage with the new sports car regulations being applied, with other manufacturers retiring, and with Formula 1 racing in its present form entering its final year.

4. The tremendous influx of work into the other departments of our business, and the wish to build up our existing machine shop equipment and capacity. The latter will, of course, enable us to compete even more effectively when we return to motorsport.

Owners of Lister cars, both in this country and abroad should have no worries concerning spares for their cars, as these will be readily available. We should like to thank those companies and organizers who have supported us in the past, and hope that when we do return in the future we may look forward to working with those organizations again.

Our last race this year will probably be the Tourist Trophy Meeting at Goodwood on 5 September.

David Brown was quite close on Lister's heels in withdrawing from sports car racing, but it is clear that he had not received the message as clearly as Lister had, for the Aston works persisted with a racing presence for a little while longer, even producing a front-engined Grand Prix car which, by the time it appeared, was well and truly out of date.

Unsurprisingly, Frank Costin left the firm, and any further development work was halted as of the day of the announcement. The works effort for the 1959 season had put Listers so far behind the competition from a relative point of view that to continue was to risk an ignominy which would eclipse the last six years of work, devaluing the efforts of so many people, particularly Archie.

On 26 July Ivor Bueb crashed badly at Clermont-Ferrand and was thrown out of his BRP Cooper-Borgward. Tragically, he failed to receive sufficient attention (but was not moved) and was to die a lingering death from massive internal injuries which finally finished him a week later. Halford had crashed in the same race, and on the day of Ivor's death the Lister team, already somewhat lowered by Brian's announced decision, were at Brands Hatch in practice for the meeting on the following Bank Holiday. To make matters worse, here Peter Blond crashed a works Costin-bodied car quite hard, and was lucky to stumble away from it. Brian abandoned the entry, the car being a complete mess anyway, and drove home. On his car radio he heard the news that Jean Behra had died at the Avus circuit after a particularly ghastly crash. When he arrived home at Cambridge, he heard from Jose that Ivor Bueb had died in France that afternoon.

There seemed little point in carrying on for the balance of the season. Out of respect for Bueb and Behra, the latter having been entertaining the thought of a works drive the next year, as well as missing Archie, a sense which never – has never – left him, Brian Lister resolved to stop racing then and there, and cancelled the Goodwood entry.

The losses of life from motor racing in the 1950s were already huge, and Brian wanted no part in it any more. The entire équipe was put up for sale in *Autosport* magazine and elsewhere. The spares, tools, jigs, body panels, assorted cars and part cars were advertised, together with their transporter, in the 21 August issue. The Ecurie Nationale Belge, after a conversation between Lister and Pierre Stasse, decided to sell the remains of their car, too. It was time to lower the boom on the works team effort. The great adventure was over.

This left Cunningham out on his own, somewhat. Listers were not the only cars he was entering in America, but Crawford and Hansgen were still proving dominant, despite problems from George Constantine in the ex-Moss Aston Martin DBR2. Elsewhere in the racing firmament, Cunningham was entering all manner of smaller-engined cars, OSCA and Stanguellini latterly, but was to revert to Jaguar metal for 1960 for his flagship effort, but not until Hansgen had won the 1959 SCCA championship for a second time in a Lister.

The six years of competition and construction had demonstrated much, and on many levels. It had proved that a small, skilled and above all committed engineering company could take on the best and win. It had proved that success in competition was not merely a function of a fat cheque book. In the view of this writer at least, it had proved that ability, not appearance, is the measure of a man.

It is a sad but oft-demonstrated fact of life that a David and Goliath rematch usually ends up with David being stomped on. What Archie Scott Brown and Brian Lister had shown, comprehensively and on a shoestring, was that such isn't always the case. Archie's acceptance into a world which prized excellence above all things, and allowed him to achieve things which would simply not be permitted now, provides a subsequent generation with an embarrassing counterpoint to its own notions of fairness. Instead of fairness, we have political correctness; instead of trust, we have palsied regulation.

Archie Scott Brown does not appear in the *Dictionary of National Biography*, even in the Scottish edition, which is surely shameful. But by those whose lives he touched, either through his racing or his personality, he will not be forgotten. For him to accomplish what he did was nothing short of extraordinary. In a world where people, many of them sportsmen, calculate their own narrow interest down to very fine tolerances indeed, it is all too easy to forget people like Archie.

Epilogue

DESPITE the fact that the events described in this book took place no more than 40 years ago, most of the racing circuits are much changed; Spa in particular is still a very fast course, but much shorter and safer now. The start line is near where Archie, and Seaman before him, crashed. Brands Hatch, Silverstone and Oulton Park have been hugely modified. Snetterton, where Archie's commemorative bas-relief can still be found, and where a memorial race is still run, is closer to its original condition than the others, except Goodwood, which is frozen in time, having been closed to racing since the 1960s. It may re-open.

If you can navigate your way around Cambridge (best done on foot) then much that is in this book can still be seen. Archie and Jay's first little flat at Hills Road is still a flat, and their subsequent house in Portugal Place is still very pretty. There is a plaque on the wall outside, but oddly it does not commemorate Archie.

Lister's moved out of the Abbey Road works. They now operate from a neat building in Church End, Cherry Hinton, just outside Cambridge, and Brian Lister still runs it. As two managers of the firm, Martin Murray and Malcolm Webdale, have just invested substantially in the firm and, it is hoped, may buy more of its equity, Brian is finally considering slowing down a little. The Abbey Road site is still there, altered but just recognizable. George Lister and Sons Ltd is still an engineering company, but it specializes now in packaging machinery and is very high-tech indeed. In Brian's office, the first things you see, though, are Lucas's wind tunnel model of a 1955 Lister Bristol and a photograph of Archie winning at Crystal Palace in the 1957 car.

On the A604 (now the A14) between Cambridge and Huntingdon you can still see Archie's Autodel garage, adjacent to a motel and Little Chef. It is a Texaco filling station now, painted an unhappy shade of red, with nothing at all in the workshop – well, perhaps something. Just down the road towards Huntingdon, you can still stroll into the Trinity Foot and enjoy a first-rate meal and good beer. The landlord remembers Archie very well; he was a schoolboy in Cambridge at the time.

Bill Scott Brown died in 1980. He and Jay never remarried, as he settled up in West Kilbride, Ayrshire and married his long-time companion. Jay stayed in Cambridge, exchanging her pretty house for a rather more functional flat. She took a succession of jobs and stayed on, preferring not to go back to Scotland. She died within weeks of Bill.

David Murray left Britain after a financial scandal and went to the Canaries. He died in 1967 in a road accident.

Don and Babs Moore are retired now and live quite near the site of the Autodel garage. Peter Riley lives a little further west, within earshot of Silverstone. Rodney Tibbs is still the motoring correspondent of what is now called the *Cambridge Evening News* and Tony Murkett lives not far from Don and Babs. Dick Barton left Listers amicably in 1960 and took a job, which he still does, at the University chemistry laboratories. Brian and Jose Lister live not far from Audley End, a few miles south of the city. During the 1980s Brian took up jazz drumming again, accompanying such US jazz stars as 'Yank' Lawson, Maxine Sullivan, 'Doc' Cheatham, Harry 'Sweets' Edison and 'Spike' Robinson. In 1990 he was featured with Ken Peplowski on a BBC2 'Jazz Parade' broadcast, which is fairly close to the top of the tree.

You can still buy a Lister today, but it would not be built by Brian or his team. Laurence Pearce of Leatherhead resuscitated the name, with Brian's permission, initially for a line of modified Jaguar sports cars, and they even built a handful of replica 'Knobblies' on new Cambridge-built chassis. These cars are therefore more authentic than many which lay claim to it. Then, at the 1993 Motor Show, the new Lister emerged. Built on a complex honeycomb alloy chassis it is ludicrously fast and uses an engine which started off as a Jaguar. Archie would have loved it; the Sultan of Brunei certainly likes his. This new Lister, the 'Storm', will certainly race.

Archie's 1957 car, MVE 303, was cut up and scrapped upon its return from New Zealand, its identity recycled into the second works car for the next year. It is perhaps a tragedy that it no longer exists, but at the time it was worth little. I am sorry to have to reveal this, as many had hoped that it would resurface, but there it is.

Roy Salvadori, Paul Frère, Henry Taylor and Lance Macklin all moved to the French Riviera some time ago, and Bruce Halford still lives down in Devon, coincidentally not very far from Marion. Stirling Moss, of course, still lives in London. One thing all these people have in common, which cements their shared experience, is the way they react when you mention Archie Scott Brown. They go quiet for a moment, then smile.

Race successes – W. A. Scott Brown

1951

4 March	CUAC Speed Trials, Bottisham 1st – 1500 cc Class (MG TD)
11 August	MGCC Race Meeting, Silverstone 4th – Novice Handicap (MG TD)

1952

2 March	CUAC Speed Trials, Bottisham 1st – 1101–1500 cc Sports and Saloon Class (Jackson Cup) (MG TD)
26 April	ECCC meeting, Snetterton 1st – 1101–1500 cc Sports Cars (MG TD) 2nd – 1101–1500 cc Sports Car H'cap (MG TD)
27 April	Cambridge '50 CC Speed Trials, Bottisham 1st – 1101–1500 cc Sports Car Class (MG TD)
3 May	AMOC Race Meeting, Snetterton 2nd – Sports Car H'cap (MG TD)
14 September	WECC Rally 2nd overall, 1st in class (MG TD)
28 September	Cambridge '50 CC Hill Climb, Great Chishill 1st – 1500 cc Class (MG TD) 2nd – FTD (MG TD)
19 October	Cambridge '50 CC Sprint, Bottisham 2nd – 1101–1500 cc Class and member of winning team (MG TD)

1953

8 March	CUAC Sprint, Bedwell Hay 3rd – over 2500 cc Class (Bugatti Type 35)
18 April	AMOC Race Meeting, Snetterton 3rd – Sports Car Race (MG TD)
25 April	ECCC Race Meeting, Snetterton 1st – up to 1100 cc Class (Tojeiro-JAP) 2nd – up to 1500 cc H'cap (MG TD) 1st – Specials H'cap (Tojeiro-JAP)
16 May	MMKMC Race Meeting, Silverstone 1st – up to 1100 cc Class (Tojeiro-JAP)

17 May	BOC National Hill Climb, Prescott 1st – up to 1500 cc Sports Car Class (Tojeiro-JAP)
25 May	Bristol MC & LCC Race Meeting, Thruxton 1st – up to 1200 cc Sports Car Class (Tojeiro-JAP) 3rd – up to 1500 cc Sports Car Class (Tojeiro-JAP)
11 October	Cambridge '50 CC Speed Trials, Bottisham 3rd – up to 1500 cc Sports Car Class (MG TD)

1954

7 March	CUAC Speed Trials, Gransden 3rd – up to 1500 cc Sports Car Class (MG TD)
21 March	ECCC Autocross 1st – up to 1500 cc Open Class (MG TD)
3 April	ECCC Race Meeting, Snetterton 1st – 1173–1500 cc Sports Car Class (Lister-MG) 1st – up to 1500 cc Sports Car H'cap (Lister-MG)
4 April	WECC Sprint, Weathersfield 3rd – 1101–1500 cc Sports Car Class (Lister-MG)
7 June	Half-litre CC Race Meeting, Brands Hatch 2nd – up to 1500 cc Sports Car Class (Lister-MG)
12 June	MCMC National Race Meeting, Oulton Park 2nd – up to 1500 cc Sports Car Class (Lister-MG)
19 June	AMOC Race Meeting, Snetterton 2nd – Sports Car Scratch Race (Lister-MG)
27 June	ECCC Sprint, Snetterton 1st – 1201–1500 cc Class (Lister-MG)
10 July	Half-litre CC Race Meeting, Oulton Park 2nd – up to 1500 cc Sports Car Race (Lister-MG)
17 July	RAC British Grand Prix, Silverstone 5th overall – Unlimited Sports Car Race and 1st – up to 2000 cc Class (Lister-Bristol) 7th up to 1500 cc Sports Car Race (Lister-MG)
24 July	Welsh MRC Race Meeting, Fairwood 2nd – up to 1500 cc Sports Car Race (Lister-MG) 1st and fastest lap – up to 2000 cc Sports Car Race (Lister-Bristol) 2nd – Unlimited Sports Car Race (Lister-Bristol)
2 August	Half-litre CC International Race Meeting, Brands Hatch 1st in heat, 2nd in final – 1500 cc Sports Car Championship (Lister-MG)
14 August	WECC International Race Meeting, Snetterton 1st and fastest lap – up to 2000 cc Sports Car Race (Lister-Bristol)
28 August	Bristol MC & LCC National Race Meeting, Castle Combe 2nd and fastest lap – Unlimited Sports Car Race (Lister-Bristol) 2nd and fastest lap – up to 2000 cc Class (Lister-Bristol)
4 September	Brighton & Hove MC International Speed Trials, Brighton 2nd – 1501–2000 cc Sports Car Class (Lister-Bristol)
5 September	Half-litre CC Race Meeting, Brands Hatch 2nd – up to 1500 cc Sports Car Race (Lister-MG) 2nd – up to 2000 cc Sports Car Race (Lister-Bristol)

11 September	Peterborough MC Race Meeting, Silverstone 1st – up to 1500 cc Sports Car Race (Lister-MG)
18 September	Half-litre CC Race Meeting, Crystal Palace 2nd – up to 1500 cc Sports Car Race (Lister-MG) 5th – up to 2000 cc Sports Car Race (Lister-Bristol)
9 October	ECCC Race Meeting, Snetterton 1st and fastest lap – 1501–2000 cc Sports Car Race and fastest lap in Sports Car H'cap (Lister-Bristol)
14 November	CUAC Driving Tests, Cambridge 4th overall (Ford Zephyr)
28 November	CUAC 'Little Rally' 1st in class (Ford Zephyr)

1955

6 Mar	CUAC Speed Trials, Tempsford 2nd – 1201–1500 cc Closed Car Class (Peugeot 203)
26 March	SMRC Race Meeting, Snetterton 1st and fastest lap – 1501–2000 cc Sports Car Race (Lister-Bristol) 2nd – Formule Libre Race (Lister-Bristol)
2 April	BRDC British Empire Trophy Race, Oulton Park 1st in final, 2nd in heat (Lister-Bristol)
11 April	BARC International Race Meeting, Goodwood 1st and fastest lap – up to 2000 cc Sports Car Race (Lister-Bristol)
16 April	Winfield Joint Committee, National Race Meeting, Charterhall 1st and fastest lap – up to 2000 cc Sports Car Race (Lister-Bristol) 1st and fastest lap – unlimited Sports Car Race (Lister-Bristol)
30 April	WH & DCC Race Meeting, Ibsley 1st – 1501–2750 cc Sports Car Race (Lister-Bristol)
28 May	WECC National Race Meeting, Snetterton 1st and fastest lap – up to 2000 cc Sports Car Race (Lister-Bristol) 1st and fastest lap – unlimited Sports Car Race (Lister-Bristol) 2nd – Curtis Trophy Formula 1 Race (Lister-Bristol) 3rd – Formule Libre Race (Lister-Bristol)
29 May	BRSCC Race Meeting, Brands Hatch 1st – Wrotham Cup, Unlimited Sports Cars (Lister-Bristol)
30 May	BRSCC Race Meeting, Crystal Palace 1st – Norbury Trophy Race for Unlimited Sports Cars (Lister-Bristol)
25 June	ECCC Race Meeting, Snetterton 2nd – Unlimited 100-mile Sports Car Race. Member of winning team (Lister-Bristol)
10 July	BRSCC Race Meeting, Brands Hatch 1st – Over 1900 cc Sports Car Race (Lister-Bristol)
30 July	BARC Race Meeting, Crystal Palace 2nd – Unlimited Sports Car Race (Lister-Bristol)
1 August	BRSCC International Race Meeting, Brands Hatch 1st and fastest lap – Kingsdown Trophy for Sports Cars over 1900 cc (Lister-Bristol)

6 August	Winfield Joint Committee International Race Meeting, Charterhall 1st – Up to 2700 cc Sports Car Race (Lister-Bristol) 3rd – Unlimited Sports Car Race (Lister-Bristol)
20 August	BARC International 9-Hour Sports Car Race, Goodwood 6th overall and 1st – Up to 1500 cc Class (Connaught, with L. Leston)
25 September	SMRC Race Meeting, Snetterton 3rd overall, 1st in Unlimited Class Invitation H'cap (Jaguar C-Type)
9 October	BRSCC Race Meeting, Brands Hatch 1st and fastest lap – Unlimited Sports Car Race (Jaguar C-Type)
26 December	BRSCC Race Meeting, Brands Hatch 1st and fastest lap – Formula 1 Air India Trophy (Connaught Formula 1)

1956

11 March	CUAC Speed Trials, Cambridge 1st – Up to 1000 cc Class (Auto-Union-DKW)
14 April	BRDC British Empire Trophy Race, Oulton Park 2nd and fastest lap – 1500–2700 cc heat (Lister-Maserati)
5 May	BRDC International Race Meeting, Silverstone 2nd – Daily Express International Trophy Race (Formula 1 Connaught) 9th overall – Unlimited Sports Car Race (Lister-Maserati) 1st in class – 1501–2000 cc Class (Lister-Maserati) 1st – Up to 1100 cc Class and member of winning team (Auto-Union-DKW)
19 May	WECC Race Meeting, Snetterton 1st in heat, 'Double Twelve' Trophy, fastest lap in final (Lister-Maserati) Fastest lap in Jaguar handicap (Jaguar XK 120 C)
20 May	BRSCC Race Meeting, Brands Hatch 2nd and fastest lap – Sports and Racing Car H'cap Race (Lister-Maserati)
23 June	BARC National Race Meeting, Aintree 3rd – Up to 1500 cc Sports Car Race (Lotus XI) 4th overall – Unlimited Sports Car Race, and 1st and fastest lap – Up to 2000 cc Class (Lister-Maserati)
8 July	EAMC Sprint, Snetterton Best time of the day, 1st – Racing Car Class (Jaguar D-Type) 1st – Over 3000 cc Production Car Class (Jaguar XK 140)
22 July	SMRC Race Meeting, Snetterton 2nd – Up to 1500 cc Sports Car Race, new class lap record (Lotus XI) New absolute circuit record, Vanwall Trophy Race (Formula 1 Connaught)
6 August	BRSCC Race Meeting, Brands Hatch 1st and fastest lap – parts 1 and 2 of Formule Libre Race, setting new Formula 1 and absolute circuit record. (Formula 1 Connaught) 1st and fastest lap – Unlimited Sports Car Race (Lister-Maserati)
18 August	BRSCC International Race Meeting, Oulton Park 5th overall – Daily Herald Trophy Race for unlimited sports cars, and 1st – Up to 2000 cc Class (Lister-Maserati)
7 October	SMRC Race Meeting, Snetterton 4th – Redex Trophy for Sports Cars, second in class (Aston-Jaguar)

14 October   BRSCC Race Meeting, Brands Hatch
1st and fastest lap – Formula 1 Race, setting new F1 and absolute circuit records (Formula 1 Connaught)
1st – Fibreglass-bodied Cars Handicap (Elva)

1957

10 March   CUAC Driving Tests
1st – Closed Car Class, and best performance of the day (Ford Zephyr)

31 March   SMRC Race Meeting, Snetterton
Fastest lap – Over 2700 cc Sports Car Race (Lister-Jaguar)

6 April   BRDC British Empire Trophy Race, Oulton Park
1st in final and fastest lap in heat (Lister-Jaguar)

22 April   BARC International Race Meeting, Goodwood
1st and fastest lap – Unlimited Sports Car Race. New sports car lap record (Lister Jaguar)

28 April   WECC Sprint, Snetterton
Best Time of the Day (Lister-Jaguar)

19 May   SMRC Race Meeting, Snetterton
1st and fastest lap – Unlimited Sports Car Race (Lister-Jaguar)
1st and fastest lap – Formule Libre Race. Set new sports car lap record (Lister-Jaguar)

10 June   BRSCC Race Meeting, Crystal Palace
1st and fastest lap – Unlimited Sports Car Race (Lister-Jaguar)

6 July   BRSCC Race Meeting, Mallory Park
3rd – Up to 1100 cc Sports Car Race (Elva-Climax)

20 July   RAC British Grand Prix, Aintree
1st and fastest lap – Unlimited Sports Car Race (Lister-Jaguar)

27 July   SMRC National Race Meeting, Snetterton
1st and fastest lap – Vanwall Trophy Formule Libre Race (Lister-Jaguar)
1st and fastest lap – over 2700 cc Sports Car Race (Lister-Jaguar)

5 August   BRSCC National Race Meeting, Brands Hatch
3rd – 1100 cc Sports Car Race (Lotus-Climax)
Fastest lap – up to 1500 cc Sports Car Race (Elva-AJB)
1st and fastest lap (new record) – Kingsdown Trophy Race for cars over 1900 cc (Lister-Jaguar)

11 August   Swedish Grand Prix for Sports Cars, Kristianstad
8th overall (Jaguar D-Type, with John Lawrence)

17 August   750 MC National Six-Hour Relay Race, Silverstone
Member of 2nd placed team (Austin A35)

1 September   SMRC Race Meeting, Snetterton
1st and fastest lap – Over 2700 cc Sports Car Race (Lister-Jaguar)
Fastest lap – Formule Libre Race (Lister-Jaguar)

14 September   BRDC International Race Meeting, Silverstone
2nd and fastest lap – Unlimited Sports Car Race (Lister-Jaguar)
Fastest lap (shared with Hawthorn) – Touring Car Race (Jaguar 3.4)

28 September   BARC National Race Meeting, Goodwood
1st and fastest lap – Unlimited Sports Car Race (Lister-Jaguar)

6 October	BRSCC Race Meeting, Brands Hatch 2nd and fastest lap – up to 1100 cc Sports Car Race heat (Elva-Climax) 1st and fastest lap in final, setting new sports car lap record (Elva-Climax) 1st – 1101–1500 cc Sports Car Race (Elva-AJB)

1958

19 January	Levin, New Zealand, International Race Meeting 2nd and fastest lap – Formule Libre Race, setting new absolute lap record (Lister-Jaguar)
25 January	International Lady Wigram Trophy, Christchurch, New Zealand 1st and fastest lap, setting new absolute lap record and record race average (Lister-Jaguar)
8 February	International Race Meeting, Teratonga Park, Invercargill, New Zealand 1st – Unlimited Sports Car Race (Lister-Jaguar) 6th – Formule Libre Race (Lister-Jaguar)
30 March	SMRC Race Meeting, Snetterton 1st and fastest lap – Unlimited Sports Car Race (Lister-Jaguar) 1st – Formule Libre Race (Lister-Jaguar)
7 April	BARC International Race Meeting, Goodwood 6th – Glover Trophy (Formula 1 Connaught)
12 April	BRDC British Empire Trophy, Oulton Park Fastest lap in heat (Lister-Jaguar) 3rd in final (Lister-Jaguar)
19 April	BRDC International Race Meeting, Aintree 4th – Formula 1 Race. (Formula 1 Connaught) 1st – Over 1100 cc Sports Car Race (Lister-Jaguar)
3 May	BRDC International Race Meeting, Silverstone 2nd – Unlimited Sports Car Race (Lister-Jaguar)
11 May	BRSCC Race Meeting, Mallory Park 1st and fastest lap – Over 1200 cc Sports Car Race (Lister-Jaguar)

Appendix B

Lister cars – competition record 1954–1959

Every effort has been made to ensure that the following is an accurate record, but some records are missing and it is impossible to guarantee that there are no errors or omissions.

Date	Event	Result	Car	Owner	Driver
1954					
3 Apr	ECCC Meeting Snetterton	1st – 1175–1500 cc Sports Car Class	Lister-MG	Works	W.A. Scott Brown
		1st – 1500 cc Sports Car H'cap	Lister-MG	Works	W.A. Scott Brown
4 Apr	WECC Sprint Weathersfield	3rd – 1101–1500 cc Sports Car Class	Lister-MG	Works	W.A. Scott Brown
23 Apr	Half-litre CC Race Meeting Brands Hatch	2nd – 1500 cc Sports Car Race	Lister-MG	Works	J. Sears
9 May	BOC National Hill Climb Prescott	3rd – 1500 cc Sports Car Class	Lister-MG	Works	J. Sears
5 Jun	WECC Race Meeting Snetterton	1st – 1500 cc Sports Car Race	Lister-MG	Works	J. Sears
		2nd – 1500 cc Sports Car H'cap	Lister-MG	Works	J. Sears
7 Jun	Half-litre CC Race Meeting Brands Hatch	2nd – 1500 cc Sports Car Race	Lister-MG	Works	W.A. Scott Brown
12 Jun	MCMC National Race Meeting Oulton Park	2nd – 1500 cc Sports Car Race	Lister-MG	Works	W.A. Scott Brown
19 Jun	AMOC Race Meeting Snetterton	2nd – Sports Car Race	Lister-MG	Works	W.A. Scott Brown
27 Jun	ECCC Sprint Snetterton	1st – 1201–1500 cc Sports Car Class	Lister-MG	Works	W.A. Scott Brown
10 Jul	Half-litre CC Race Meeting Oulton Park	2nd – 1500 cc Sports Car Race	Lister-MG	Works	W.A. Scott Brown

Date	Event	Result	Car	Owner	Driver
17 Jul	RAC Internat'l Race Meeting Silverstone	5th – Unlimited Sports Car Race	Lister-Bristol	Works	W.A. Scott Brown
		1st – 2000 cc Class	Lister-Bristol	Works	W.A. Scott Brown
		7th – 1500 cc Sports Car Race	Lister-MG	Works	W.A. Scott Brown
24 Jul	Welsh MRC Race Meeting Fairwood	2nd – 1500 cc Sports Car Race	Lister-MG	Works	W.A Scott Brown
		1st – 2000 cc Sports Car Race	Lister-Bristol	Works	W.A. Scott Brown
		2nd – Unlimited Sports Car Race	Lister-Bristol	Works	W.A. Scott Brown
2 Aug	Half-litre CC International Race Meeting Brands Hatch	1st in heat, 2nd in final, 1500 cc Sports Car Championship	Lister-MG	Works	W.A. Scott Brown
14 Aug	WECC International Race Meeting Snetterton	1st – 2000 cc Sports Car Race	Lister-Bristol	Works	W.A. Scott Brown
		3rd – 1500 cc Sports Car Race	Lister-MG	Works	W.A. Scott Brown
28 Aug	BRISTOL MC & LCC National Race Meeting Castle Combe	2nd – Unlimited Sports Car Race	Lister-Bristol	Works	W.A. Scott Brown
		2nd – 2-litre Class	Lister-Bristol	Works	W.A. Scott Brown
4 Sep	BHMC Internat'l Speed Trials Brighton	2nd – 1501– 2000 cc Sports Car Class	Lister-Bristol	Works	W.A. Scott Brown
5 Sep	Half-litre CC Race Meeting Brands Hatch	2nd – 1500 cc Sports Car Race	Lister-MG	Works	W.A. Scott Brown
		2nd – 2000 cc Sports Car Race	Lister-Bristol	Works	W.A. Scott Brown
11 Sep	Peterborough MC Race Meeting Silverstone	1st – 1500 cc Sports Car Race	Lister-MG	Works	W.A. Scott Brown
18 Sep	Half-litre CC International Race Meeting Crystal Palace	2nd – 1500 cc Sports Car Race	Lister-MG	Works	W.A. Scott Brown
		5th – 2000 cc Sports Car Race	Lister-Bristol	Works	W.A. Scott Brown
25 Sep	BARC International Race Meeting Goodwood	2nd – 2000 cc Sports Car Race	Lister-Bristol	Works	S. C. Moss
9 Oct	ECCC Race Meeting Snetterton	1st – 1501–2000 cc Sports Car Race	Lister Bristol	Works	W.A. Scott Brown

1955

Date	Event	Result	Car	Owner	Driver
26 Mar	SMRC Race Meeting Snetterton	1st – 1501–2700 cc Sports Car Race	Lister-Bristol	Works	W.A. Scott Brown
		2nd – Formule Libre Race	Lister-Bristol	Works	W.A. Scott Brown

Date	Event	Result	Car	Owner	Driver
2 Apr	BRDC British Empire Trophy Oulton Park	1st. Final 2nd – Heat Two 5th – Heat Two 6th – 1501–2700 cc Class, Final	Lister-Bristol Lister-Bristol	Works W. Black	W.A. Scott Brown J. Sears
11 Apr	BARC Internat'l Race Meeting Goodwood	1st – Up to 2000 cc Sports Car Race	Lister-Bristol	Works	W.A. Scott Brown
16 Apr	ECCC Race Meeting Snetterton	1st – 1101–2000 cc Sports Car Class	Lister-Rover	Murkett Bros Ltd	A. Murkett
16 Apr	Winfield Joint Committee Nat'l Race Meeting Charterhall	1st – Up to 2700 cc Sports Car Race 1st – Unlimited Sports Car Race	Lister-Bristol Lister-Bristol	Works Works	W.A. Scott Brown W.A. Scott Brown
30 Apr	WH & DCC Race Meeting Ibsley	1st – 1501–2750 cc Sports Car Race	Lister-Bristol	Works	W.A. Scott Brown
7 May	BRDC Internat'l Race Meeting Silverstone	3rd – 1501–2000 cc Class, Unlimited Sports Car Race	Lister-Bristol	O. Issard-Davies	A. Moore
28 May	WECC National Race Meeting Snetterton	1st – 2000 cc Sports Car Race 1st – Unlimited Sports Car Race 2nd – Curtis Trophy Formula 1 Race 3rd – Formule Libre Race	Lister-Bristol Lister-Bristol Lister-Bristol Lister-Bristol	Works Works Works Works	W.A. Scott Brown W.A. Scott Brown W.A. Scott Brown W.A. Scott Brown
29 May	BRSCC Race Meeting Brands Hatch	1st – Unlimited Sports Car Race	Lister-Bristol	Works	W.A. Scott Brown
30 May	BRSCC Race Meeting Crystal Palace	1st – Unlimited Sports Car Race 5th – Unlimited Sports Car Race	Lister-Bristol Lister-Bristol	Works Six Mile Stable	W.A. Scott Brown N. Cunningham-Reid
30 May	BARC Internat'l Race Meeting Goodwood	5th – 2000 cc Sports Car Race 6th – 2000 cc Sports Car Race	Lister-Bristol Lister-Bristol	O. Issard-Davies J. Green	A. Moore D. Hampshire
25 Jun	ECCC Race Meeting Snetterton	2nd – 100 mile Unlimited Sports Car Race	Lister-Bristol	Works	W.A. Scott Brown
26 Jun	BOC Hill Climb Prescott Hill	2nd – 1501–3000 cc Sports Car Class	Lister-Bristol	K. Eaton	K. Eaton
10 Jul	BRSCC Race Meeting Brands Hatch	1st – Over 1900 cc Sports Car Race	Lister-Bristol	Works	W.A. Scott Brown
16 Jul	RAC/BARC Int'l Race Meeting Aintree	1st – 1501–2000 cc Class, Unlimited Sports Car Race	Lister-Bristol	J. Green	D. Hampshire

Date	Event	Result	Car	Owner	Driver
23 Jul	AMOC Race Meeting Silverstone	2nd – Sports Car Handicap Race	Lister-Bristol	Six-Mile Stable	N. Cunningham-Reid
		1st Class Award Regularity Trial	Lister-Bristol	Six-Mile Stable	N. Cunningham-Reid
30 Jul	BARC Race Meeting Crystal Palace	2nd – Unlimited Sports Car Race	Lister-Bristol	Works	W.A. Scott Brown
1 Aug	BRSCC Internat'l Race Meeting Brands Hatch	1st – Over 1900 cc Sports Car Race	Lister-Bristol	Works	W.A. Scott Brown
6 Aug	Winfield Joint Committee Int'l Race Meeting Charterhall	1st – Up to 2700 cc Sports Car Race	Lister-Bristol	Works	W.A. Scott Brown
		3rd – Unlimited Sports Car Race	Lister-Bristol	Works	W.A. Scott Brown
		3rd – Up to 2700 cc Sports Car Race	Lister-Bristol	Six-Mile Stable	N. Cunningham-Reid
20 Aug	BARC Internat'l Sports Car Race Goodwood	9th Overall & 1st 1500–2000 cc Class	Lister-Bristol	J. Green	D. Hampshire/ P. Scott-Russell
		3rd – 1500–2000 cc Class, 13th Overall	Lister-Bristol	Works	A. Moore/W. Holt
28 Aug	MAC Hill Climb Shelsley Walsh	1st – Up to 2000 cc Sports Car Class	Lister-Bristol	K. Eaton	K. Eaton
3 Sep	BARC Internat'l Race Meeting Aintree	1st – 2000 cc Class Unlimited Sports Car Race	Lister-Bristol	Six-Mile Stable	N. Cunningham-Reid
4 Sep	BRSCC Race Meeting Brands Hatch	1st – over 1900 cc Sports Car Race	Lister-Bristol	Six-Mile Stable	N. Cunningham-Reid
		3rd – over 1900 cc Sports Car Race	Lister-Bristol	W. Black	J. Sears
11 Sep	BOC Hill Climb Prescott Hill	2nd – 1501–3000 cc Sports Car Class	Lister-Bristol	K. Eaton	K. Eaton
11 Sep	ECCC Sprint Snetterton	1st – Class E	Lister-Bristol	W. Black	J. Sears
17 Sep	BRSCC Race Meeting Silverstone	1st – 2000 cc Sports Car Race	Lister-Bristol	W. Black	J. Sears
		2nd – 2000 cc Sports Car Race	Lister-Bristol	O. Issard-Davies	A. Moore
25 Sep	SMRC Race Meeting Snetterton	1st – Unlimited Sports Car Race	Lister-Bristol	W. Black	J. Sears
1 Oct	BMC & LCC Meeting Castle Combe	3rd – 2000 cc Sports Car Race	Lister-Bristol	R. Salvadori	R. Salvadori
		4th – 2000 cc Sports Car Race	Lister-Bristol	W. Black	J. Sears
9 Oct	BRSCC Meeting Brands Hatch	2nd – Over 2000 cc Sports Car Race	Lister-Bristol	W. Black	J. Sears

Date	Event	Result	Car	Owner	Driver
1956					
14 Apr	BRDC British Empire Trophy, Oulton Park	2nd – Heat 2	Lister-Maserati	Works	W.A. Scott Brown
		6th – Heat 2	Lister-Bristol	O. Issard-Davies	A. Moore
		7th – Heat 2	Lister-Bristol	A.J. Nurse	A.J. Nurse
5 May	BRDC Internat'l Race Meeting Silverstone	1st	Lister-Maserati	Works	W.A. Scott Brown
		2nd	Lister-Bristol	O. Issard-Davies	A. Moore
		3rd – 1500–2000 cc Class, Unlimited Sports Car Race	Lister-Bristol	A.J. Nurse	A.J. Nurse
12 May	M&MKMC Race Meeting Silverstone	1st – Up to 2500 cc Sports Car Race	Lister-Bristol	A.J. Nurse	A.J. Nurse
		2nd – Unlimited Sports Car Race	Lister-Bristol	A.J. Nurse	A.J. Nurse
19 May	WECC Race Meeting Snetterton	1st – 2nd Heat, Unlimited Sports Car Handicap	Lister-Maserati	Works	W.A. Scott Brown
20 May	BRSCC Race Meeting Brands Hatch	2nd – Sports & Racing Car Handicap	Lister-Maserati	Works	W.A. Scott Brown
21 May	BARC Race Meeting Goodwood	2nd – Unlimited Sports Car Race	Lister-Bristol	O. Issard-Davies	A. Moore
21 May	NSCC Race Meeting Mallory Park	1st – 1501–2000 cc Sports Car Race	Lister-Bristol	A.J. Nurse	A.J.Nurse
		2nd – Formule Libre Race	Lister-Bristol	A.J. Nurse	A.J. Nurse
		6th – 1501–2700 cc Sports Car Race	Lister-Bristol	A. Churchley	A. Churchley
2 Jun	LCMC Race Meeting Oulton Park	1st – Up to 3000 cc Sports Car Race	Lister-Bristol	A.J. Nurse	A.J. Nurse
		3rd – Racing Car Handicap	Lister-Bristol	A.J. Nurse	A.J. Nurse
		2nd – 2000 cc Sports Car Race	Lister-Bristol	A.J. Nurse	A.J. Nurse
9 Jun	NSMC Race Meeting Oulton Park	3rd – Formule Libre Handicap	Lister-Bristol	A.J. Nurse	A.J. Nurse
10 Jun	750 MC Race Meeting Brands Hatch	1st – 2000 cc Sports Car Race	Lister-Bristol	Six Mile Stable	N. Cunningham-Reid
23 Jun	BARC Race Meeting Aintree	Unlimited Sports Car Race: 1st – 2000 cc Class and 4th overall	Lister-Maserati	Works	W.A. Scott Brown
		2nd – 2000 cc Class	Lister-Bristol	Six-Mile Stable	N. Cunningham-Reid
		3rd – 2000 cc Class	Lister-Bristol	O. Issard-Davies	A. Moore

Date	Event	Result	Car	Owner	Driver
23 Jun	MMEC Race Meeting Silverstone	1st – 2000 cc Sports Car Race	Lister-Bristol	A.J. Nurse	A.J. Nurse
		2nd – Unlimited Sports Car Race	Lister-Bristol	A.J. Nurse	A.J. Nurse
14 Jul	RAC/BRDC Internat'l Race Meeting Silverstone	2nd – 1500–2000 cc Unlimited Sports Car Race	Lister-Bristol	O. Issard-Davies	A. Moore
21 Jul	AMOC Race Meeting Silverstone	2nd – Over 1500 cc Sports Car Race	Lister-Bristol	Six-Mile Stable	N. Cunningham-Reid
		2nd – Unlimited Sports Car Race	Lister-Bristol	Six-Mile Stable	N. Cunningham-Reid
6 Aug	BRSCC Race Meeting Brands Hatch	1st – Over 1900 cc Sports Car Race	Lister-Maserati	Works	W.A. Scott Brown
6 Aug	NSCC Race Meeting Mallory Park	2nd – 1501–2700 cc Sports Car Race	Lister-Bristol	A.J. Nurse	A.J. Nurse
18 Aug	BRSCC Race Meeting Oulton Park	5th – Unlimited Sports Car Race	Lister-Maserati	Works	W.A. Scott Brown
		1st – 2000 cc Class	Lister-Maserati	Works	W.A. Scott Brown
		2nd – 2000 cc Class	Lister-Bristol	Ecurie Bullfrog	J. Horridge
2 Sep	SMRC Race Meeting Snetterton	1st – 1501–2700 cc Class, Unlimited Sports Car Race	Lister-Bristol	Ecurie Bullfrog	J. Horridge
16 Sep	NSCC Race Meeting Mallory Park	3rd – 1501–2700 cc Sports Car Race	Lister-Bristol	A.J. Nurse	A.J. Nurse
		3rd – Formule Libre Race	Lister-Bristol	A.J. Nurse	A.J. Nurse
30 Sep	HDLCC Sprint Staverton	1st – 1101–2000 cc Sports Racing Car Class	Lister-Bristol	A.J. Nurse	A.J. Nurse
6 Oct	NSMC Race Meeting Silverstone	Up to 2700 cc Sports Car Race: 2nd	Lister-Bristol	O. Issard-Davies	A. Moore
		3rd	Lister-Bristol	A.J. Nurse	A.J. Nurse
		4th	Lister-Bristol	Ecurie Bullfrog	J. Horridge
		4th – Formule Libre	Lister-Bristol	O. Issard-Davies	A. Moore
		2nd – Racing Car Handicap	Lister-Bristol	O. Issard-Davies	A. Moore
		6th – Sports Car Handicap	Lister-Bristol	Ecurie Bullfrog	J. Horridge
7 Oct	SMRC Race Meeting Snetterton	3rd – Up to 2500 cc Sports Car Race	Lister-Bristol	Ecurie Bullfrog	J. Horridge
14 Oct	BRSCC Race Meeting Brands Hatch	3rd – Fibreglass Bodied Cars Handicap	Lister-Bristol	Ecurie Bullfrog	J. Horridge

Date	Event	Result	Car	Owner	Driver
1957					
6 Apr	BRDC British Empire Trophy Oulton Park	1st – Over 2000 cc Heat and 1st overall	Lister-Jaguar	Works	W.A. Scott Brown
		4th – 1201–2000 cc Heat	Lister-Maserati	O. Issard-Davies	A. Moore
22 Apr	BRSCC Race Meeting Brands Hatch	1st – 2000 cc Sports Car Race	Lister-Bristol	Ecurie Bullfrog	J. Horridge
22 Apr	NSCC Race Meeting Mallory Park	1st – 2000 cc Sports Car Race	Lister-Bristol	G. Baird	G. Baird
22 Apr	BARC Internat'l Race Meeting Goodwood	1st – Unlimited Sports Car Race	Lister-Jaguar	Works	W.A. Scott Brown
28 Apr	WECC Sprint Snetterton	Best time of day	Lister-Jaguar	Works	W.A. Scott Brown
5 May	BOC National Hill Climb Prescott Hill	1st – 1601–3000 cc Sports Car Class	Lister-Bristol	W. Bradley	W. Bradley
18 May	M & MKMC Race Meeting Silverstone	2nd – Up to 2500 cc Sports Car Race	Lister-Maserati	O. Issard-Davies	A. Moore
		2nd – Unlimited Sports Car Race		O. Issard-Davies	A. Moore
		2nd – Up to 2500 cc Sports Car Race (II)		O. Issard-Davies	A. Moore
		2nd – Unlimited Sports Car Race (II)		O. Issard-Davies	A. Moore
		3rd – Up to 2500 cc Sports Car Race (II)	Lister-Bristol	G. Baird	G. Baird
19 May	BRSCC Race Meeting Brands Hatch	2nd – 1100–2000 cc Sports Car Race	Lister-Bristol	Ecurie Bullfrog	J. Horridge
19 May	SMRC Race Meeting Snetterton	1st – Unlimited Sports Car Race	Lister-Jaguar	Works	W.A. Scott Brown
		1st – Formule Libre Race	Lister-Jaguar	Works	W.A. Scott Brown
25 May	LCMC Race Meeting Oulton Park	3rd – Up to 3000 cc Sports Car Race	Lister-Bristol	Ecurie Bullfrog	J. Horridge
9 Jun	BRSCC Race Meeting Brands Hatch	5th – 1101–2700 cc Sports Car Race	Lister-Bristol	Ecurie Bullfrog	J. Horridge
10 Jun	BRSCC Race Meeting Crystal Palace	1st – Unlimited Sports Car Race	Lister-Jaguar	Works	W.A. Scott Brown
10 Jun	NSCC Race Meeting Oulton Park	1st – 1501–2700 cc Sports Car Race	Lister-Bristol	G. Baird	G. Baird
		4th – Formule Libre Race	Lister-Bristol	G. Baird	G. Baird

Date	Event	Result	Car	Owner	Driver
22 Jun	SUNBAC Race Meeting Mallory Park	1st – 1501–2000 cc Sports Car Race	Lister-Bristol	G. Baird	G. Baird
		1st – Over 1500 cc Sports & Racing Car Race	Lister-Bristol	G. Baird	G. Baird
30 Jun	Winfield Joint Committee Race Meeting Charterhall	1st – 1500–2700 cc Sports Car Race	Lister-Bristol	F. Elliott	F. Elliott
13 Jul	Leinster Trophy Wicklow, Eire	6th – Heat 2 of Trophy Race	Lister-Bristol	Ecurie Bullfrog	J. Horridge
20 Jul	RAC/BARC Int'l Race Meeting Aintree	1st – Unlimited Sports Car Race	Lister-Jaguar	Works	W.A. Scott Brown
5 Aug	BRSCC Race Meeting Brands Hatch	1st – Unlimited Sports Car Race	Lister-Jaguar	Works	W.A. Scott Brown
24 Aug	MGCC Race Meeting Silverstone	1st – Novice Handicap, Heat A	Lister-Jaguar	N. Hillwood	N. Hillwood
1 Sep	SMRC Race Meeting Snetterton	1st – Over 2700 cc Sports Car Race	Lister-Jaguar	Works	W.A. Scott Brown
		3rd – Over 2700 cc Sports Car Race	Lister-Jaguar	R. Walsh	T. Kyffin
1 Sep	Winfield Joint Committee Race Meeting Charterhall	3rd – Up to 2000 cc Sports Car Race	Lister-Bristol	F. Elliott	F. Elliot
		1st – 1501–2700 cc Sports Car Race	Lister-Bristol	F. Elliott	F. Elliott
8 Sep	Darlington MC Speed Trials Croft	2nd – Up to 2000 cc Class	Lister-Bristol	F. Elliott	F. Elliott
		2nd – Sports Car Racing Car Class	Lister-Bristol	F. Elliott	F. Elliott
14 Sep	BRDC Internat'l Race Meeting Silverstone	2nd – Unlimited Sports Car Race	Lister-Jaguar	Works	W.A. Scott Brown
		2nd – Up to 2700 cc Class	Lister-Maserati	O. Issard-Davies	A. Moore
22 Sep	NSCC Race Meeting Mallory Park	2nd – Heat 2 Formule Libre Race	Lister-Bristol	G. Baird	G. Baird
22 Sep	Yorkshire SCC Sprint Meeting	1st – Over 1501 cc Sports/Racing Car Class	Lister-Bristol	F. Elliott	F. Elliott
28 Sep	BARC National Race Meeting Goodwood	1st – Unlimited Sports Car Race	Lister-Jaguar	Works	W.A. Scott Brown
6 Oct	BMRC Sprint Meeting Winfield	1st – 1501–3000 cc Sports Car Class	Lister-Bristol	F. Elliott	F. Elliott
		1st – Unlimited Sports Car Class	Lister-Bristol	F. Elliott	F. Elliott
		3rd – Racing Car Class	Lister-Bristol	F. Elliott	F. Elliott

Date	Event	Result	Car	Owner	Driver

1958

Date	Event	Result	Car	Owner	Driver
19 Jan	Levin, NZ International Race Meeting	2nd – Formule Libre Race	Lister-Jaguar	Works	W.A. Scott Brown
25 Jan	International Lady Wigram Trophy Race Christchurch, NZ	1st	Lister-Jaguar	Works	W.A. Scott Brown
8 Feb	International Race Meeting Teratonga Park Invercargill, NZ	1st – Unlimited Sports Car Race	Lister-Jaguar	Works	W.A Scott Brown
		6th – Formule Libre Race	Lister-Jaguar	Works	W.A. Scott Brown
23 Mar	WECC National Speed Trials Snetterton	1st – 1501–3000 cc Sports Car Class	Lister-Bristol	J. Randle	J. Randle
30 Mar	SMRC Race Meeting Snetterton	1st – Unlimited Sports Car Race	Lister-Jaguar	Works	W.A. Scott Brown
		1st – Formule Libre Race	Lister-Jaguar	Works	W.A. Scott Brown
7 Apr	SWAC Castle Hill Climb	1st – Up to 2000 cc Sports Car Class	Lister-Bristol	J. Randle	J. Randle
12 Apr	BRDC British Empire Trophy Race, Oulton Park	3rd – In Heat	Lister-Jaguar	Works	W.A. Scott Brown
		3rd – In Final	Lister-Jaguar	R. Walsh	W.A. Scott Brown
19 Apr	BARC Internat'l Race Meeting Aintree	1st – Over 1100 cc Sports Car Race	Lister-Jaguar	Works	W.A. Scott Brown
		3rd – Over 1100 cc Sports Car Race	Lister-Jaguar	Ec. Ecosse	M. Gregory
20 Apr	Lothian CC Sprint Winfield	Best time of the day	Lister-Bristol	F. Elliott	F. Elliott
		1st – Unlimited Cars	Lister-Bristol	F. Elliott	F. Elliott
		1st – Class 2 Open Cars	Lister-Bristol	F. Elliott	F. Elliott
		1st – Class 3 Open Cars	Lister-Bristol	F. Elliott	F. Elliott
27 Apr	Winfield Joint Committee Race Meeting, Charterhall	1st – 1501–3000 cc Sports Car Race	Lister-Bristol	F. Elliott	F. Elliott
3 May	BRDC Internat'l Race Meeting Silverstone	1st – Over 1500 cc Sports Car Race	Lister-Jaguar	Ec. Ecosse	M. Gregory
		2nd – Over 1500 cc Sports Car Race	Lister-Jaguar	Works	W.A. Scott Brown
		Team Award	Lister-Jaguar	Ec. Ecosse	M. Gregory
		Team Award	Lister-Jaguar	P. Whitehead	P Whitehead
		Team Award	Lister-Jaguar	ENB	F. Rousselle
11 May	BRSCC Race Meeting Mallory Park	1st – Over 1200 cc Sports Car Race	Lister-Jaguar	Works	W.A. Scott Brown
		1st – Over 1200 cc Sports Car Race	Lister-Jaguar	R. Walsh	B. Halford

Date	Event	Result	Car	Owner	Driver
18 May	Spa Sports Car Grand Prix Spa, Belgium	1st 6th 9th	Lister-Jaguar Lister-Jaguar Lister-Jaguar	Ec. Ecosse ENB P. Whitehead	M. Gregory F. Rousselle P. Whitehead
26 May	BARC Race Meeting Goodwood Handicap Race	1st – Sports Car Scratch Race 1st – Sports Car	Lister-Jaguar Lister-Jaguar	P. Whitehead R. Walsh	P. Whitehead B. Halford
5 Jul	BRSCC Race Meeting Crystal Palace	1st – Unlimited Sports Car Race I 1st – Unlimited Sports Car Race II 2nd – Unlimited Sports Car Race I 2nd – Unlimited Sports Car Race II	Lister-Jaguar Lister-Jaguar Lister-Jaguar Lister-Jaguar	Works Works R. Walsh R. Walsh	I. Bueb I. Bueb B. Halford B. Halford
5 Jul	RSAC Hill Climb 'Rest and be Thankful'	3rd – 1500–2000 cc Sports Car Class	Lister-Bristol	J. Randle	J. Randle
12 Jul	RUAC Leinster Trophy Race	1st – Unlimited Sports Car Class	Lister-Jaguar	P. Whitehead	P. Whitehead
19 Jul	RAC/BRDC Int'l Race Meeting Silverstone	1st – Unlimited Sports Car Race 1st – Over 2000 cc Class 6th – Unlimited Sports Car Race 3rd – Over 2000 cc Class	Lister-Jaguar Lister-Jaguar Lister-Jaguar Lister-Jaguar	Works Works R. Walsh R. Walsh	S.C. Moss S.C. Moss. B. Halford B. Halford
27 Jul	SMRC Race Meeting Snetterton	1st – Over 2700 cc Sports Car Race 2nd – Over 2700 cc Sports Car Race 3rd – Over 2700 cc Sports Car Race 1st – Formule Libre Race 3rd – Formule Libre Race 4th – Formule Libre Race	Lister-Jaguar Lister-Jaguar Lister Jaguar Lister-Jaguar Lister-Jaguar Lister-Jaguar	Works Works R. Walsh Works Works R. Walsh	W. Hansgen R. Jensen B. Halford W. Hansgen R. Jensen B. Halford
4 Aug	NSCC Race Meeting Mallory Park	4th – Over 1500 cc Sports Car Race 5th – Over 1500 cc Sports Car Race	Lister-Bristol Lister-Bristol	J. Randle F. Elliott	J. Randle F. Elliott
4 Aug	BRSCC Race Meeting Brands Hatch	1st – Unlimited Sports Car Race 2nd – Unlimited Sports Car Race 3rd – Unlimited Sports Car Race	Lister-Jaguar Lister-Jaguar Lister-Jaguar	Works Works R. Walsh	I. Bueb R. Jensen B. Halford

Date	Event	Result	Car	Owner	Driver
7 Sep	SMRC Race Meeting Snetterton	1st – Scott Brown Memorial Trophy (Formule Libre)	Lister-Jaguar	Works	I. Bueb
		1st – Unlimited Sports Car Race	Lister-Jaguar	Works	R. Jensen
20 Sep	MCMC Int'l Race Meeting Oulton Park	2nd – Unlimited Sports Car Race	Lister-Jaguar	Works	I. Bueb
		1st – Over 2000 cc Class	Lister-Jaguar	Works	I. Bueb
		3rd – Unlimited Sports Car Race	Lister-Jaguar	R. Walsh	B. Halford
		2nd – Over 2000 cc Class	Lister-Jaguar	R. Walsh	B. Halford
		5th – Unlimited Sports Car Class	Lister-Jaguar	ENB	A. Pilette
21 Sep	CWMC Hill Climb	2nd – FTD	Lister-Bristol	J. Randle	J. Randle
		1st – over 1500 cc Sports Car Class	Lister-Bristol	J. Randle	J. Randle
27 Sep	NSMC Race Meeting Silverstone	2nd – Up to 2000 cc Class, Formule Libre Race	Lister-Bristol	J. Randle	J. Randle
4 Oct	WHMC Sprint Rhydymwyn	1st – Sports Cars Over 1500 cc	Lister-Bristol	J. Randle	J. Randle
5 Oct	Darlington MC Race Meeting Catterick	1st – 1501–3000 cc Sports Car Race	Lister-Bristol	P. Melville	P. Melville
		2nd – 1501–3000 cc Sports Car Race	Lister-Bristol	F. Elliott	F. Elliott
11 Oct	SMRC Race Meeting Snetterton	2nd – Unlimited Sports Car Race	Lister-Jaguar	R. Walsh	B. Halford
		2nd – Over 1100 cc Sports Car Class	Lister-Jaguar	R. Walsh	B. Halford

1959

Date	Event	Result	Car	Owner	Driver
22 Mar	SMRC Race Meeting Snetterton	1st – Over 3000 cc Sports Car Race	Lister-Jaguar	Ec. Ecosse	R. Flockhart
		2nd – Formule Libre Race	Lister-Jaguar	Ec. Ecosse	R. Flockhart
		2nd – Over 3000 cc Sports Car Race	Lister-Jaguar	D. Wilkinson	J Bekaert
		3rd – Formule Libre Race	Lister-Jaguar	D. Wilkinson	J. Bekaert
30 Mar	BARC Int'l Race Meeting Goodwood	1st – Unlimited Sports Car Race	Lister-Jaguar	Works	I. Bueb
		2nd – Unlimited Sports Car Race	Lister-Jaguar	J. Seiff	P. Blond
30 Mar	NSCC National Race Meeting Mallory Park	1st – Over 1200 cc Sports Car Race	Lister-Jaguar	Border Reivers	J. Clark
		1st – Formule Libre Heat			
		1st – Formule Libre Final	Lister-Jaguar	Border Reivers	J. Clark

Date	Event	Result	Car	Owner	Driver
30 Mar	WCMC Hill Climb Trengwainton	FTD 1st – 2000 cc Sports Car Class 2nd Open Championship	Lister-Bristol	J. Randle	J. Randle
4 Apr	WECC National Sprint North Weald	BTD 2nd – 1501–3000 cc Sports Car Class	Lister-Corvette Lister-Bristol	R. Brightman J. Randle	R. Brightman J. Randle
11 Apr	BRDC Race Meeting Oulton Park	4th – Unlimited Sports Car Race	Lister-Jaguar	Works	I. Bueb
18 Apr	BARC Internat'l Race Meeting Aintree	3rd – Unlimited Sports Car Race 6th – Unlimited Sports Car Race	Lister-Jaguar Lister-Jaguar	Ecurie Ecosse Border Reivers	M. Gregory J. Clark
Apr	BRSCC Race Meeting Snetterton	2nd – Formule Libre Race, Part 1 1st – Formule Libre Race, Part 2	Lister-Jaguar Lister-Jaguar	D. Wilkinson D. Wilkinson	J. Bekaert J. Bekaert
Apr 25	Winfield JC Race Meeting Chartershall	1st – over 1500 cc Sports Car Race	Lister-Jaguar	Border Reivers	J. Clark
Apr	JDC/AMOC Race Meeting Brands Hatch	1st – Unlimited Sports Car Race 1st – Jaguar Race 1st – Martini Trophy	Lister-Jaguar Lister-Jaguar Lister-Jaguar	D. Wilkinson D. Wilkinson D. Wilkinson	J. Bekaert J. Bekaert J. Bekaert
2 May	BRDC Internat'l Trophy Meeting Silverstone	3rd – 3000 cc Sports Car Race	Lister-Jaguar	Works	I. Bueb
May	M&MKMC Race Meeting Silverstone	1st – Unlimited Sports Car Race (1&2) 2nd – Unlimited Sports Car Race (1&2)	Lister-Jaguar Lister-Jaguar	D. Wilkinson P. Mould	J. Bekaert P. Mould
May	SMRC Race Meeting Snetterton	1st – Over 3000 cc Sports Car Race 3rd – Formule Libre Race	Lister-Jaguar Lister-Jaguar	D. Wilkinson D. Wilkinson	J. Bekaert J. Bekaert
18 May	BRSCC National Race Meeting Crystal Palace	4th. over 1500 cc Sports Car Race 5th – over 1500 cc Sports Car Race	Lister-Jaguar Lister-Jaguar	Works Works	I. Bueb B. Halford
18 May	BARC National Race Meeting Goodwood	2nd – Whitsun Trophy 3rd – Whitsun Trophy 3rd – Handicap Race	Lister-Jaguar Lister-Jaguar Lister-Jaguar	D. Wilkinson E. Ecosse E. Ecosse	J. Bekaert P. Blond P. Blond
18 May	CWMC Hill Climb	1st – Over 1500 cc	Lister-Bristol	J. Randle	J. Randle
23 May	AMOC National Race Meeting Silverstone	1st – Sports Car Scratch Race 1st – Jaguar Race 3rd – Jaguar H'Cap	Lister-Jaguar Lister-Jaguar Lister-Jaguar	P. Mould P. Mould P. Mould	P. Mould P. Mould P. Mould

Date	Event	Result	Car	Owner	Driver
30 May	WECC Race Meeting Snetterton	1st – Double Twelve Trophy Race	Lister-Jaguar	D. Wilkinson	J. Bekaert
		2nd – F. Libre Race	Lister-Jaguar	D. Wilkinson	J. Bekaert
		2nd – Double Twelve Trophy Race	Lister-Jaguar	W.F. Moss	W.F. Moss
		1st – 3000 cc Class Trophy Race	Lister-Jaguar	P. Mould	P. Mould
30 May	BRSCC Race Meeting Rufforth	1st – Sports Car Race	Lister-Jaguar	Border Reivers	J. Clark
		2nd – F. Libre Race			
Jun	LCMC Race Meeting Oulton Park	2nd – Unlimited Sports Car Race	Lister-Jaguar	P. Mould	P. Mould
		2nd – Daily Mirror Trophy Race	Lister-Jaguar	P. Mould	P. Mould
Jun	NSCC Race Meeting Silverstone	1st – Over 1200 cc Sports Car Race	Lister-Jaguar	D. Wilkinson	J. Bekaert
		1st – F. Libre Heat	Lister-Jaguar	D. Wilkinson	J. Bekaert
		2nd – F. Libre Final	Lister-Jaguar	D. Wilkinson	J. Bekaert
		2nd – Over 1200 cc Sports Car Race	Lister-Jaguar	P. Mould	P. Mould
Jun	ECCC Race Meeting Snetterton	1st – F. Libre Race	Lister-Jaguar	D. Wilkinson	J. Bekaert
Jun	MMEC Race Meeting Silverstone	1st – Unlimited Sports Car Race	Lister-Jaguar	P. Mould	P. Mould
		2nd – Racing Car H'cap	Lister-Jaguar	P. Mould	P. Mould
Jun	BARC Race Meeting Aintree	1st – Unlimited Sports Car Race	Lister-Jaguar	D. Wilkinson	J. Bekaert
		2nd – H'Cap Race	Lister-Jaguar	D. Wilkinson	J. Bekaert
Jun	BARC Race Meeting Mallory Park	2nd – over 1200 cc Sports Car Race	Lister-Jaguar	P. Mould	P. Mould
Jul	National Hill Climb 'Rest-and-be-Thankful'	1st – 2000 cc Sports Car Class	Lister-Bristol	J. Randle	J. Randle
5 Jul	Winfield J.C. Race Meeting Charterhall	1st – Over 1500 cc Sports Car Race	Lister-Jaguar	Border Reivers	J. Whitmore
		1st – Over 1500 cc Racing Car Race	Lister-Jaguar	Border Reivers	J. Whitmore
		3rd – Over 1500 cc Sports Car Race	Lister-Jaguar	A.R. Miller	A.R. Miller
11 Jul	Lothian CC Hill Climb Bo'ness	Best Time of Day	Lister-Jaguar	Border Reivers	J. Clark
		1st – Over 2000 cc Sports Car Class	Lister-Jaguar	Border Reivers	J. Clark
11 Jul	Leinster MC Race Meeting Dunboyne	1st – Goodyear Trophy Race	Lister-Jaguar	D. Wilkinson	J. Bekaert

Date	Event	Result	Car	Owner	Driver
18 Jul	British Grand Prix Meeting Aintree	4th – Unlimited Sports Car Race	Lister-Jaguar	Border Reivers	J. Clark
		2nd – Over 2000 cc Class	Lister-Jaguar	Border Reivers	J. Clark
		5th – Unlimited Sports Car Race	Lister-Jaguar	Works	B. Halford
		3rd – Over 2000 cc Class	Lister-Jaguar	Works	B. Halford
		6th – Unlimited Sports Car Class	Lister-Jaguar	Works	I. Bueb
		4th – Over 2000 cc Class	Lister-Jaguar	Works	I. Bueb
18 Jul	Int'l Hill Climb Bouley Bay	1st – 1101–2000 cc Sports Car Class	Lister-Bristol	J. Randle	J. Randle
26 Jul	SMRC Race Meeting Snetterton	1st – 1101–3000 cc Sports Car Race	Lister-Jaguar	P. Mould	P. Mould
		2nd – Over 3000 cc Sports Car Race	Lister-Jaguar	W.F. Moss	W.F. Moss
26 Jul	BMRC/B&DMC Sprint Winfield	1st – Racing Car Class	Lister-Jaguar	Border Reivers	J. Clark
		1st – Unlimited Sports Car Class	Lister-Jaguar	Border Reivers	J. Clark
		2nd – Unlimited Sports Car Class	Lister-Jaguar	Border Reivers	J. McBain
2 Aug	NSCC Race Meeting Mallory Park	2nd – Over 1201 cc Sports Car Heat	Lister-Jaguar	Border Reivers	J. Clark
		2nd – Over 1201 cc Sports Car Final	Lister-Jaguar	Border Reivers	J. Clark
		3rd – F. Libre Heat	Lister-Jaguar	Border Reivers	J. Clark
		3rd – Over 1201 cc Sports Car Heat	Lister-Jaguar	P. Mould	P. Mould
Aug	BRSCC Race Meeting Brands Hatch	1st – Over 3000 cc Sports Car Race	Lister-Corvette	M. Anthony	M. Anthony
		3rd – Over 3000 cc Sports Car Race	Lister-Jaguar	G.M. Jones	G.M. Jones
Aug	Border MRC Race Ouston	1st – Unlimited Sports Car Races 1&2	Lister-Jaguar	Border Reivers	J. Blumer
Aug	WECC Race Meeting Snetterton	2nd – F. Libre Race	Lister-Jaguar	W.F. Moss	W.F. Moss
		1st – Jaguar Race	Lister-Jaguar	W.F. Moss	W.F. Moss
		3rd – F. Libre Race	Lister-Corvette	R. Brightman	R. Brightman
Aug	M&DMC Race Meeting Thornaby	1st – F. Libre Race	Lister-Jaguar	Border Reivers	J. Blumer
Aug	TEAC Hill Climb Stapleford	1st – 1501–2000 cc Sports Car Class	Lister-Bristol	J. Randle	J. Randle
Aug	BARC Race Meeting Aintree	1st – Sports Car Handicap	Lister-Bristol	K.W. Yeates	K.W. Yeates

Date	Event	Result	Car	Owner	Driver
Sep	BHMC Brighton Speed Trials	1st and new record – Unlimited Sports Cars	Lister-Corvette	M. Anthony	M. Anthony
		1st and new record – 2000 cc Class	Lister-Bristol	J. Randle	J. Randle
Sep	SMRC Race Meeting Snetterton	1st – Over 1100 cc Sports Car Race	Lister-Jaguar	W.F. Moss	W.F. Moss
Sep	D&DMC Race Meeting Thornaby	2nd – Over 1500 cc Sports car Race	Lister-Bristol	F. Elliott	F. Elliott
Sep	D&DMC Race Meeting Catterick	3rd – 1501–3000 cc Sports Car Class	Lister-Bristol	F. Elliott	F. Elliott
13 Sep	NSCC Race Meeting Mallory Park	1st – Over 1201 cc Sports Car Race	Lister-Jaguar	Border Reivers	J. Clark
		3rd – F. Libre Race	Lister-Jaguar	Border Reivers	J. Clark
		2nd – Over 1201 cc Sports Car Race	Lister-Jaguar	W.F. Moss	W.F. Moss
13 Sep	Peterborough MC Race Meeting Silverstone	3rd – Over 1500 cc Sports Car H'cap	Lister-Jaguar	D. Wilkinson	J. Bekaert
		1st – F. Libre Race	Lister-Jaguar	D. Wilkinson	J. Bekaert
		1st – Over 1500 cc Sports Car Race	Lister-Jaguar	D. Wilkinson	J. Bekaert
		3rd – H'Cap Race	Lister-Jaguar	D. Wilkinson	J. Bekaert
		2nd – Over 1500 cc Sports Car Race	Lister-Jaguar	P. Mould	P. Mould
		3rd – F. Libre Race	Lister-Jaguar	W.F. Moss	W.F. Moss
Sep	JDC/BDC Race Meeting Silverstone	2nd – Jaguar H'cap	Lister-Jaguar	D. Wilkinson	J. Bekaert
		1st – Jaguar Race			
		3rd – Jaguar H'cap II			
		1st – Open H'Cap			
Sep	BARC Race Meeting Goodwood	3rd – H'cap Race	Lister-Bristol	K.W. Yeates	K.W. Yeates
Sep	BRSCC Race Meeting Rufforth	1st – Unlimited Sports Car Race	Lister-Jaguar	P. Mould	P. Mould
		3rd – Unlimited Sports Car Race II			
Oct	NSMC Race Meeting Silverstone	2nd – Sports Car H'cap	Lister-Bristol	J. Randle	J. Randle
		1st – 1100–2700 cc Sports Car Race			
		3rd Sports Car H'cap	Lister-Jaguar	D. Wilkinson	J. Bekaert
		1st – F. Libre Race	Lister-Jaguar	D. Wilkinson	J. Bekaert
		1st – Unlimited Sports Car Race	Lister-Jaguar	P. Mould	P. Mould
Oct	LCMC Race Meeting Oulton Park	2nd – Sports Car Race	Lister-Jaguar	S.J. Diggory	S.J. Diggory
		1st – Sports Car Race	Lister-Jaguar	S.J. Diggory	C. Escott

Date	Event	Result	Car	Owner	Driver
Oct	WECC Hill Climb Stapleford	2nd – 3000 cc Sports Car Class	Lister-Bristol	J. Randle	J. Randle
		2nd – 2500 cc Racing Car Class	Lister-Bristol	J. Randle	J. Randle
		1st – 3000 cc Sports Car Class	Lister-Jaguar	P. Mould	P. Mould
		1st – Unlimited Sports	Lister-Jaguar	D. Wilkinson	J. Bekaert

Appendix C

Lister race successes in America

1958

Date	Event	Result	Car	Owner	Driver
20 Apr	SCCA President's Cup Marlboro, Md	1st – Class C Modified	Lister-Jaguar	Cunningham	W. Hansgen
4 May	SCCA National Race Virginia Int'l Raceway Danville, Va	1st – Class C Modified	Lister-Jaguar	Cunningham	W. Hansgen
13 May	SCCA National Race Cumberland, Md	1st – Class C Modified	Lister-Jaguar	Cunningham	W. Hansgen
1 Jun	SCCA National Race Bridgehampton, NY	1st – Class C Modified	Lister-Jaguar	Cunningham	W. Hansgen
		2nd – Class C Modified	Lister-Jaguar	Cunningham	E. Crawford
15 Jun	SCCA National Race Lime Rock, Conn.	1st – Class C Modified	Lister-Jaguar	Cunningham	W. Hansgen
		5th – Class C Modified	Lister-Corvette	Clark-Bowden	F. Windridge
5 Jul	SCCA National Race Lime Rock, Conn.	1st – Class C Modified	Lister-Jaguar	Cunningham	E. Crawford
		2nd – Class C Modified	Lister-Jaguar	Cunningham	W. Hansgen
17 Aug	SCCA National Race Montgomery, NY	1st – Class C Modified	Lister-Jaguar	Cunningham	W. Hansgen
1 Sep	SCCA National Race Thompson, Conn.	1st – Class C Modified	Lister-Jaguar	Cunningham	W. Hansgen
20 Sep	SCCA Grand Prix Watkins Glen, NY	1st – Class C Modified	Lister-Jaguar	Cunningham	E. Crawford
		2nd – Class C Modified	Lister-Jaguar	Cunningham	W. Hansgen
5 Oct 5	SCCA Autumn Meet Virginia, Danville, Va	1st – Class C Modified	Lister-Jaguar	Cunningham	W. Hansgen

At the end of the 1958 season, Hansgen (11,600) and Crawford (6,800) were first and second in the points standings of the SCCA. Fred Windridge was 13th with 600.

Date	Event	Result	Car	Owner	Driver
1959					
19 Apr	SCCA President's Cup Marlboro, Md	1st – Class C Modified	Lister-Jaguar	Cunningham	W. Hansgen
3 May	SCCA National Race Virginia, Danville, Va	1st – Class C Modified	Lister-Jaguar	Cunningham	W. Hansgen
		1st – Class B Modified	Lister-Scarab	Clark-Bowden	F. Windridge
17 May	SCCA National Race Cumberland, Md	1st – Class C Modified	Lister-Jaguar	Cunningham	W. Hansgen
		2nd – Class C Modified	Lister-Jaguar	Cunningham	F. Windridge
31 May	SCCA National Race Bridgehampton, NY	1st – Class C Modified	Lister-Jaguar	Cunningham	W. Hansgen
		1st – Class B Modified	Lister-Corvette	Clark-Bowden	F. Windridge
		3rd – Class C Modified	Lister-Jaguar	Cunningham	J. Fitch
7 Jun	SCCA Pacific Coast Championship Races Laguna Seca, Calif.	2nd – Class C Modified	Lister-Jaguar	J. Flaherty	J. Flaherty
20 Jun	SCCA Road America Elkhart Lake, Wis.	1st – Class B Modified	Lister-Corvette	Clark-Bowden	F. Windridge
4 Jul	SCCA National Race Lime Rock, Conn.	2nd – Class C Modified	Lister-Jaguar	Cunningham	B. Cunningham
		2nd – Class E Modified	Lister-Bristol	Colombosian	R. Colombosian
		3rd – Class E Modified	Lister-Bristol	Kahmer	R. Kahmer
9 Aug	SCCA National Race Montgomery, NY	2nd – Class C Modified	Lister-Jaguar	Cunningham	P. Forno/ W. Hansgen
		3rd – Class E Modified	Lister-Bristol	Walsh	J. Walsh
7 Sep	SCCA National Race Thompson, Conn.	2nd – Class C Modified	Lister-Jaguar	Cunningham	W. Hansgen
13 Sep	SCCA National Race Road America 500 Elkhart Lake, Wis.	1st – Class C Modified	Lister-Jaguar	Cunningham	W. Hansgen/ E. Crawford
		3rd – Class C Modified	Lister-Jaguar	Cunningham	J. Fitch/P. Forno
26 Sep	SCCA National Race Watkins Glen, NY	1st – Class C Modified	Lister-Jaguar	Cunningham	W. Hansgen
15 Nov	SCCA National Race Daytona Beach, Fla.	2nd – Class C Modified	Lister-Jaguar	Cunningham	W. Hansgen
		3rd – Class C Modified	Lister-Jaguar	Cunningham	E. Crawford

At the end of the 1959 season Hansgen led the C Modified points standings with 68, Crawford was equal fourth with 16, Cunningham sixth with 14, Fred Windridge seventh with 8 and Fitch and Forno joint tenth with 6 points. Windridge was also second equal in Class B, with 10 points.

In 1960 Bud Gates took fourth place in Class B Modified with 22 points, driving a Lister-Corvette, with Floyd Askov fifth with 8 points, courtesy of his Lister-Buick. In Class C, Ed Hugus (Lister-Jaguar) took fourth place with ten points.

1961 saw a small resurgence; Pete Harrison (Lister-Chevrolet) headed C Modified with 56 points. Art Huttinger (Lister-Corvette) was second with 30 and Bob Colombosian, having swapped his Lister-Bristol for a Lister-Buick, finished fourth with 16. Charles Jefferson managed sixth with his Lister-Jaguar.

The 1962 season was dominated in C Modified by Chapparals, with Gene Hobbs (Lister-Corvette) the highest points scorer with 17. Donald Adams, Art Huttinger, Howard Keck, Ed Lowther, Howard Quick, Harold Ulrich and Peter Harrison all managed points, though. Many of these cars, immaculately restored, race today. Brian Lister is the first to admit that they are much closer to perfect than he could ever get them – it is a great tribute that people even try.

Lister works production records

TECHNICALLY, this is not part of Archie's story, but in a sense every car which came out of the Abbey Road works had something to do with him. The cars are listed by chassis number and original appearance; many of them look very different now.

Chassis	Year	Engine	Bodywork (style and maker)	Owner	Reg. No.	Remarks
BHL 1	1953	MG	Barchetta-Wakefield	Works	MER 303	–
BHL 2	1954	Bristol	Barchetta-Wakefield	Works	MVE 303	Scrapped – became '57 works car, driven by Archie.
BHL 1	1956	Maserati	Flat-iron-Wakefield	Works	MER 303	Recycled as Lister-Maserati.
BHL 2	1957	Jaguar	Flat-iron-Wakefield	Works	MVE 303	Used Lister-Bristol works identity, driven by Archie.
BHL 3	1955	Bristol	Lucas-Wakefield	Issard-Davies	VPP 9	First Lucas-designed car. exchanged with works for Lister-Maserati.
BHL 3	1958	Jaguar	Knobbly-W & P	Works	VPP 9	Destroyed at Spa. Scrapped
BHL 4	1955	Bristol	Lucas-Wakefield	Black	4 CNO	–
BHL 5	1955	Bristol	Lucas-Wakefield	Green	HCH 736	Written off and recycled as:
BHL 5	1957	Jaguar	Gomm-Gomm	Equipe Devone	HCH 736	Driven by Halford, Clark.
BHL 6	1955	Bristol	Barchetta-Wakefield	Eaton	SNX 590	Later glass fibre bodied.
BHL 7	1955	Bristol	Lucas-Wakefield	6 Mile Stable	NVE 732	–
BHL 8	1955	Rover	Barchetta-Wakefield	Murkett Bros	OER 271	Later rebuilt.
BHL 9	1955	Bristol	Flat-iron-Wakefield	–	–	–
BHL 10	1955	Bristol	Flat-iron-Wakefield	–	–	–
BHL 11	1955	Bristol	Flat-iron-Wakefield	–	–	–
BHL 12	1956	–	Chassis only	Hillwood	673 LMK	Jaguar engine – Gomm body.
BHL 13	1956	Bristol	Flat-iron-Wakefield	–	VAV 450	–

Chassis	Year	Engine	Bodywork (style and maker)	Owner	Reg. No.	Remarks
BHL 14	1956	Bristol	Flat-iron-Wakefield	Baird	JCH 888	–
BHL 15	1956	Bristol	Flat-iron-Wakefield	Markoff	–	Later Jaguar engine.
BHL 16	1956	Bristol	Chassis only	–	–	–
BHL 17	1956	Bristol	Flat-iron-Wakefield	von Klein	–	–
BHL 18	–	–	–	–	–	Not built?
BHL 19	–	–	–	–	–	Not built?
BHL 20	1956	–	Chassis only	–	–	–
BHL 2	1958	Jaguar	Knobbly-W & P	Works	VPP 9	Used identity of Spa wreck.
BHL 2	1958	Jaguar	Knobbly-W & P	Works	MVE 303	Used identity of '57 car.
BHL 2.59	1959	Jaguar	Costin-W & P	Works	not reg'd	1959 Le Mans entry.
BHL 3.59	1959	Jaguar	Costin-W & P	Works	not reg'd	1959 Le Mans entry.
BHL 101	1958	Jaguar	Knobbly-W & P	Cunningham	–	1958 SCCA entry Hansgen.
BHL 102	1958	Jaguar	Knobbly-W & P	Cunningham	–	1958 SCCA entry Crawford.
BHL 103	1958	Jaguar	Knobbly-W & P	P. Whitehead	NBL 660	–
BHL 104	1958	Jaguar	Knobbly-W & P	Ecurie Ecosse	341 SG	1958 Ecosse entry – Gregory.
BHL 105	1958	Jaguar	Knobbly-W & P	Ecurie Nat. Belge	–	1958 ENB entry.
BHL 106	1958	Chevrolet	Knobbly-W & P	Cunningham	–	–
BHL 107	1958	Chevrolet	Knobbly-W & P	Kelso Aerodynamic	–	–
BHL 108	1958	Chevrolet	Knobbly-W & P	Jim Hall	–	–
BHL 109	1958	Jaguar	Ecosse-W & P	Ecurie Ecosse	–	'Monzanapolis' car. Parts combined with ch. 104 to make hybrid, KTU 254.
BHL 110	1958	Chevrolet	Knobbly-W & P	Imported by Carsten	–	–
BHL 111	1958	Jaguar	Ecosse-W & P	A. Miller	GM 9639	Originally 2.5 litre XK unit, then Chevrolet. Sold engineless to Ham. Now 3.8.
BHL 112	1958	Jaguar	Knobbly-W & P	Imported by Cunningham	–	–
BHL 113	1958	Jaguar	Knobbly-W & P	Imported by Shelby	–	–
BHL 114	1958	Chevrolet	Knobbly-W & P	Mrs Henry Clark Bowden	–	1958 Fred Windridge car. Used several engines.
BHL 115	1958	Chevrolet	Knobbly-W & P	Hallahan	–	–
BHL 116	1958	Jaguar	Knobbly-W & P	Jack Flaherty	–	–
BHL 117	1958	Jaguar	Knobbly-W & P	Imported by Shelby	–	–

Chassis	Year	Engine	Bodywork (style and maker)	Owner	Reg. No.	Remarks
BHL 118	–	–	–	–	–	Not built?
BHL 119	–	–	–	–	–	Not built?
BHL 120	1958	Jaguar	Knobbly-W & P	P. Mould	YOB 575	–
BHL 121	1959	Chevrolet	Costin-W & P	J. Ewer	–	–
BHL 122	1959	Jaguar	Costin-W & P	–	–	–
BHL 123	1959	Jaguar	Costin-W & P	Cunningham	–	–
BHL 124	1959	?	Costin-W & P	–	–	–
BHL 125	1959	Chevrolet	Costin-W & P	R. Brightman	–	–
BHL 126	1959	Jaguar	Costin-W & P	W. Moss	–	–
BHL 127	1959	Chevrolet	Costin-W & P	–	–	–
BHL 128	1959	Chevrolet	Costin-W & P	Imported by Shelby	–	–
BHL 129	1959	Chevrolet	Costin-W & P	Imported by Shelby	–	–
BHL 130	1959	Chevrolet	Costin-W & P	M. Anthony	TUF 1	–
BHL 131	1959	Chevrolet	Costin-W & P	Connors	–	–
BHL 132	1959	Chevrolet	Costin-W & P	–	–	–
BHL 133	1959	Chevrolet	Costin-W & P	Saul	–	–

There are many cars about which are rebuilt around a door handle pull or a handful of rivets; I give them no place in this listing, not because they are not good cars (it would be impertinent of me to make such a pronouncement) but no car is included which is not thought to possess a chassis built at the Lister works. For reasons which are clear, I must say that this is merely my version of the facts. All records of detailed production seem to be lost and the only reason that this appendix is included at all is that it has relevance to the Lister story. Great assistance in preparing this list was given by Phillipe Renault and Jonathan Evans.

Glossary of Automobile Clubs and event organisers

AMOC	Aston Martin Owners' Club
BARC	British Automobile Racing Club
BDC	Bentley Drivers' Club
B&DMC	Berwick & District Motor Club
BHMC	Brighton & Hove Motor Club
BMCLCC	Bristol Motor Cycle & Light Car Club
BMRC	Border Motor Racing Club
BOC	Bugatti Owners' Club.
BRDC	British Racing Drivers' Club
BRSCC	British Racing & Sports Car Club
C50CC	Cambridge 50 Car Club
CUAC	Cambridge University Automobile Club
EAMC	East Anglia Motor Club
ECCC	Eastern Counties Car Club
½ LCC	Half-Litre Car Club
HDLCC	Hampshire & Dorset Light Car Club
JDC	Jaguar Drivers' Club
LCC	London Car Club
LCMC	Lancashire and Cheshire Motor Club
MAC	Midlands Auto Club
MCMC	Mid-Cheshire Motor Club
MGCC	MG Car Club
MMKMC	Maidstone and Mid-Kent Motor Club
NSCC	Nottingham Sports Car Club
NSMC	North Staffordshire Motor Club
RAC	Royal Automobile Club
RSAC	Royal Scottish Automobile Club
RUAC	Royal Ulster Automobile Club
SCCA	Sports Car Club of America
SMRC	Snetterton Motor Racing Club
SUNBAC	Sutton Coldfield & North Birmingham Automobile Club
SVRA	Sportscar Vintage Racing Association of America
SWAC	South Wales Automobile Club

WECC   West Essex Car Club
WHDCC   West Hants and Dorset Car Club

Others are, I trust, self-explanatory, or lost to us.

Bibliography

Jim Clark, *Jim Clark at the Wheel* (Arthur Barker Ltd, 1964)

Paul Frère, *Starting Grid to Chequered Flag* (B. T. Batsford Ltd,1962)

Anthony Hall, *Maserati 250F* (Haynes Publishing, 1990)

Geoffrey Healey, *Austin Healey* (Haynes Publishing, 1977)

Denis Jenkinson, *The Racing Driver* (B. T. Batsford Ltd, 1962)

Charles Johnson, *To Draw a Long Line* (Bookmarque Publishing, 1989)

Chris Nixon, *Racing with the David Brown Aston Martins*, Vols I and II (Transport Bookman, 1980)

Doug Nye, *Powered by Jaguar* (Motor Racing Publications, 1980)

Doug Nye, *Cooper Cars* (Osprey, 1983)

Dennis Ortenburger, *Flying on Four Wheels* (Patrick Stephens Ltd, 1986)

Roy Salvadori & Anthony Pritchard, *Roy Salvadori – Racing Driver* (Patrick Stephens Ltd, 1985)

Andrew Whyte, *Jaguar Sports, Racing and Works Competition Cars from 1954* (Haynes Publishing, 1987)

Index